PORN ROW

Also by Jack McIver Weatherford

Tribes on the Hill: An Investigation into the Rituals and Realities of an Endangered American Species, the Congress of the United States

PORN ROW

by

Jack McIver Weatherford

ARBOR HOUSE NEW YORK

Manufactured in the United States of America

10 9 8 7 6 5 4 3 2 1

Library of Congress Cataloging in Publication Data

Weatherford, J. McIver.
  Porn row.
  Bibliography: p.
  1. Washington (D.C.)—Moral conditions. 2. Sex
oriented businesses—Washington (D.C.) 3. Pornography—Social aspects—Washington (D.C.) 4. Prostitution—Washington (D.C.) I. Title.
HN80.W3W4   1986   363.4'7'09753   86-1187
ISBN: 0-87795-798-3

for
Walker Pearce
with love and appreciation

Contents

Preface

This book began serendipitously. Late one night I appeared on a talk show in New York City where I was discussing congressional politics by virtue of having worked in the Senate and written a book about it—topics that I thought were of great interest to everyone. Just off stage, but easily within my view, the technical crew in the studio watched a pornographic film the entire time I was talking. I tried to be enlightening, wise, and witty with the host and to respond with great authority to call-in questions from an audience scattered all along the East Coast. But I lost my train of thought each time I mentioned the president's new thrust, the widening gap between the parties, the rise and fall of the economy, or just the underdog in the last election.

At other public appearances I had been annoyed by the "sex element" in other people's irrelevant reactions to what I was talking about: An interviewer in Los Angeles wanted to know about Ted Kennedy's "sexcapades"; a caller asked about a cabinet member's mistress; and interviewers frequently brought up the various congressional sex scandals involving pages, strippers, prostitutes, secretaries, and call girls. I always tried to sidestep such subjects and get back to what I thought of as "the issues," but on the New York show that 2:00 A.M., seeing those porn films while talking, I realized that many people were a lot more interested in sex than politics. As naïve and self-evident as some readers may find that observation, I was puzzled by it, honestly and genuinely puzzled by it.

The incident made me realize something else as well. I had

never seen real pornography. I thought that I was knowledgeable, and to me pornography came in three styles: *Playboy,* which was revealing; *Penthouse,* which was even more revealing; and *Playgirl,* which was the alternative to the other two. Of course, I knew more blatant kinds existed, but I had never really seen any. The film the technicians were watching was part of a wholly different sexual world, and therein arose the theme for this book.

In contrast to the other sciences, observation of the subject is not enough in anthropology. Even observation supplemented by interviews is rarely sufficient; anthropology demands participation in the world being studied. To understand a people, one must literally walk in their shoes, eat their food, share their daily routine, laugh at their jokes, and come as close as possible to being one of them. It is only through this process of enculturation and socialization that a researcher comes to understand the subjective as well as the objective sides of the culture.

When I began, I thought this project would be easy. My work in anthropology had already taken me into many different settings around the world. I had hiked the Inca road through the Andes, researched a nuclear power plant in Bavaria, visited in the mud huts of the Masai of Kenya, canoed the jungle rivers of Ecuador, and worked in the Congress of the United States. Until starting this research, however, I had never been inside a pornography store or massage parlor, or seen a live sex show—any of which I could easily have done in any moderate-size city anywhere in my own country. Once I started this new venture, I found the natives more inscrutable than Washington politicians, more savage than Ecuadorian headhunters, and, in the end, more tragic than any other people I had ever encountered.

As every writer and researcher knows, a book is a collaborative process that involves many people, not just the writer. The person with whom I first discussed the idea for this book was fellow writer Rochelle Jones, who continued throughout the study and the writing to offer help and encouragement. Next came a long talk with Lois Wallace, who supported the idea fully and helped me launch the project. As my agent, she also continued to work throughout the whole process with me. My editor, Ann Harris, worked very closely with me in the final months of writing and is due more credit than I can acknowledge.

As an anthropologist, I owe a great debt to my academic colleagues. Kevin Avruch and Peter Black helped me map out the initial research plan; and throughout my work in the porn store, Eleanor Gerber telephoned me constantly to give advice and to keep me in touch with the outside world. For that I owe her a great personal as well as intellectual debt. My colleagues at American University were supportive during the writing process, and I particularly thank Ruth Landman, William Leap, Dolores Koenig, and Brett Williams. I had a tremendous amount of help from David McCurdy, Anna Meigs, and Anne Sutherland, my three fellow anthropologists at Macalester College. Kay Crawford and Barbara Wells-Howe of Macalester also assisted me in various stages of the work. I appreciate the manuscript-reading and comments by Marc Swartz, Freya Manfred, Thomas Pope, Ester Newton, Hans Christoph Buch, and Ray Durgnat. And thanks are due to Z. I. Giraldo, who was brave enough to visit me "in the field" and polite enough to pretend that I was not doing anything odd.

Special friends who helped in various ways include Dan Davis, Lee Owens, and John and Nancy Neubauer. The women of PRIDE in Minneapolis gave freely of their time and information, and I also appreciate the cooperation of Rebecca Rand. As always, the staff of the Library of Congress was a great aid to me in every stage of the work. I also appreciate the encouragement as well as jokes made at my expense by my former boss John Glenn and by my colleagues on his staff. They all said they would visit me at work, but they did not seem to have the right stuff.

In every step of this project, from the initial idea through the research and the writing of the book, I was aided by my wife, Walker Pearce, who stuck by me the whole way. Her

PREFACE

humor and good sense helped to keep it all in perspective. The final product bears her influence throughout. In appreciation, this book is dedicated to her.

No government money was used for any part of this study.

PORN ROW

One

JUNK-FOOD SEX

"This is a goddamn porn store, not a museum. If you want to look at naked women for free, go to the Smithsonian." As he snarled at the customers, George knocked solidly on the door-jamb with the sawed-off broom handle he always carried inside the store. A few customers smiled meekly, as though trying to take his outburst as an odd but well-intentioned bit of humor. Others suddenly became invisible behind the revolving paperback rack, and several of them slipped sheepishly into the private peep booths in the back room.

Turning away from his momentarily routed audience of customers and back again to me, George brushed back the handful of sandy hair that always fell over his forehead, in much the same automatic way that the men coming out of the peeps perfunctorily checked their zippers after watching a private showing of a porn film. "Now remember," George began telling me in a schoolteacherish manner, the broom handle tucked under his arm like a swagger stick, "when you're in here alone at night, this is *your* damn store, and *you* gotta control it—not the customers, not the girls, not the hustlers, the queers, the dope dealers, or the pimps. It's up to you to show them that you can keep all of them in line and at the same time keep peace among them while they're in here."

To demonstrate how to keep control at all times, George turned toward a couple just emerging from one of the sixteen peep booths in the back. Then he looked at me to make sure I was watching the chubby woman as she straightened her pants, brushed her legs off, and combed her hair with open fingers. A man followed behind her, already wearing an expression that said "I don't know her and I never saw her before in my life."

George screamed at her from across the room. "What in the fuck is your fat ass doing back in here? I told you two weeks ago that you are barred from here!"

"But I've been here every day this week and nobody said a word," the woman protested in a tightly controlled voice, walking slowly toward George on her way to the front door.

"I don't care how many times you've been back in here, *I* said you were barred." George headed back toward the peep booth that she had just left, still shouting at her. "Look at the goddamn mess you left in my booth! Your trick rag is on the seat, and there's newspaper stuck to the floor from where you gave that dude his blow job."

Now safely at the door, the woman raised her voice sharply. "The newspaper was on the floor when I got here. And if you would mop up the goddamn cum off the floor sometime, the paper wouldn't stick to it like that."

"It's whores like you that spit that damn cum all over the floor," George retorted.

"You son of a bitch. You don't know who you're calling a whore. I'll have you know I've been working an undercover assignment for the police around here, and I know more about your ass than you know about mine."

"You've been a whore a lot longer than I've worked down here—don't hand me that cop shit. You just give 'em blow jobs to let you work and you try to turn in the better-looking hookers to get the competition off the streets. Where's your damn badge?"

"It's in my damn purse, but I ain't about to show it to you, cocksucker. You don't know who you're dealing with. I can

2

have your damn job any day because I know the Man." Now in a full rage, she stood in the open door so that people on the street as well as in the shop could hear her. "I better not see your white motherfucking ass on the street alone at night or I'm likely to cut your goddamn throat from ear to fucking ear." She let the door swing shut as she marched on down the street.

Back at the counter, George leaned forward and continued his lecture as if he had never interrupted it. "See, even though some of them have been around a long time and can talk a mean streak, you still gotta let them know every once in a while that you're in control here and you can let anybody you want come in or keep them out." He paused, furrowed his eyebrows, and asked, "You understand what I mean now, don't you?"

I did not understand. I did not understand anything at all. Mostly, I did not understand what I was doing there in the middle of this place called the Pink Pussy within sight of the White House, where I assumed that Ronald and Nancy Reagan were having a good night's sleep like any two normal human beings.

This was my first night on the job. Such was my reward for doggedly scouring the red-light district for a month in search of work. I wanted to investigate the Sex Strip from the vantage point of a participant and not a mere interloper. In my quest, I haunted the businesses along Fourteenth Street, the Washington Strip lined with brightly flashing marquees, each gaudier than the next. They screamed out the earthy pleasures of the erotic books at City News, the nude dancers at the Utah Steak House, exotic massages at the Swedish House, and lots of men at the Potomac Baths. Amid the glitter of the sex joints rose the golden arches of McDonald's and neon signs proclaiming the delights of the hamburgers in Burger King, the fried chicken at Church's, the chili dogs at the Dairy Queen, the taco salads at Wendy's, the roast beef sandwiches at Roy Rogers, potato salad at Kentucky Fried Chicken, and chocolate chip cookies at the H-Street Bakery. Twenty-four hours a day, the Strip offered every available pleasure of contemporary sexuality and appetite. The visitor could have a Big Mac with one of Kim's great blow jobs; a chocolate shake with a 'Round the World; home-made cole slaw and finger-licking fried shrimp with a hand job by Victoria; or a simple chocolate-dipped ice cream cone and a fast fuck.

Day after day I had tramped up and down the Strip looking for a job. Usually the manager was not around when I arrived, or there was simply no job to be had, or at best someone asked me to fill out a card with my name and phone number on it. Only once did I get the opportunity to complete a one-page application. Yet every day I read carefully all the job listings in each of the newspapers on sale in the porn stores and in the coin boxes chained to lampposts throughout the Strip. I followed the leads given to me by old friends and new acquaintances, and I spent as much time as I could hanging out in the Strip bars and the fast-food places scattered throughout the area.

Then one Tuesday morning the phone rang unexpectedly and a man identifying himself as manager of the Pink Pussy offered me a job if I could start work within three hours. I had never heard of his store and had not looked for work there; later I heard that he had gotten my name from one of the other stores where I had applied.

The Pink Pussy was not even on the main Strip. It stood amid a clutch of abandoned storefronts and apartment buildings around the corner, on a small spur off the Strip. It was a sleazier and gaudier version of Fourteenth Street. By night it had more blacks and Asians than whites, but during the day the influx of office workers kept it mainly white. The whores on the Strip in front of the Pink Pussy looked older, fatter, skinnier, and more haggard and worn out than the sharp ones up the Strip. The few businesses nearby had more iron bars protecting the windows, and the sidewalk was strewn with broken glass, hamburger wrappers, condoms, and cigarette butts. Buildings that appeared abandoned were sleeping quarters for a large assortment of locals, shooting galleries for the sale and use of drugs, and hidden spots for hurried sexual encounters.

The businesses on this part of the Strip bespoke a more gruesome poverty and lower status than those on the sparkling main Strip. More young boys with long, stringy hair and ran-

4

dom gaps in their tobacco-stained teeth loitered in front of a basement gay bar to hustle themselves to pedestrians and to men who cruised slowly past in their cars. A once grand theater in art-deco style now showed martial arts and triple-X-rated films.

On the subway ride downtown to the Pink Pussy, I carefully rehearsed my cover story about being a free-lance writer struggling to make a living and needing to take a night job. I cut the story to fit precisely the jagged space between ethnographic practicality and anthropological ethics. As a covert anthropologist doing free-lance undercover work, I did not want to endanger my cover, but at the same time I did not want to violate too grossly the constraints of my discipline. As it happened, I was saved the need to use the story at all.

"Al from City News tells me you're a writer. I hope that means you can fill out a cash-receipts form at night." With that the manager, who was a foot shorter than George but thirty pounds heavier, skimmed lightly over my so-called occupation and went on to what were for him the much more important questions of whether I could do the work and whether I lived on a bus line that supplied steady transportation both day and night, as well as Sundays and holidays. (The Pink Pussy does not close even for Christmas.) So long as I could get to work and do the work, he did not care what my occupation was, and he certainly did not want to hear my story about why I was ending up working in a dirty-book store. I soon learned that the guy working in the Wide World of Sex next door to the Pink Pussy also held a Ph.D., his in literature from Berkeley, and he claimed to have attended the Iowa Writers' Workshop. He bragged about his work and claimed to be writing a novel about a prostitute and a gay hustler falling in love. He never did show me any of his often-promised drafts or the short stories he had written for the Iowa Workshop.

Like him and like me, everyone on the Strip had some other, more important identity. Actresses worked behind the bars, models worked for call-girl services, laid-off teachers danced nude on the bar, consultants between jobs sold porn, graduate students in psychology tended bar, and cosmetologists gave erotic massages. To outsiders these people might appear to be society's derelicts, but each told a story of another, *real* identity that would soon whisk her or him away to a different setting. One was waiting for a wealthy benefactor to die; another would soon marry a rich man from out of town, as soon as he straightened out a few details; someone else claimed to be the mistress of a powerful government official who wanted to marry her but could not divorce his wife without causing a public scandal. One man was waiting for the GI Bill to approve his new course of study or for credits to be transferred in from Broken Elbow Community College. All the rest were getting together enough money to open their own bar, restaurant, nursery, computer company, beauty parlor, video arcade, auto body shop, video rental shop, record store, modeling agency, acting studio, tanning salon, aerobics clinic, gym, travel bureau, or talent-booking agency. By comparison, my own moonlighting as a writer ranked rather low in prestige and very low in creativity as a cover story or as a life's ambition.

Before assigning me to George for training, the manager lectured me on punctuality—I had to be at work fifteen minutes before my shift began—and on not using alcohol or drugs while working. Any shortfall in the day's cash statement at the end of the day had to be made up from my own pocket that night; otherwise it would be deducted from my pay *with* interest. On the other hand, he granted covert permission to keep any excess money in the till from overcharged or shortchanged customers. This helped compensate for having to work fifty-four hours a week while being paid for only forty-two at the near-minimum-wage rate of $3.56 per hour with no benefits of any kind. If I ever cheated the Company in any way, I would be fired on the spot. Each week a person would be sent in as a disguised checker to monitor my handling of money and merchandise.

The manager explained that because he was responsible for a number of different stores and other types of businesses in the neighborhood, he would not be working with me on a daily basis. But he hastened to add that he would still know everything that happened and everything that I might do even when I thought I was alone. "I'll be right here when you least expect it, because I work night and day." He paused, but I could think of nothing to say. "And remember," he started again, "there are no secrets down here, at least not from the Company. Any questions?"

"Yeah. What's the name of the Company, anyway?"

"This store is the Pink Pussy, but it belongs to *the* Company. That's the only name it has, *the* Company, and that's who you work for now."

I subsequently learned that the Company is headquartered "up north" and stretches south as far as the Carolinas and sometimes Florida. Appropriately enough, the Company is headed by the Man, a figure of near-mythic proportions around the Strip but about whom no one seems to know anything very certain beyond the often-repeated observation that he always wears very expensive lizard cowboy boots.

At that moment I was not yet thinking about the boots the Man wore. Instead I was fighting off the image of my sinking into the Potomac River wearing a large pair of cement shoes in punishment for a $3.18 shortage in the cash register. The unexpected fear encouraged me to pay close attention to George's on-the-job training in how to run the shop. I realized very quickly that he preferred the doing-and-showing method to the slower, Socratic techniques based on discussion and thought.

Perched on my stool by the cash register, which afforded a commanding view of the entire store and all the hidden mirrors, I listened closely and took furious mental notes as George explained the organization of my new workplace. Going clockwise around the room from the front door, he pointed first to the section of swingers' magazines. These list the names, vital statistics, and telephone numbers of young women and couples beneath their pictures. Supposedly the women and the couples want to engage in free love and relish any type of sexual bizarreness. In truth, if the ads are real, the women are looking for paying customers; but many of the ads are fabrications of the publisher, designed to titillate and tease the reader into buying the magazine. According to George, it did not matter whether the entries were real or not, because people bought the magazines for their own fantasies. Men wanted to know that somewhere nearby, beautiful young women eagerly awaited their embraces and wished to fulfill any and all of their sexual desires. The magazines also let those who wanted to think of themselves as buying a mere dating guide satisfy their hunger for pornography.

Nestled close to the "swingers" were the magazines variously known as "soft porn," and "tits and ass," or simply "T&A." Each T&A magazine featured a solitary woman who posed throughout the magazine in all manner of sexual positions, using props such as dildoes, bananas, lollipops, gearshifts, and vibrators to simulate masturbation. Magazines that showed another person assisting in any way belonged in the neighboring "hard-core" section, known more generally as "fuck books." These depicted women with males, with other women, or with any combination of partners. No matter how many people appeared, the sequence of activities remained the same, beginning with undressing, and moving through mutual masturbation, fellatio, cunnilingus, coitus, and sodomy, with a scattering of orgasms. The only variations from one magazine to the next seemed to be the background scenery and sometimes the tattoos visible on the male models.

Pointing out the various hard-core magazines, George walked across to the far corner of the room and rattled a rack with his stick. This rack contained the gay magazines, featuring only males and transvestites. George announced decisively that as soon as the Company made him manager, he was shipping all the gay magazines over to one of the gay stores. He did plan to keep the "TVs," his term for the transvestite magazines, which he said sold fairly well but gave the store the wrong kind of image.

On the wall closest to where I sat at the register were the various types of kinky magazines, lined up neatly next to one another. The sadomasochism books, or S&M, featured whips, unlike the bondage-and-discipline (B&D) magazines, which did not usually feature whipping, spanking, or strangling. The miscellaneous row offered magazines devoted to water sports, enemas, diapering, and related fetishes, the significance of which I would not understand until much later in my work.

"Any questions?" George asked, pleased by his quick but thorough tour of the room.

"What about *Playboy* and all that?" I asked, in the manner of a serious student who had stayed up the entire night preparing for this class.

"We sell only pornography here, not news. If somebody wants that shit, tell them to go to a newsstand or maybe to the Christian Science Reading Room or somewhere. No store down here sells that—or *Penthouse, Oui, Hustler,* or any of that crap. People down here want to buy pictures of *sex,* not something to read in the Library of Congress."

Having disposed of my question, Professor George moved on to the long, brightly lit display case in front of me. He pointed his stick at the different shelves that separated the pills and potions, the lubricants and body oils, and the large array of rubber goods, toys, and drug paraphernalia and head supplies. In a locked case behind me were the films and videos, arranged so that their covers could be seen but not touched. They, too, fell into categories of soft- and hard-core, or more simply "teases" and "fuck films."

His lecture now complete, George sat down on the counter, lit up a Marlboro, asked a young guy loitering in the peep-show section to run pick us up some drinks from Burger King, and handed him $2. Turning back to me, he asked, "Now, you think you got all this?"

Of course I did not, though my mind was already swirling with the typologies and taxonomies of pornography, customers, and films with which I could fill dozens of matrices to be published in a nice article in the *American Anthropologist.* But of more immediate concern was the issue of the Company, since the image of cement shoes kept jutting into my neatly constructed typologies. Sex could wait; I needed to know where I fitted into this mess.

Taking a drag on his cigarette, George explained, without explaining too much, that about one-half the businesses on the Strip belonged to the Company. These included pornography, film, and other businesses. All businesses that served drinks or food, as well as those that involved pinball or video games, belonged to other companies or to small entrepreneurs. About half of the pornography stores and theaters also belonged to other people. In addition, the Company owned the wholesale suppliers for all the goods we sold except the dope paraphernalia. Another arm of the Company supplied the films for the peep shows and managed them. These wholesalers served all the businesses on the Strip, whether they belonged to the Company or not. George considered this a bad practice. He claimed the Company's delivery men always gave the best materials to the other stores because the store owners tipped them for this service. The delivery men then brought all the rejects and well-thumbed magazines over to the Pink Pussy. George told me he frequently complained because this system hurt the Company, but despite his protests, only occasionally would they send him a set of new releases before letting the independent stores have them.

George, who was quite voluble when he wanted to be, seemed to choose his words much more cautiously when detailing the Company to me. He had barely begun to sidestep my barrage of questions, however, when a neatly dressed young woman walked into the store and came directly over to where he was perched on top of the display counter. She asked him a question, and he said, "Lady, don't ask me. Can't you tell that a man like me would never be working in a dive like this? I just came in on my break from OMB." And he jumped off the counter and went to the far side of the store, allowing me ample room to take charge.

My only sales experience had been as a Christmas clerk in the men's department of J.C. Penney's during high school, and one disastrous summer week selling encyclopedias door to door. Summoning my best shopping-mall smile, I said, "Yes, ma'am, what can I do for you?"

"I need a present for a shower for a woman in my office who's getting married, and I sort of, like, wanted to get her a funny present—something a little different from the standard towels and all." She looked around the wall display and the counter without allowing herself to focus on any single item.

"Have something special in mind, like rubbers? A movie?" I asked.

"The shower theme is Bedroom Boutique. You know, all the presents are supposed to have something to do with the bedroom, because some other girls are giving her a kitchen-and-dining-room shower. Our shower is all sheets and nighties and things like that, but I thought I could find something else here."

"Great, how about a dildo? We have a whole line here on the back. And of course we have them in all the colors, too. Let's see here . . . they range from ebony jet through bittersweet, milk chocolate, Puerto Rican tan, and Nordic thunder." I grabbed a sample of each and spread them out on the counter in front of her. "Now let's see. . . . Some of these come uncircumcised, too, and some have batteries. This model has a crank to make the head wiggle separately from the body. And this one has a pump. I'm not exactly sure how this works, if it pumps something in or something out . . ."

"Well, never mind that. It sounds too messy anyway. I just want a medium in regular; nothing really fancy, you know."

"They range from $4.95 for the four-inch one up to $47.95 for the eighteen-inch one. That's plus tax, of course. So maybe you want a twenty-dollar kind in medium tan. That's about nine inches long."

"That sounds right, or maybe just a fifteen-dollar one. No one will really use it," she said.

"Sure," I agreed, "but you want one big enough for everyone at the party to see it when she opens the present. The joke's spoiled if everyone hollers, 'Oh, what is it, anyway?' They might think it's just another potato peeler or toilet brush."

"Okay, then I'll go for the eighteen-dollar one—it's plenty big." She searched through her purse for her wallet.

"Now, would you like some lubricant to go with that?" I continued. "We have a great set of flavors here: lemon, strawberry, wild cherry, piña colada, and plain."

"How about banana daiquiri? She loves those daiquiris, and that's what we're having at the shower. Plus they're going to Cancun on their honeymoon, and a daiquiri would be just perfect."

"No, I don't think we have that one, but the piña colada is really pretty close, and I think everyone in Cancun has switched to piña coladas now. You know, native boys just climb up the coconut trees along the beach there and make the drinks for honeymooners. She'll love this one." I decided I was bordering on the unctuous and tried to restrain myself before I got too carried away with my salesmanship.

The first major sale of my new career totaled nearly $25, and I felt reasonably confident that I had not lost that old Penney's touch. But as soon as the lady was out the door, with my wishes for her to "have a nice day and come back to see us," a scowling George headed straight at me.

"Who the fuck you think you are? Gucci Pucci or somebody?" George spat out the words with contempt. "That little act might work over on Connecticut Avenue, but this is the damn Sleaze Strip you're on now, buddy."

"What are you talking about?" I demanded indignantly. "I got her to buy a medium-size dildo, and it was more than she wanted to spend."

"That's not the point." George slipped back into his lecture mode. "You'll never see her again. Next time she'll be afraid you might ask her how the big dildo worked out. People come in here to be anonymous. She probably bought the damn thing for herself anyway, and next week she'll want a bigger one or a faster one. But she'll be damned if she comes in here to see *you* again. She'll go to another store. You let the customer ask the questions and you answer them. That's all you do. They want quick information, not a whole rigmarole like you were the Avon lady or something."

George was right in that I never saw that customer again, but I never really believed she would have come back anyway. Much later in the evening he demonstrated the correct way to make a sale when a somewhat drunk man came over to the counter and asked him, "How much's the Spanish fly?"

"Five ninety-eight," George answered.

"Is it them pills or little powders?"

12

"We got both."

"Do the pills really work like the other stuff?"

"Read the box. It says right here, 'Genuine Simulacrum Spanish fly, imported from Taiwan.' You think Customs would let fake stuff in the country?"

"How much is that other kind?"

"All $5.98."

"I'll try the one in the red box."

"The cherry-flavored?"

"Oh, no, I mean the coffee ones."

The man paid his money. George rang up the sale, gave him his receipt, and bagged the purchase without a "Thank you" or a "Come again." After the man walked out the door, George looked at me and said, "He'll be back in a week, as soon as he gets a new girlfriend."

George was right, though it was a while before I realized the man came in habitually and always asked roughly the same questions about the Spanish fly. That night, however, all this was still very new, and I was profoundly impressed with the psychological and cultural knowledge of this master of salesmanship.

I forgot my newly learned taxonomies and classificatory schemes as I imagined my future as the Carlos Castaneda of pornography reporting what I'd learned about human nature from this shaman of sleaze. *The Teachings of George Santorini* and *A Separate Piece* rose up in my mind, and already I visualized *The Road to the Pink Pussy* clutched in the hands of eager young anthropology students around the world.

As I fantasized, George turned his attention to a young hooker who was just emerging alone from one of the back booths, wearing a rabbit-fur jacket and hot pink high-heeled shoes. "You sold much pussy today, honey?" he asked her.

"Never enough. I sold about as much as you have dick, sweetheart," she replied, and kissed him on the cheek as she sauntered by him. "But no matter how much I sell, there is always lots more for you, baby."

"You know I don't like used stuff," George came back at her.

"If you're man enough, you can get past the used part and then it's all new stuff." On that note, she slipped out the door with an exaggerated wink and a leer at him.

As though to compensate for being too friendly in front of his rookie porn clerk, George rattled his stick along the racks and shouted into the room, "If you want to see meat, go to the Safeway. If you want to buy a dirty book, then bring it on up to the counter."

By the time I left George and the Pink Pussy that first night, I felt that I had learned a lot and I was having some fun. But far more impressive to me now is how little I knew. Back then, I saw the Strip as just a slightly different version of the standard American culture that I thought I knew so well, but it proved to be a far different and far more serious world.

On that first day it never even occurred to me to wonder why I'd been given the job. I was so interested in hiding the fact that I was an undercover anthropologist there to study their world and its people, I never suspected what the manager and George were trying to hide from *me*. Only later did I find out that the clerk before me had been murdered. He was taken down to the basement one night and forced to kneel, and his brains were shot out of his head. I often stared at the spot in the basement where it had happened. I concentrated on the smudges where his knees had rested and then where his skull had cracked as it hit the floor. I searched out the marks of his brains on the crumbling wall. I tried to separate the moisture stains on the floor from the bloodstains and the thousands of other substances etched into the floor in the unchronicled history of that dungeon.

Mostly, I wondered why he had been shot. Some said it was robbery, but little seemed to have been missing. Others said he had gotten involved with dope or that he had crossed the Company. Still others insisted he was rubbed out by another company, or that he simply knew too much. Later, all of this was to become much more important to me. But on my first night, I was happily ignorant of it.

14

Two

THE BEAT OF THE STRIP

During the first week, I worked an irregular schedule with either George or the manager there to train me. One morning I opened the shop and worked until late afternoon; the next day I came to work in the afternoon and worked through the night. Then I split the shifts and worked the busiest parts of each. As the manager said, this let me "get a real feel for the rhythm of the place. To understand your job, you have to understand the whole store—and to understand it, you have to understand the Strip. This isn't Embassy Row down here, you know."

I certainly agreed that it was not Embassy Row, but I could not yet discern what he called "the rhythm of the place." To me it was a cacophony of hustling, bustling people, cars cruising back and forth blowing their horns, hookers loitering and talking animatedly with each other. Within a few days, however, I perceived a definite ebb and flow to the day's events, as regular and predictable as an instinctual cycle. Within a month, I internalized the cycle and I awoke, ate, relaxed, slept, and lived by it. It became second nature, just as the nine-to-five workday was for the bureaucrats in town.

If there is ever a time when the Strip can be said to be in its "natural state," that time is the early morning when the

15

district most belongs to the people who live and work there. The Strip pauses to catch its breath after closing the late-night bars and sending the last loiterers home in cabs. The daytime customers are still home in bed, and virtually all commerce ceases just before the daily cleanup begins. The night shift of whores, pimps, strippers, porn clerks, and police sits down for cups of coffee and eggs on muffins at the same laminated tabletops with the day shift of masseuses, porn clerks, and police coming to work. Over free refills of coffee and complimentary copies of the *Washington Post* or *USA Today*, the hookers catch up on gossip about each other and the dumb tricks they had the night before; the policemen rehash the arrests and the almost big events of their shift; and other habitués just try to stay awake a little longer in order to do some errand, go to the doctor, or appear in court, before they can go home and sleep through the afternoon.

Blue-collar neighborhoods have pubs and taverns where the community gathers in the evening for beer and television. The affluent suburbs have the cocktail hour at the club. Inner-city professional districts have their trendy bars with lush plants and fashionable but rapidly changing mixed drinks. The Strip uses area coffee shops, McDonald's, and other fast-food places for a social breakfast routine at the close of its workday.

The Pink Pussy opens for the day around 10:00 or 10:30, depending on the arrival of the day clerk after his usual breakfast meeting with the store manager at McDonald's. After breakfast the manager leaves to start his rounds of the other stores under his supervision, and precisely at 10:30 Mac and John, the two oldest men working on the Strip, drive up in their long black limousine and park in front of the Pink Pussy. For years these two ancients have arrived together every morning to pick up customers wanting a ride out to the Maryland racetracks. Mac drives and John directs. Both dress impeccably and very conservatively by Strip standards. They wear coats and ties every day, along with hats and well-polished shoes. For the colder mornings, they have thick wool overcoats; and for the rainy days, tan raincoats.

As soon as they arrive, Mac heads across the street to pick

16

up coffee for John and himself, while John comes into the Pink Pussy and asks if I have any messages for him. Even though he does not work for the Pink Pussy or to my knowledge for any part of the Company, John treats the store as his own office. I tell him that Hugh wants him to telephone and that a man with a scar over his left eye wants a ride but may not get to the store until a few minutes after 11:00 A.M. Using the pay telephone, John makes a few calls, and then waits for slow Mac to return with the coffee. When Mac returns, the two of them settle down to read the morning news, drink their coffee, and wait for their customers. When the weather is nice, Mac enjoys waiting out front with the customers, but usually they all loiter around inside the shop. The men almost never buy anything other than cigarettes, but occasionally one will drop a quarter or two in the peeps to kill time. Finally, at 11:00 or 11:15, John stands to leave and all the men head for the limousine. Mac and John have provided this service for as long as the racetracks have operated. Mac claims that in the 1920s he drove for President Herbert Hoover before the White House and Secret Service bought their own fleet of cars.

About the time that Mac barges headlong into the Pennsylvania Avenue traffic, the first dancers begin arriving on the Strip for the lunch shift. By some legal quirk, only bars with restaurants can feature live, nude dancers, so the shows usually begin their first set at 11:45, in time for lunch. Frequently when they have a few extra minutes before reporting to work, one or two of the dancers pop into the Pink Pussy to pick up rolling papers or pipe screens, or to check out any new equipment. Violet, a petite blonde with long legs, became a frequent visitor, often slipping into one of the peeps in the back for an early-morning smoke before facing the tables of pawing bureaucrats and the job of dancing around plates of meat loaf heaped with mashed potatoes or platters of baked chicken served in a nest of french fries.

One morning when I was working the early shift, Violet came in to dress and paint her fingernails in a large mirrored room just off the display area behind the rack of hard-core magazines. We hollered back and forth across the intervening

17

room while she prepared for work; then she came out, wearing a small G-string, a fringe-covered halter, and a tall red feather attached to a headband. She walked across the room and handed me her large makeup kit. "Honey, do me a big favor and look in the side pouch and see if I brought some little scissors with a curved end. My fingernails are wet and I don't want to ruin them." As she asked, her whole body bobbed up and down and she tried to speed the drying of her fingernails by shaking her hands in the air as though slinging off water. I could not find her scissors, which provoked a mournful plea. "Oh, please find me a pair somewhere. If you do, I'll show you something that's guaranteed to knock your dick hard before you can open your zipper."

Violet reached past me to turn up the volume on the radio, began dancing in the middle of the room, and then, like a trained acrobat, suddenly jumped onto the glass top of the display counter, which I feared might break. I clapped for her new trick and resumed the search for the scissors.

"That's not the surprise, you dumb fart. Look at this." Facing me, only a couple of feet from my eyes, she snatched down her G-string. "What do you think? Do you just love it or what?" There against her well-tanned skin, I saw a mound of flaming red pubic hair cut in the shape of a heart. The color matched her new feather and fingernails. "Lena and I did it last night with hot wax," Violet explained. "It's bound to bring in lots of tips between now and Valentine's Day, unless, of course, all the other girls in the place copy it, like they did those Santa Claus decals I wore on my ass at Christmas." As I complimented her on it, I located a pair of scissors in the drawer beneath the cash register. Even though they were somewhat rusty, she proceeded to use them to trim the bottom point of the valentine slightly. "You know," she continued, "Lena stuck this great little red arrow through it last night, but every time I put on my pants, the damn thing stuck me right in the clit, so I ripped that sucker right out. But it snatched out a couple of pubes with it and messed up the point."

After Violet repaired the damage, she returned the pair of scissors. Still perched on top of the display counter and naked below the waist, she looked me right in the eye and asked, "Do you see anything unusual? Anything at all?"

I looked hard but saw nothing that might be considered unusual on a living valentine. Then she grabbed her inner thighs and pulled them apart for more exposure of her genitals. "How about now?" Finally, she kicked one leg to the right and then the other to the left. "And now?" she repeated.

Satisfied that I saw nothing unusual, she slipped her G-string back on, pulled up her bikini pants, and explained: "I just started my damn period this morning—naturally—and I didn't know if you could see my string or not. Of course, I thought of dyeing it red, too, and letting it just blend in, but I was out of red dye already. You men sure are crazy the way you get so upset by a little pussy blood, especially when you're eating."

Dressed again, Violet jumped from the counter and checked herself in the mirror. Using the long scarlet nail on her little finger, she extracted a dark chunk of food from between her teeth, gathered her kit, and opened the door to leave just as a customer entered. Violet smiled sweetly at him and in a little girl's quizzical voice asked, "Why are you coming in to look at all this paper stuff when you can come over to the Western Beef House and see the real thing?" The man chuckled, embarrassed, and said he'd try to drop by there later in the day. Satisfied with his answer, Violet smiled brightly. "When you come in, be sure to ask for me—Violet—and I'll show you a special surprise for Valentine's," she told him, waved at both of us, and was off to work.

By the time Violet and the other women started their first shift, the construction workers had begun pouring out of the huge building projects engulfing the Strip. They were ready for lunch. Except for special celebrations, when they went to one of the joints for a show and lunch, they usually shied away from places like the Western Beef House because of the high prices. Picking up finger food from the carry-out businesses or bringing their own sandwiches, the workers often congregated on the benches lining the small green median in the center of the street. Instead of yelling at Violet and her friends on stage, they yelled at the women office workers scurrying through the area on their way to pick up lunch or to catch the subway. Some of the women passed regularly enough for the men to note and shout comments on any change in hairstyle or new piece of clothing. Most women ignored them, but the hookers sometimes tore into the guys.

"Hey, stud, how about putting your money where your mouth is!"

"Give those amateurs a break and try a pro."

"My mama always told me that men with big mouths had little dicks."

"Can't you get laid at home, big boy?"

"If you got it, baby, flaunt it; if not, shut up."

Usually the men laughed uproariously, and one of them might retort with his own version of street banter.

When the weather was too wet, too cold, or too hot to sit outside comfortably, the men moved into the porn stores. They took their lunches back to the peeps and watched a show while munching. Despite the noise and excitement they generated in small groups along the street, I never had a construction worker cause trouble in the store. Usually they were sedate, did not talk to one another, and slipped in and out of booths like children in church. Even when some of the local secretaries or other women came into the store, the construction workers always backed away and leered silently.

These "tourist women," as such outsiders were called even when they worked very close to the Strip, had to be watched carefully, for in their naïveté they could easily upset the social equilibrium of the store. The most dangerous situations arose when they wandered into the back room of peep booths, which was reserved for men and the women they brought with them. The store had a strict rule prohibiting unescorted women and transvestites from going to the back. Even though I did not always abide by the rule with Violet and some of her friends, especially during the slow mornings, I did observe the rule carefully with secretarial types and other curious tourist women from outside. Such a woman could easily open the wrong door and incur the wrath of a man or couple in the midst of a sex act. Even more likely, she would be harassed by the men, who assumed that any woman venturing into that world was fair game.

I was careful to prevent such harassment inside the store, but I saw it frequently on the streets. Sometimes it was malicious, as when a group of men surrounded a woman's car and started bouncing it up and down while shouting vulgar propositions at her. At other times it was accompanied by a display of humor, but even the humor had an undercurrent of viciousness and generated real fear.

One afternoon a chartered bus stopped across the street from the Pink Pussy to discharge a load of Catholic high-school girls on a class trip from Boston to the nation's capital. Apparently the driver assumed that a McDonald's so close to the White House must be a perfectly safe site. As soon as the bus stopped, street dudes climbed all over the bus or through the windows like locusts on a wheat wagon. They escorted the young girls into the restaurant, offered them dope, pulled out bottles of alcohol, and tried to get their hotel-room numbers.

The nuns rushed around frantically, pushing some of the young men back out of the bus windows and others through the front door. One fat man in his twenties grabbed a nun by the waist and offered her a drink of something in a paper cup. A transvestite came up to another nun, rubbed the sleeve of her dress, and asked her if it came from Filene's basement. A small crowd of observers gathered, laughing and urging the men on to more outrageous behavior.

The guard from McDonald's came out to help the nuns restore order, but he soon had to go back inside, where the local boys and the visiting girls were now playing hide-and-seek, and the girls were shrieking that boys were in the bathroom with them. Then a police car arrived, the jokes trickled off, the observers wandered on down the street, and order returned. Finally the bus took off toward the White House with all the girls safely aboard with their burgers and fries and a few of the street guys hanging on to the sides and windows.

To make sure that no such madcap activities got started in the back of the Pink Pussy, I adhered to the rule about women in the peeps, even though it was a discriminatory policy. During lunchtime the back was almost exclusively male, since very few men brought in hookers for quick noontime sex. Most men entered the booths alone and left alone after fifteen or twenty minutes. Since Washington is a bureaucratic city and government workers tend to take longer lunch breaks, there was ample time for everyone to get in and out without lines building up in front of the favorite peep shows or customers crowding the aisles. Business stayed brisk from shortly before noon until well after 2:00, but rarely was there a real rush. Most of the people who came in watched the peeps; very little merchandise was sold. Men picked out books or magazines that they asked me to hold for them until after work. Even with the purchases wrapped in a plain brown bag, most men did not want to carry such materials back to their jobs.

By 2:30 in the afternoon, the last of the government workers finished lunch, shopping, and socializing, and returned to work. This began the siesta time on the Strip. Some days I closed the shop long enough to get lunch, or I found somebody to pick up food and bring it back to me. During this time the nude dancers also finished their stints and joined the changing of the guard, which was a miniature version of the early-morning change. Once again handfuls of locals could sit down over coffee, hamburgers, and apple turnovers to talk. But the siesta break was not nearly as relaxed as the early breakfast. Many people had new jobs to hurry off to. Some of the girls merely changed from a shift in one restaurant or bar to a shift in another, or to one of the massage parlors. In between, others rushed home to rest or to pick up their children from school.

I took my lunch back to the shop. Usually I could count on eating it in peace and quiet, but sometimes I felt obligated to share it with one of the men returning from the racetrack. Lou dropped them off in the middle of the afternoon. Those who had had a successful bet on the horses immediately scampered away to celebrate or paused only long enough to repay loans from one of the loan sharks waiting at the store. The men who lost at the track that day were usually eager to share any fries or chips offered from my lunch. Regular horse-racing fanatics could borrow a dollar or two from me, since I knew they would be back to play the horses again and would repay me. If I did not lend them the money, they borrowed larger amounts at exorbitant interest rates from the loan sharks, a group that I never learned to like or trust.

The first wave of government workers on flexible time schedules began leaving their offices around 3:30. They filtered into the Strip gradually, reaching a peak just after 6:30 when the congressional offices closed. Much of the commotion came simply from the heavy auto traffic passing through the area, but many of the commuters were also customers. The men who came into the Pink Pussy, who stopped in at the Texas Beef House, or went into the massage parlors were not the biggest tippers of the day, but they were in many regards the best customers of the day. They came fast, they came regularly, and they left. They did not loiter, nurse slow drinks, browse through books for too long, provoke foreign-policy discussions, or ingest too much alcohol or too many drugs to reach orgasm. Most of the men coming in at this time of day wanted to get home before very late, and they appreciated rapidity and efficiency of service in food, pornography, alcohol, or sex. The folks working the Strip appreciated the same dispatch.

The street corners and traffic circles began filling with two long lines of girls dressed in a pageant of costumes befitting a Hollywood spectacle. Other women modeled in front of the massage parlors and beckoned men inside for nude body rubs. Late afternoon also attracted the male hustlers, their blue-jeans uniforms making them look dull and unimaginative next to the peacock spread of the women. Other young men also went to work as night dancers in two of the restaurants, which switched from nude women by day to nude men at night.

Quickly the afternoon rush became the peak evening hours, and the noise of the Strip turned to high. The barkers in front of the bars shouted louder. The porn stores raised the volume of their radio speakers. More lights were turned on to brighten the marquees, and even the car engines seemed to race more loudly than during the day. The rush-hour automobiles filled with harried but gawking commuters passing through the Strip gave way to the slower cruising cars returning to the city after dinner in the suburbs of Virginia and Maryland.

Only after dark did the pimps and the dope pushers finally arrive, fashionably late. Like lords of the night, the pimpmobiles cruised the city streets and alleys, checking business. In marked contrast to the ostentation of the pimps, the dope sellers descended with great stealth, moving through the night in search of quiet, dark, yet still fairly public places to work. They followed a circuit from the porn stores, where they could meet up on the peep booths, to the back of a parking lot, to the dark edge of the park, over to the deserted lower level of a condemned parking garage, and back to the porn stores again. The fast-food places emitted far too much light for them to do their work; the bars and restaurants had bouncers to keep them out; and by unwritten law of the Strip, they did not crowd the space of the hookers on the street—to do so could upset the whole business basis of the Strip, and in the end hurt their dope trade as much as the legitimate operations.

For a long time I never had reason to know any of the dope pushers. Theirs seemed to be a separate though intertwined world that crossed mine only when they used the back rooms of the shop. I found their aloofness exaggerated, but they caused me little trouble. Then one night a dealer I knew as Dodge, but had never talked to, came in to see me rather than to use the store.

"Look here," he began. "You're always drinking those damn club sodas with Violet's crew, and I need to talk to you about that. You know, people say that anyone who drinks that stuff with nothing in it is either in Alcoholics Anonymous or else queer. What's your story, anyway? You on Antabuse or what?"

"I'm not on anything," I answered, trying to chuckle to conceal my ignorance of Antabuse. Only later did I learn it is a medication used in the treatment of alcoholics that makes them sick whenever they use alcohol.

"You can't tell me that you don't breathe a little smoke sometimes, or maybe take a toot off coke. How about free coke that somebody else pays for? I mean, I know you guys don't make much money in these smut stores, but even you can afford to use some free stuff, can't you? Even Violet gets her share of free dope around."

I continued to smile and shake my head, filling the pauses with inconsequential utterances, but I felt confused and unable to keep up my side of what was supposed to be a conversation. I assumed that he wanted to sell me some drugs and was trying to find out which kind I might want. Sensing that he was not quite communicating with me, Dodge straightened up and switched to a much more serious, almost businesslike tone. "Look here, I've got a buddy who needs some clean piss. He has to report for his urine test tomorrow morning. It's not really important who the piss is from, so long as it has no drug traces and it comes from a man. Have you used any alcohol or any drugs at all for six weeks?"

I shook my head, but tried to do this in a noncommital way because I was unsure whether I should be getting involved in this matter at all. The signal was enough for Dodge, however, who scrambled through the garbage and extricated an only slightly crumpled cup, which he brought over to me. "Could you just fill this about halfway, man?"

"I—er—I went just before you came in," I stalled, trying to make it sound like a confession.

Dodge looked at me imploringly. "Hey, come on, man, this is really important. Like, could you just try! Even a little bit. Do it behind the counter; nobody'll look. If you're shy and all that, I'll stand by the door and keep everybody out. I know how it is, 'cause I get piss-shy when anyone stands too close to me, too."

"Honestly, I just went. You can't get blood out of a turnip, you know."

"Oh, fuck it!" For a moment Dodge looked disheartened, but then he brightened up again. "Hey, dude, I'll get you something to drink. What you want? A cola? Coffee? Root beer? Hey, you like tea, I know. I'll get you tea. Just hold on." With that, he flew out the door and up the street toward Roy Rogers. He returned with iced tea in a container so large it looked more like a milk carton. He set it squarely in front of me on the counter and said, "I'll be back before you close."

True to his word, Dodge returned within two hours, and I

gave him the sealed container filled with fresh, still-warm urine. Looking me straight in the eye as he took it, he asked, "Now you're sure about this, Jack? I mean, you ain't even touched a drop of drink or a gram of any kind of dope at all in six weeks? Of course, I trust you, but this guy is sort of a mean motherfucker and he doesn't want to go back to the penitentiary at all."

So saying, he pointed outside to his double-parked car and the hulking shadow that filled the front seat and darkened the small window on the passenger side. "Not only would he be upset, but his whole . . . well, you know, we don't really mean to say *gang*, but his *associates* would also be pissed. You know, the guys at the far end of the avenue with the big bikers. Nobody likes to get them peeved—certainly not me, anyway."

"I'm clean, I'm telling you. Absolutely clean."

"Not even a little toke after work one night, which maybe you forgot about the next morning? Nothing at all?"

"Look," I said, getting tired of Dodge's questions and not thinking about the future user of my urine and how his friends might or might not like it, "you just come back tomorrow and let me know that he passed just fine, okay?"

"Don't worry. I'll be here tomorrow. This could develop into a nice friendly relationship. It never hurts to have friends." With that, Dodge left, apparently satisfied that I was not lying to him.

Dodge did not return the next day, but word quickly spread around on the Strip that *I* had passed the urine test. Soon I was swamped with too many free iced teas. To avoid the caffeine jitters, I had to pour them out and drink ice water instead. Over the next few months, the urine connection brought me more contacts, more information, and more customers than anything else I ever did on the Strip. Because I did not charge for the urine, people had to take a little more time to cultivate a talking relationship with me, spend time with me at one of the bars, or stop in for a friendly chat at the store. The only problem with my urine was that I was finally drinking so much liquid just to produce urine that people decided it was getting weaker. I did not notice any deterioration, but to preserve its strength, or at least its reputation, I gave out less. This made the people who wanted clean urine all the more anxious to develop a good relationship with me.

The late-night appearance of the drug pushers caused me few problems, but their customers provoked a great deal of aggravation during my tenure at the Pink Pussy. They hung around the porn shops nervously waiting for the next appearance of their contact and pestering me with questions about the whereabouts of Spike, Black Bob, or Toad, or asking if I had seen a green Monte Carlo on the block that night. Sometimes they passed out in the booths, stumbled into customers, or vomited on the floor, but the worst nuisance was their incessant stealing. Even a simple porn book, especially one with a sealed cover, earned them enough to buy some cigarettes or maybe a beer. I soon learned that in dealing with these erratic junkies, I fared best if I led with the stick. Several times I used the stick to force a junkie to return a book or to pull it out from under his jacket. George once chased one all the way down the street to get back a magazine. Generally the junkies did not want any trouble, so they returned stolen goods as soon as they were caught with them. Still, each merchandise inventory revealed a few books or magazines missing from the stock.

If the addicts could not steal from you, they tried to sell stolen goods to you. They disgorged an endless stream of car radios, Sony Walkmans, suitcase-size radios, cassette players, briefcases, car tools, umbrellas, calculators, designer glasses, table silver, telephones, travel clocks, and purses. They always claimed to have color television sets, video equipment, personal computers, stereos, and cameras stashed someplace nearby. At times the Strip seemed like a free port of electronic and leather goods.

A tremendous amount of jewelry and name-brand watches also popped up nightly in the store, but very often they were fakes. The fourteen-karat-gold necklace turned the wearer's neck green in a matter of hours, and the diamond-studded Cartier, Longines, or Seiko watch fell apart within a day. The junkies knew that outsiders would gladly pay $20 or even $30 for such junk, assuming they were buying a stolen original at a fraction of its true value. All too often, even the counterfeit would be stolen by someone else, who then offered it for sale as the genuine article without ever knowing he had stolen a fake.

As the hour grew late, business in the Pink Pussy dwindled. Fewer men entered, and fewer of those who did brought women with them to trick with in the back booths. Most whites retreated into the better-lit main Strip or to their homes, leaving our part of the area to blacks and to the occasional whites safely ensconced in their locked cars. By midnight I began the ritual of closing the now-deserted store. I vacuumed the front area and swept out all the peep booths in back, gathering the debris into large plastic trash bags. I mopped down the floor in each booth, cleaned off the screens and seats, and sprayed a heavy dose of a sickly sweet deodorizer in each booth. I closed out the cash register, calculated the daily sales, arranged $20 worth of change for opening the following morning, and tallied the number of quarters I had given in change to the men entering the peeps.

Having extinguished the marquee and interior lights, I then waited in the darkness by the door with a large plastic bag into which I had dumped all the smaller bags of trash. This was my big crime of the day. I stared across the street past the remaining hustlers and into the interior of McDonald's, searching for the guard. Having locked him firmly in my sights through the plate-glass front of the restaurant, I followed him with my eyes until he was upstairs in the farthest corner of the place. Then I dashed quickly out the door of the Pink Pussy, locking it as I went, and, lugging the large bag of garbage behind me, made my way across the street and into the alley beside McDonald's. I crept through the dark alley carefully, but not so quietly that I startled anyone in the middle of any type of business or transaction. At the end of the alley, I paused to see if any McDonald's employees were outside or if their back door stood open. If all was clear, I dashed over to their large trash dumpster and stuffed my bag of garbage into it as deeply as I could. Mission accomplished, I walked calmly back up the alley and onto the street, where I paused to talk with some of the late-night crowd.

Because the Company was too cheap to pay for garbage service, this routine was a daily part of the job.

On particularly warm nights, when the McDonald's guard liked to stand out in front of the restaurant and talk to the hookers under the guise of watching for double-parking, I sometimes felt trapped forever in the doorway of the Pink Pussy with my bag of trash. But invariably someone saw me at last and managed to distract the guard by playing with his nightstick or complaining loudly about some soggy french fries. I sneaked past them on my mission, but I then owed someone a favor.

Returning to the shop for the last time, I gathered the daily report, money, and credit-card receipts and stuffed them all into a small canvas satchel. Then I switched on the burglar alarm, locked the front door, and walked the four blocks to the all-night store where I turned in my paper work and money. Occasionally I teamed up with someone else for the walk, but usually I made it alone, walking down the very middle of the street. Too many times I had helped clean a bleeding and confused man who had been mugged on one of these streets around the Strip, a hooker who had been knocked in the head by a drunk trick, or a kid who had been grabbed and beaten for no obvious reason by a bunch of other kids. The walk was one of unrelieved darkness along a block with broken streetlights, past boarded-up storefronts, dark alleys, closed shops, and makeshift enclosures fencing off large construction sites. Yet no one ever bothered me on my nightly trek with the money. Perhaps this was because I walked in the middle of the street, or because most regulars on the Strip assumed that I carried a gun, or simply because I was known to work for the Company. I never knew the reason, but I always appreciated it.

Three

SEX WITHOUT PARTNERS

Every day I dispensed from $100 to $300 in quarters for the peep shows. Each customer had to show that he had eight quarters with him; otherwise he had to get that amount in change before entering the peeps. Eight quarters comprised the cost of seeing a sixteen-minute film at the rate of a quarter for each two minutes. The management did not want men going into the booth, becoming excited, and not having enough quarters to finish the film. During the time the customer left the booth for additional change, he might well lose interest or the urge to continue with the show.

No matter how many magazines, expensive dildoes, and sexual toys I might sell in a day, the money never rivaled that of the peeps. Even in this small store, which required only one man per shift to operate it, approximately $6,000 a month passed through the peeps—all of it in quarters. This represented about 12,000 minutes of pornographic film per month.

The importance of the peeps and what they meant to the audience are evidenced less by these statistics than by the debris I cleaned out of the booths at night. I swept out hamburger wrappers, drink cups, sanitary napkins, sperm-filled prophylactics, whiskey bottles, old french fries, ripped hose, syringe needles, bloody underwear, cigarette butts, and small packets of ketchup, mustard, and mayonnaise. The most common items of all were the sperm-coated napkins from Burger King, Kentucky Fried Chicken, and Roy Rogers.

Whenever I turned off the radio in the shop, I heard the constant squishing sounds of men masturbating in the booths. Set against the background whine of the film projectors as they looped the same film through again and again were the sounds of solitary sex: a man breathing harder and sighing almost painfully; another making a slapping sound as he jerked his hand back and forth across his penis. Some customers used commercial lubricants to intensify the feeling and reduce the friction of masturbating. Others used saliva. I quickly learned to differentiate among the sounds.

If listening was not enough for me to know what was happening (and it usually was), I could easily see into the booths. They were open at the top, and surreptitiously placed mirrors permitted me to watch the booth interiors as I sat at the front cash register. Numerous hidden openings for the film projector or the coin-box slots provided new perspectives and angles of vision as I walked the aisle. As dark and seemingly private as the peeps area appeared, it was in truth an open stage for anyone who knew where to look. Some customers also made their own openings from one booth to another, and occasionally an irate man would verbally attack someone he caught spying on him. But for the most part, these customer-devised openings were obvious and easily covered with a raincoat or stuffed with a paper bag by anyone who spotted them.

Through the course of my months at the Pink Pussy, I discovered how varied the act of masturbation is. One of the construction workers, a married man in his late twenties, liked to watch white and black women having sex while he masturbated, using a double-handed grip on his penis similar to the way one holds a golf club. A slightly older man in tie and sport coat masturbated with only one hand while standing facing the screen. A young guy frequently ate his fast-food dinner in the booth, holding his hamburger with one hand and jerking his penis with the other. A thin, middle-aged man enjoyed listening

31

to headphones while sitting completely naked in the booth and rubbing his penis with his open palm. Some men masturbated without removing their penises from their clothing, rubbing them through the cloth or sticking their hands into their pants. Others simply opened their zippers and pulled their penises out. Still others pulled their pants down and fondled the anal area with one hand while masturbating with the other.

The Pink Pussy thrived from the masturbation business. The store provided the place, the privacy, and the visual aids for the male masturbator. But just as people sometimes like to go out to a restaurant and other times prefer a quiet dinner at home, so too could customers at the Pink Pussy consume their pornography on the premises or take it as carry-out. That the magazines were bought primarily to help in masturbation was apparent when the customers referred to them as "jerk-off mags," "cum books," "one-armed reading," "meat beaters," and "squirt books." Occasionally men claimed to look at such books as a prelude to sex with a female, but most men who were willing to talk admitted that the books were sources of visual images used in their solitary sex acts.

The toy section also contained devices that were primarily aids to masturbation. Instead of using his own hand, for example, the customer could use the vinyl opening in one of the inflated female dolls. These dolls came in a variety of racial types with or without acrylic hair attached to the head or the pubic area. Each doll possessed an anal, vaginal, and oral cavity of appropriate size for the user to insert his penis and rub it back and forth. More sophisticated models had electric vibrators and suction pumps to increase the sense of authenticity and to disguise the act of masturbation as something more social.

The mascot of the Pink Pussy was a large rubber head we named Daisy, which always sat on the counter next to the cash register. Daisy had orange-blond hair, blue eyes, and very large, rounded red lips that opened into a nice long throat. Daisy had no body, but coming out of the back of her head was a twenty-inch wire hooked onto batteries and a vibrator. The man who took her home could thrust his penis into her and feel the electrically-induced vibrations. Many nights I talked to Daisy; I became rather attached to her. From time to time I sold replicas of her, but the one sitting on the display counter seemed unique. One night a Salvadoran bought an inflatable doll that proved to be punctured, and when he brought it back, we were out of replacement dolls in that color. So instead he bought Daisy, and I never saw her again.

For the man who did not want to buy the whole body or even a Daisy-style head, we stocked a variety of plastic, rubbery devices that slipped over the hand like a glove and gave it a slight resemblance to a vagina. These, too, came in a variety of skin tones and different shades of acrylic hair. As a rule they looked far less realistic than the male penises lined up next to them.

For the man interested in mechanical devices but reluctant to put his penis into anything electrical, the Pink Pussy offered a vacuum masturbator guaranteed to make the penis grow the more it was used. The device consisted of a large plastic tube, one end of which had a hole large enough for the insertion of the penis. The other end was connected to a small manual pump that created a vacuum in the tube when squeezed. The tugging of the vacuum against the penis alternated with the release of air that flowed over the penis. The faster the man pumped, the quicker the pressure inside rose and fell, stimulating him to ejaculation.

I suspected (but could never be certain) that many of the lubricating creams and lotions sold in the store ended up being used in masturbation as often as in copulation. Certainly many of the men bought the creams and used them there in the booths. Some of the creams carried the warning that they were for external rubbing only and should not be used inside the anus, vagina, or mouth.

We also carried a smaller but still substantial line of female masturbatory devices. Some of them, such as the vibrators and dildoes, could be used either as part of a sexual encounter with a partner or alone in masturbation. Ben wa balls, for example, were small metal balls made to be inserted into the vagina; as the woman walked or moved about, the balls generated sexual sensations. Small battery-powered eggs could be inserted for the same effect. Such devices were much easier to use by oneself than as an adjunct to copulation, but I had no way of knowing how often and in what ways the customers actually employed them.

During my time working at the Pink Pussy, there appeared to be a steady increase in the sale of masturbatory materials. Much of this seemed to correlate directly with the growing fear of AIDS. A minority of men who had frequented prostitutes began doing so less often; instead, they masturbated with a film in the booth. Some men who claimed not to have been users of pornography in the past began buying it as a substitute for sexual encounters that were no longer safe. It was not clear, however, to what extent the fear of AIDS increased masturbation and to what extent AIDS was being used as an excuse for masturbating rather than going out with women. Even if the fear of AIDS was not a direct cause of increased masturbation, it helped men to be less ashamed of the practice. AIDS was bringing masturbation "out of the closet," so to speak.

Other businesses on the Strip, not only the Pink Pussy and the porno stores, catered in varying degrees to masturbation. Pornographic theaters showing a variety of triple-X-rated films twenty-four hours a day functioned as little more than very large peep booths. They offered feature-length pornography on a big screen with all the sound effects of the act and with background music as well. The theaters also supplied much more comfortable seats. By choosing a seat that left ample distance between him and the other customers, each man had adequate space to masturbate alone. Shyer men put a coat or jacket over their laps to give themselves even more privacy.

Some customers go to such theaters primarily *because* of the lack of privacy and for the opportunities they thus offer for exhibitionism. Such customers want to be seen masturbating and sometimes even rise up out of their seats to display their erections more prominently. Because these men take particular delight in showing themselves to women, the theaters usually offer free admission or some other special incentive to attract females into this otherwise male enclave. But in the absence of females, any audience can be acceptable. Sometimes several men in a section of the theater masturbate in unison, like kids on a camping trip. Seeing and being seen is simply one element in the array of sexual thrills many of these customers share.

Theaters have become much more innovative, seeking to compete with high-quality home-video pornography and the sexual channels available on cable and satellite-transmitted television. To keep the customer from masturbating at home in front of the television set, the theaters often supplement the film with live acts performed between screen showings. The customer sees a strip show involving one or more women in much the same kind of performance given by Violet and her co-workers in the restaurants. In the theaters, however, men can masturbate, an act more difficult to accomplish when surrounded by tables of people eating lunch. The dancers in the theaters coax the men on with comments and gestures, but one of the hazards for the women performers who get too close to their audience is that some customers sling sperm from their hands onto the stage. Even if it misses her and lands on the floor, it may cause her to slip while dancing. But if the woman stays too far away, she will not receive any tips from the men. When the man tips the dancer, he may then be able to fondle her and even get her to fondle him, although such contact is strictly illegal.

Some theaters feature live performances by the actual women who star in the film. Thus, after watching a woman's sexual antics on screen, a man can watch her perform in the flesh. Depending on the severity of police surveillance at any given time, two women or a man and a woman may dance together and simulate various sexual acts.

Certain theaters bill themselves as private clubs and charge a membership fee in addition to the admission price. This enables them to present much more explicit performances, since the law traditionally gives more latitude to acts performed "in private." The homosexual theater "clubs" feature naked dancing boys who not only perform sex acts with one another on stage but also allow members of the audience to fellate and fondle them while the other members masturbate.

A customer who enjoys the live shows but does not want to be a part of a public spectacle can choose to be in one of a number of booths surrounding a central stage. As long as he inserts quarters, he can watch through a small window as one or more women perform erotic dances or sex acts. Some booths also have a telephone so that the customer, for an additional fee, can converse with one of the women on the other side of the window. This personalizes her performance for him. Another variation on the same booth has an arm-size hole next to the window, permitting the man to stick in one hand and, provided he offers the performer the appropriate tip, feel her body with one hand while he masturbates with the other. These types of businesses have experienced steady growth with the increased threat of AIDS. They present a relatively clean form of prostitution, allowing the man to come as close as possible to actual copulation and giving him much of the pleasure without the risk of AIDS.

The line between such shows and outright prostitution fades in these encounters, especially when some of the performers work as prostitutes in between acts. Some businesses permit this on-site prostitution as a side income for the poorly paid dancers; others try to keep it to a minimum and make the woman leave the premises with the trick.

Even for the streetwalkers and prostitutes not working in live sex shows, masturbation of the customer, rather than copulation, generates a large part of their business. They frequently use the peep booths in the Pink Pussy to give "hand jobs." The commonest request of all from the male customers, however, was for a blow job. As several women explained to me on repeated occasions, the way they give a blow job makes it just "a wet hand job." The woman grasps the penis with one hand and places her mouth over the head of the penis to keep both penis and hand lubricated with saliva. All the pressure comes from her hand, with an occasional flick of the tongue or kiss of the lips to vary the sensations and simulate a real blow job. As the women themselves admit, they could never have the jaw and lip energy to bring so many men to orgasm in one night. Still, to most of the men, it is a blow job and seems superior to what they can get at home or from their girlfriends. So long as the pressure is tight and wet around the penis, men can rarely tell the difference.

The fastest-growing prostitution market in the mid-1980s, however, comes in the form of sex by telephone. The customer dials a number, gives his credit-card number, and is then connected with a woman who talks through any fantasy he wishes to hear. She pretends to be or do anything that excites him. She will play a mean, domineering mistress, a hurt little girl, or a sex-hungry blonde; or, if he wants, she will shower him with vulgar words or let him shower her with them. Such businesses around the country now have toll-free numbers to encourage long-distance calls from places that lack similar services. The rancher on the outskirts of Bozeman, Montana, whose house is surrounded by three feet of snow in a strong wind at minus fifty degrees, can frolic with a phonemate in Los Angeles and have a fantasy romp with her along the palm-lined beaches of Santa Monica. An aeronautics factory worker in Washington State can have a raunchy talk with an ersatz Dallas Cowgirl cheerleader in Texas. A government worker in Augusta, Maine, can fling for a half-hour with a Puerto Rican girl in New York City, or a Louisiana teacher can indulge his fantasy with a buxom blond Viking woman from Wisconsin. The fantasy potential seems limitless, but at heart the only real sex act involved is masturbation by the solitary male at his end of the phone. Like sex with Daisy, the voice on the phone is merely a prop that helps the man pretend that he is doing something more than merely masturbating.

All societies known to anthropology have apparently practiced at least some masturbation. Ancient Peruvian pottery depicts it, as do Japanese woodprints, West African carvings, and prehistoric European cave paintings. Virtually every study ever made, however, indicates that the rate of masturbation appears to be much higher in the Western industrialized nations, particularly in the United States, than in any of the traditional or primitive societies. Even in the numerous non-Western societies in which masturbation is openly encouraged in children, the rates for adults seem to be lower. Only in the West does masturbation seem to function as a major source of sexual gratification for other than a very small minority of adults. As the natives of the Trobriand Islands explained to Bronislaw Malinowski, only very ugly people or albinos need to masturbate.

Many factors underlie this adoption of masturbation by adults in Western society, among them child-rearing practices and sex-training techniques. The ways in which young people learn about sex and their initial sexual experiences determine in part how they experience it later in life and what kinds of sexual experiences they will enjoy. The methods used in North America and northern Europe today contrast starkly with the traditional methods of child training in many other societies. Just how great the differences can be and just how important they are for children in various societies can be seen by comparing Western techniques with those used in a much simpler society. The range of diversity in the ways in which a society produces sexual adults is shown by contrasting the very repressive approach of the West with the very permissive approach of a people such as the Muria, a tribal group living in scattered villages of east central India.

At dusk in the Muria villages, mothers call in their children while husbands return home from the fields for the evening meal. The young people then gather in their own special house, called a *ghotul*, where they sing, dance, and flirt in much the way any group of adolescents might do anywhere in the world. As the evening proceeds, boys and girls begin to give one another massages with special oils that they rub all over the body. The massages slowly turn into more intimate touching and feeling of the other's body, and if both agree, they make love, or spend the night just caressing each other, or sleep snuggled closely together. The next night the scenario remains the same, but each person finds a new partner for the night's activities, thus ensuring that no one is ever left out or that one couple does not spend too much time together.

The *ghotul* is a significant part of Muria life and education.

For the parents, it helps keep adolescent children out of the house and out of mischief. The parents then have privacy and can devote themselves to the younger children and to each other.

For the adolescent, the *ghotul* provides a constant source of entertainment with friends and a tremendous amount of pleasure. It is also a training ground for marriage and for becoming a good sex partner. From singing and dancing on through massages and tickling to petting and coitus, the sexual sequence assumes an organized format that adolescents learn in its entirety. Slowly and step by step, they learn to make love and all the arts that are a part of it. They learn it by doing it, without the need for locker-room jokes, fumbled attempts in the back seat of a car, or years of frustrated curiosity.

Among the Muria, the older adolescents teach the younger ones. This usually means that the older female instructs the younger male. Before she is ready for coitus, the young girl learns her own body by inserting her fingers into her vagina and slowly stretching it. Then, when she feels ready to copulate, she takes the initiative, but lovemaking includes much more than mere copulation. Etiquette requires that on the first night of sleeping together, a couple not copulate; instead, each must get to know the other's body. They learn every curve and crevice of the partner's anatomy and how the other person responds to different types of touches. How quickly does he become erect, and how long does he maintain it? How much does she lubricate? Does she like to have her thighs massaged with oil? Does he like to have his nipples flicked with the tongue?

During this process, the younger ones also watch older couples discreetly for more information, and thus they slowly acquire the necessary knowledge. In the end everyone knows everything that everyone else knows, but each new element has been learned in its own time and at its own pace. Because the female always sets the pace, the male always follows. Thus, the boys work hard to attract the attention of the girls. A boy spends time frizzing his hair and attaching feathers to it; he bathes frequently and hangs bells from his body. Because beauty is seen primarily as being a part of motion, the bells are used to call attention to the way the boy moves and thereby attract the admiration of the older females.

The first time a boy penetrates a female, he does it gradually as part of the play and the rubbing together of bodies; but this does not necessarily lead to complete copulation. Similarly, for the girl, there is no dramatic first experience, no bleeding, and no sudden tearing of the hymen. As the couple progresses to full intercourse, the female lies on the bottom and wraps her legs around the boy. In this fashion, her legs push and pull slightly on his body and thus direct him and help keep him in the appropriate rhythm. The sexual act is never complete until the female as well as the male is satisfied. No matter how much the male enjoys it, he must never lose sight of the injunction that he owes the female pleasurable intercourse for her labor in menstruation and in childbirth. Because God gave women those labors, He also gave women the right to complete sexual satisfaction from the male.

Even though there is some rivalry among the males to be chosen by various females and to be popular and good lovers, the system works against competition. No couple may spend more than a few nights together; then they are expected to change partners. This rotation of partners allows each male and each female to know each in turn, thus preventing anyone from being neglected and ensuring that everyone has an opportunity to learn from everyone else. No one is to be left in ignorance. By the same token, every male-female relationship among unmarried people is expected to be sexual. The concept of a platonic relationship between a boy and a girl amuses the Muria. As their proverb says, "Thirst is not quenched by licking dew."

The Muria consider it bad for young people *not* to have sex, and for them teenage pregnancy does not seem to be a problem. Despite the possibilities of pregnancy, other issues are more important. In their explanation of the world, sex is a powerful force, and if it is stored too long inside the person, it may emerge in strange and harmful ways. To prevent such harm, sexual desires need to be exercised constantly. The *ghotul* meets the sexual needs of all the unmarried individuals; after marriage, copulation should be with one's mate only.

When the time comes, the families arrange the marriages of the young people. Occasionally a couple gets to know each other so well in the *ghotul* that they insist on being married, but research shows that in the long run these marriages are not as durable as those arranged by the parents. For the couple in the arranged marriage, both divorce and adultery are virtually unknown. Each spouse is already well trained in how to be a good mate, and each understands his or her duty toward sex as well as toward other domestic tasks and responsibilities. Just as important, there is no mystery in sex. Both partners have had sex with all the other people of their age in the community, thus there is no alluring mystery as to what someone else may be like in bed. Nor is there any great difference in sex partners, since they have all learned the same things. Young people leave the *ghotul* confident of their own abilities and knowing that everyone else is about equally competent. They do not need to search for better sex partners than the ones they marry.

The educational experience of the Muria contrasts vividly with the experience of an adolescent in industrial society. Rather than learning about the body with a partner surrounded by other couples, the contemporary youth learns about it alone, and often in the bathroom or bedroom. At about the age of thirteen or fourteen, the average American boy does not have an older girlfriend to guide him gingerly through the various phases of lovemaking. Instead, he is at home alone, finding what sensual pleasures he can in the bathtub stroking his genitals. Rather than learning how to massage someone with different types of oil, he learns how it feels to masturbate with shampoo versus soap or his mother's hand cream.

In due time, his explorations and fondling of himself lead to his first orgasm. Some boys already know what to expect from having talked to other guys about masturbation or from seeing others do it. For many, however, the first orgasm is a shock, in which a mass of white goo shoots out of the penis, and the penis then goes limp and hurts when touched; all the good feeling is gone. Remembering his solitary ignorance, one man described the feeling of his first adolescent ejaculation as having shot out the marrow of his bones and thinking that he would probably die. Another feared he had broken his penis from rubbing it too much, and that the sperm was probably composed of his white blood cells.

Such misconceptions do not last long, of course. The boy lives, and within another day, if not hours, his penis works just fine again. From a book, or more likely from a friend, he learns that what happened to him happens to all guys, and that it will happen again and again.

For the young girl, no such orgasmic trauma is likely to occur. From fingering, rubbing, or squeezing her genitals, she discovers the diverse pleasurers they offer, but she does not have the problems of erection or ejaculation to contend with. She also has the opportunity to masturbate in more varied ways than the young males. She can get a thrill from sitting on top of the washing machine as it spins, from sliding down the banister, or from riding a horse or on the back of a large dog. She can stimulate her genitals with her hand, by flexing her thighs, by sitting on the heel of her foot, or by using any number of objects.

In time, both the young boy and the girl develop their own habitual masturbation styles, whichever most easily brings them to orgasm. This masturbatory act becomes the primary mode of sexual satisfaction for the typical adolescent during the five to ten years before a full-time sexual liaison develops with another person. For boys, the waiting period will be three to four years longer than for the typical girl. This extended period of adolescent masturbation is the primary sexual training ground for people in industrial societies.

What the young boy or girl learns is to please himself or herself and to read his or her body. Each acquires sexual habits that will have an enduring influence on all later sexual interactions. Through masturbation, the male learns to respond to the very tight stimulus of the hand, which is quite different from the looser flesh inside the vagina. He also learns to be quick. The aim of masturbation is orgasm, and because the child is always threatened with the angry voice of his mother at the bathroom door, or with his father catching him "playing with himself" between the sheets, he learns to be fast about it. Once learned, this habit is hard to break, even when he might want to train himself to slow down. While the Muria boy learns through several years of practice in the *ghotul* to sustain coitus until the female is satisfied, the American boy learns merely to rush through the act and get to the climax as quickly as possible.

Masturbation is also a physiological process that accustoms one to a certain procedure. The muscles, blood vessels, and nerve cells of the body become fine-tuned for a repetitive process, to the point where the average person has a tremendous amount of difficulty if he or she tries to masturbate with the left hand after learning to do it with the right. Whereas the simple switch from right-handed to left-handed masturbation proves very difficult, the Muria, by contrast, learn to reach orgasm with a wide variety of partners, each having a slightly different physiology and slightly different pattern of movement. Muria youths learn coitus and may occasionally masturbate, but Western youths learn masturbation even though they may occasionally have coitus.

Years of masturbation by the American female can lead to numerous difficult adjustments when she begins regular copulation. She must switch sexually from rubbing her clitoris, the most common form of masturbation, to having a penis inserted in the vagina. Manual or oral stimulation of the clitoris by her partner may or may not supplement the act of intercourse, but the shift is still a major one. The two experiences—solitary sex versus sex with a partner—are very different, and the transition is sometimes difficult to complete successfully. By contrast, women in societies such as the Muria learn from the beginning to reach orgasm with penetration.

Often American adolescents go through a period of heavy petting, in which the couple rubs against each other and manipulates one another's genitals while kissing. Frequently, a teenage girl will masturbate her boyfriend or even allow him to penetrate her with a finger, but the couple may choose not to engage in complete coitus. Through these noncopulatory sex acts, common among adolescents, each person does learn something about the partner and something about sex as a social act. Still, the orgasm, when it occurs, frequently comes through masturbation or rubbing of the genitals rather than through coitus. Even if the hand belongs to the other person, the act is still masturbation. This heavy emphasis on non-copulatory acts has also become institutionalized in Western societies for adults. It serves as a prelude to copulation and thus often goes under the name of "foreplay," as if the act of copulation somehow required a warm-up period.

During the initial years of adulthood, when coitus is new, the novelty of the act may be enough to overcome the problems of changing from masturbation to copulation, but in time problems arise. As the female's vagina becomes less firm and tight with age, her partner may experience greater difficulty maintaining an erection or attaining an orgasm. Problems of impotence, premature ejaculation, and lack of orgasm may all be connected with the early form of solitary sex training.

Whereas the Muria and many other tribal people learn to copulate or to make love at an early age, people in industrial society learn to masturbate and to fantasize. Particularly for males, fantasy becomes an integral part of sex, and the fantasy often settles on pornographic images such as those for sale in the Pink Pussy. Through the years of adolescent masturbation, the young man becomes more accustomed to responding to such images than to real flesh. Even when real flesh is available, it rarely comes up to the standards of his favorite fantasy. A man may then find himself relying on fantasies during coitus as well as during masturbation. Whether aroused through his own hand or through the vagina of a partner, the man's primary stimulation often continues to come from the images dancing behind his eyelids.

Western society devised pornography as a means of sustaining and elaborating upon the fantasies that are so important in the solitary sexual lives of modern industrial people. Many societies—from Japan, India, and Peru to ancient Rome and Egypt—developed erotic arts that some people might consider pornography, but in these societies sexually explicit pictures and pottery were not used as an aide to masturbation but to stimulate the desire for coitus, frequently with religious overtones directed toward fertility. Pornography even of this type has little place in a society such as the Muria, where adolescents learn about sex as a social act from an early age and thus have no need to develop the art of solitary masturbation and the fantasies that induce it.

Working in the Pink Pussy, I was surprised to learn that many of the men to whom I doled out all those quarters each night expressed a dislike for pornography in general although they sought one variety of it in particular. The man who could not have an orgasm without looking at big breasts ignored everything else in the store. Another, who fantasized about blond pubic hair, showed no interest in big breasts unless they happened to be on a woman who also had blond pubic hair. The man who liked pictures of transvestites thought that the customer who bought pictures of young men was sick, and the men who liked bondage had no common interest with the men who wanted the soft-core magazines. Often it seemed that the men who liked to read written stories had little interest in the picture magazines. Each man had a narrow range of fantasy and showed interest only in the precise kind of pornography that sustained this fantasy; as far as he was concerned, the rest was trash. There were no connoisseurs of pornography as a whole, no little old men in raincoats who got equal thrills from bondage, incest, and interracial rape. Even within the extreme monotony of pornography, there was a marked specialization of fetishes and fantasies that kept the users separate and isolated in their antisocial pleasures.

Pornography is a fetish, or a collection of fetishes. As such it is simply a very explicit aid to fantasy and thereby to masturbation.

Four

THE NEWEST VICE

In contrast to the major role that masturbation plays in the sex lives of contemporary Westerners, it appears to have been of far less importance even in the West until about 200 years ago. From the beginning of art, and later the invention of writing, in the Mediterranean area, much interest was shown in the topics of copulation, virginity, circumcision, adultery, and castration, but masturbation received only scant attention. When it was mentioned or depicted at all, it was given little emphasis.

The great physician Hippocrates, for example, recorded information about a large number of sexual concerns, but he mentioned masturbation only in pointing out that young boys tug on or play with their genitals a great deal, a practice that he thought might stem from kidney stones and painful urination. Hippocrates maintained that young girls do not do this because they have large urethras and can more easily pass off sediments that might otherwise build into kidney stones.

With the strong Greek penchant for commenting on, analyzing, dissecting, satirizing, and categorizing all aspects of human life, including a great deal of attention to sexual subjects, it seems likely that masturbation would have found a more significant place among Greek medical texts, philosophical treatises, codes of law, or theatrical productions, unless, of course, it simply did not occur very often. In fact, the Greeks probably had ample opportunities for sexual encounters without recourse to self-help. From the beginning of sexual development, young men had access to servant girls, harlots, hetaerae, and slaves. In addition, a boy probably had older boys or men showing sexual interest in him, and he may have had relationships with them or with other boys younger than himself. With so many sources of sexual gratification and sexual activity beginning at so young an age, it seems likely that masturbation did not figure very importantly in the sexual development of Greek males.

According to both literary and archaeological evidence, masturbation may have been much more common for females among the ancient Greeks. A large number of dildoes, called *olisbos* in Greek, were "made either of wood or padded leather and had to be liberally anointed with oil before use." Literary references to these objects were frequent, usually comical, and derogatory. The widespread practice of female masturbation probably arose from the unusual situation in which a society glorified the love of boys over the love of women.

Unlike the Greek writings, ancient Christian and Jewish scriptures are virtually silent on the topic of masturbation. In the eighteenth century, when masturbation began to emerge in the West as a topic of growing importance, clerics had to devise some very elaborate interpretations of biblical language in order to condemn the practice. The Bible clearly sets forth strong condemnations of and punishments for a variety of sexual acts, such as fornication, adultery, homosexuality, prostitution, incest, bestiality, coitus interruptus, and variations on these acts, but masturbation is never even alluded to. In order to condemn it, clerics extended the biblical condemnation of Onan's ejaculating outside his wife's body to condemn masturbation as well.

According to the account in the thirty-eighth chapter of Genesis, Onan had to copulate with Tamar, his brother's widow. In the patriarchal society of the Jews, a wife belonged to her husband's patrilineage, and if her husband died, she was passed on to his next oldest brother in a system known as the levirate. This remains the custom of a number of pastoral patrilineal people today, such as the Nuer tribesmen of the Sudan.

Onan, however, rebelled against this, since any children he helped Tamar to conceive would be acknowledged as the children of his dead brother and not as his own.

> Onan knew that the seed would not be his, and it came to pass, when he went in unto his brother's wife, that he spilled it on the ground, lest he should give seed to his brother. And the things which he did displeased the LORD: whereupon he slew him also. (Gen. 38, 9, 10.)

When the clerics of the eighteenth century noticed the lack of a biblical condemnation for what they knew must be a sin, they deduced that the sin of Onan included masturbation as well as this form of birth control. By contrast, traditional Jewish interpretations have insisted that Onan died for violating the levirate, not for masturbation or for coitus interruptus. In 1727, Ephraim Chambers published the first *Cyclopaedia* or *Universal Dictionary of Arts and Sciences,* in which he listed the sin under "Onania" and "Onanism." He noted these were new words, "terms which some late empirics have framed, to denote the crime of self-pollution."

The "late empirics" mentioned by Chambers probably refers to the 1710 booklet *Onania, or the heinous Sin of Self-pollution, and all its frightful Consequences in both Sexes Considered,* by an anonymous clergyman. The booklet went through nineteen English editions, as well as French and German translations. The religious denunciation of the practice of onanism was soon followed by a thorough scientific and medical denunciation by the Swiss physician Samuel Auguste André David Tissot, who wrote a whole treatise against it in the 1760s. With both science and religion using the new term and condemning the practice, masturbation soon became the primary root of most evil.

The newly found vice of onanism was, of course, not new, but it was becoming much more common, particularly in the century that followed these writers. The changes brought by industrialization made the issue more acute. The later age of marriage, increased sexual segregation in work, longer schooling, grueling apprenticeships, the separation of individuals from their families and their removal from their rural communities to cities were all aspects of the Industrial Revolution that increased the frequency of masturbation. Deprived of other sexual outlets, young people, especially males, turned more and more to sexual self-satisfaction. Thus, a practice that was of minimal importance in primitive society, and of almost as little significance in agricultural society, suddenly became a major source of sexual gratification in industrial society.

From approximately the middle of the nineteenth century until the eve of World War I, European and American society experienced paroxysms of antimasturbation hysteria. Convinced that their children would go insane, grow hair on their palms, catch tuberculosis or cancer, or possibly become murderers, parents and doctors experimented with a bevy of concepts and techniques designed to stop the pernicious act of masturbation. Almost every aspect of child rearing and child training, from the way children ate and slept to what they wore and said, was modified to protect the child from masturbation. As recently as 1918, the Children's Bureau of the United States Department of Labor issued a pamphlet telling parents that infants and small children should sleep in nightclothes with extra-long sleeves that could be pinned to the bedding to keep them from fondling their genitals. The legs of their sleepwear should also be pinned to the sheets or tied to opposite sides of the crib so that children would not rub or flex their legs against their genitals and thus accidentally discover masturbation.

Doctors also decided that children should sleep on their backs to prevent the genitals from rubbing against the mattress, and children past infancy were made to sleep with their hands outside of the covers to guard against fondling. This very awkward sleeping position still appears regularly as the appropriate position for children in Hollywood films and television programs, although children in reality do not sleep that way.

In addition to these elementary techniques, approximately

two dozen antimasturbation devices were registered in the United States Patent Office between 1861 and 1932. The simpler ones were nothing more than large penis rings with needles, spikes, or saw teeth attached to the interior of the ring. Fitted around the penis, the ring caused only minor discomfort to the boy so long as he did not rub his hand against his penis, roll over on his stomach or side when in bed, or (worst of all) get an erection; the erect penis immediately pushed into the teeth or pins of the ring. The use of any of these devices assumed, of course, that there was no such thing as a "spontaneous erection" during the night and that all erections were based on the conscious or unconscious attempt of boys to seek physical pleasure. Some boys simply learned to endure the pain as the price of pleasure, and in time some of them came actually to enjoy the pain as a pleasurable aspect of sex.

With the invention of the galvanization process, a rust-proof safety pin was patented that could safely be used to pin the foreskin closed over the head of the penis, protecting it from direct stimulation by the hand or any other object. Every few days the pin had to be removed and reinserted into a fresh wound; otherwise the old wound might become insensitive to pain and thus no longer be an effective preventive of masturbation.

These devices were made primarily for children and for the insane, but there were others to be used for both adults and children. Male and female versions of the chastity belt proved effective contraptions for keeping the hands away from the genitals. Even with openings for the elimination of bodily wastes, however, the belts were not very sanitary. Another simple device sealed the penis inside a splint that opened at the end to allow urination but kept the sensitive organ separated from the hand by a sheath of wood, metal, and cloth. The tight construction also prevented the penis from becoming erect.

The medical community seized every new technological development and tried to harness it to the service of humankind through the prevention of masturbation. Electricity quickly found a variety of innovative uses. One electric invention rang a bell if the penis erected during the night; this warned the endangered wearer and his entire family of the perilous situation. Another invention reversed the flow of current to give an electric shock to the offending organ as soon as it started to erect. Special electric nozzles were manufactured to be inserted into the anus and into the urethra of both men and women, where the full impact of the shock could be focused on the most sensitive parts of the body. These devices served a moral as well as medical function by punishing the sinner who came close enough to the act to become sexually excited.

Indirect descendants of these early forms of therapy survived into the twentieth century in a variety of guises. Electric shocks became a standard part of aversion training for rats running a maze as well as for patients trying to overcome sexual abnormalities of various types. At the other end of the theoretical continuum in psychological thought from these Skinnerian models, shock treatment applied to the brain and the entire body became a standard and often misused treatment in psychiatric institutions. Electric shocks to the genitals and other areas of the body are also still used throughout the world by authoritarian regimes and terrorists to torture political prisoners.

These mechanical devices were used throughout the West, but in America the quest to prevent masturbation also focused on diet. Sylvester Graham of West Suffield, Connecticut, set about reforming the whole nutritional basis of American society as a way to prevent masturbation and other sexual "diseases." In addition to the elimination of alcohol, Graham advocated the use of a very coarsely ground whole-wheat flour to cure masturbation. Marketed under the name of Graham flour, it is still widely used in the United States today and is best known as the primary ingredient of the graham cracker, which remains a favorite of small children. Between 1834 and 1848, Graham's book on the medical and moral problems arising from such sexual practices and indulgences as masturbation went through ten editions, but the twentieth century has not been as kind to Graham's book as to the crackers made with his flour.

Later the search for foods for children that would prevent an unwholesome interest in sex led to the notion that they should eat more cold foods than warm ones. Hot porridges, grits, and similar breakfast foods heated the body and thus induced thoughts of sex and lust. To avoid this, new breakfast cereals were developed to be eaten with cold milk and thus keep the children's thoughts away from sex. These cold cereals were fortified with extra vitamins and nutrients to further enhance children's health. Despite the changes in diet, however, youngsters continued to masturbate and still managed to grow into the tallest generations in recorded history, proving that masturbation does not stunt growth.

During the nineteenth century, surgery became a rapidly growing area of medicine. The invention of new antiseptics and anesthesia, together with the copious experience provided to surgeons by the numerous wars of that century, made surgery much less hazardous and more efficient. When not using their skills on battle casualties, doctors looked among the civilian population for new diseases to which they might apply this recently improved form of treatment. Masturbation, being one of the major "diseases," quickly came to mind. Around the year 1858, the clitoridectomy was introduced in London as a way of preventing masturbation in females as well as precluding excessive sexuality in adult women. The less radical forms of clitoridectomy involved slicing off only the clitoris or possibly just the sensitive tip. Variations and elaborations of the operation removed sensitive tissue from the labia as well. Cauterization of the clitoris and labia, as well as of the inner thighs, were all utilized for the eradication of masturbation.

To supplement clitoridectomies, infibulation was introduced: Both sides of the labia were sewn together, closing off access to the clitoris and the vagina, and leaving only a small opening for the discharge of urine and menstrual blood. A variation of infibulation was tried on males: The foreskin was stitched together much like the labia. Some men persisted in having erections, thus ripping open the stitches, while some of the females were so sex-crazed that they tore through the stitches in the labia in order to rub the clitoris or stimulate the vagina. This called for even more drastic measures. Medical science next introduced the technique of scraping the two sides of the labia, or of the interior part of the foreskin on the male, and letting the raw tissue grow together. Thus, the clitoris and vagina of the female were hidden by a long scar that sealed them shut, and the male penis was permanently encased behind the foreskin. For the male who persisted and tore through the scar tissue, a portion of the head of the penis was cut away, and in truly extreme cases the entire penis was amputated on the assumption that it was better for such people not to reproduce anyway.

Surgeons then began to look for new ways to prevent masturbation from ever beginning, in the belief that once it started, it was almost impossible to stop. Thus, female clitoridectomy was extended from being a cure for women who masturbated to being a preventive for girls who had not yet done so.

While clitoridectomy was a logical preventive for the female, no logical preventive for the male was immediately available until some unknown innovator thought to borrow circumcision from the Jews and Moslems, who practiced it for religious reasons. It was reasoned that exposing the head of the penis would toughen it and make it less sensitive. Masturbation techniques for uncircumcised boys usually involve grasping the foreskin in the hand and rubbing the foreskin back and forth across the head of the penis. The hand clutches the foreskin but does not touch the head of the penis directly. It was assumed that without this foreskin, the male would not be capable of masturbating.

Circumcision of males also solved a hygienic difficulty. Boys were not allowed to wash the foreskin, because the act of washing might generate sinful feelings in the boy and lead him to discover masturbation. Without a foreskin, however, the whole problem of cleanliness was solved. Smegma—the secretions that can accumulate beneath the foreskin—did not have the chance to collect, and the boy did not need to retract the foreskin in order to wash the genitals.

In 1870 approximately 8 percent of the males in the United States were circumcised—mostly among the upper classes, who could afford medical attention and could thus indulge in this new fad. By 1910 the figure had risen to 56 percent, having spread from the upper to the middle class, which historically has had a penchant for adopting anything that improves hygiene and promotes sexual morality. The increased popularity of circumcision was due partly to the publication in 1891 of the medical text *Circumcision as Preventative of Masturbation,* and partly to the propaganda efforts of the Orificial Surgical Society. Formed in 1890 principally to promote genital surgery as a way of preserving mental and physical health, the group operated for forty years, during most of that time affiliated with the American Medical Association, but publishing its own journal. The rate of circumcision continued to climb until recent years, when it seems to have reached a peak somewhere above 80 percent of all males in the United States.

The circumcision fad also swept through the other English-speaking nations: Great Britain, Canada, New Zealand, South Africa, and Australia. In Canada and Australia the rates probably never reached a full majority of the males, and in the mid-1970s hovered around 44 percent. The figure in Great Britain today has dropped to around 1 percent of the males, and except for those who practice it for religious reasons, these are mostly upper-class males since the National Health Service no longer pays for it as a routine procedure as it does in Canada.

The widespread acceptance of circumcision in the United States is attributed partly to the fundamentalist Christianity practiced in large parts of the country. Because such sects interpret the Bible literally, they believe that what God told the Jews in Genesis remains valid today, so that circumcision should be an important part of Christian practice. Even Catholic immigrants from mainland Europe, where the practice was never widespread, found it easy to have their sons circumcised when told to do so by physicians in their new country. After all, Christ had been circumcised, and the Catholic church still celebrates the holy day of that circumcision. Moreover, the foreskin of Jesus was the only piece of his body that did not ascend into heaven, and thus the only relic of his earthly existence he left behind. Circumcision was a practice that was not inconsistent

54

with some of the Catholic immigrants' beliefs, and if circumcision made the child more American, most parents did it gladly.

Today circumcision is the most commonly performed surgical procedure in the United States. In one century it has grown from a practice limited to some tribal and religious groups, such as Jews and Moslems, to being the norm in the United States, New Zealand, and among the whites of South Africa, and is common in Canada and Australia.

However, circumcision is no longer considered a preventive of masturbation, and masturbation is no longer viewed as the cause of insanity, epilepsy, cancer, or anything else. This does not mean that the medical and paramedical professions have lost interest in masturbation; on the contrary, masturbation is now trumpeted as a cure for everything from headaches to all types of sexual dysfunctions. "Inorgasmic" women are taught to masturbate or to allow their mates to masturbate them as a way of becoming "orgasmic." Instead of selling devices to prevent masturbation, most major department stores and drugstores stock a full array of vibrators to facilitate it. Manuals and pamphlets explain to parents that it is acceptable behavior, and other pamphlets explain how to do it and not feel sinful or guilty.

American pornography not only caters to an audience of masturbating men but frequently features pictures of women masturbating. Erotic drawings, sculpture, and pottery in other societies usually focus on the coital act, depicting lovers in some form of embrace, or preparing for it. By contrast, American pornography shows women fondling their genitals, rubbing the labia or clitoris, or inserting objects such as a finger or a vibrator into the vagina. Most of the short pornographic films in the Pink Pussy showed nothing more than a woman masturbating. Some of the longer video tapes showed no more than this either, and even those that included other sex acts usually featured at least one long masturbatory sequence. Most cultures of the world would find this funny, silly, sad, or embarrassing, but they would not find it sexually stimulating.

One of the younger customers in the Pink Pussy explained why he wanted to see only pictures of women fondling themselves alone. "If there is a man in the picture with her, I can't really relate to her. He is some kind of a rival or something in the way and she prefers him over me. But if she only has her finger, then I figure that I am what she really wants, and I can get off on that." So he masturbates while looking at pictures of women who masturbate.

An Italian anthropologist remarked to me that it is only natural that people who like to jog as much as Americans do would also like to masturbate. Italians, he explains, would get too lonely doing either because Italians always need someone to talk to; therefore they prefer to play soccer and have babies.

The lone runner, shutting off the rest of the world with earphones, symbolizes much of the narcissistic self-absorption of our society, as do so many current sports, from wind and water surfing through hang gliding and scuba diving. This same theme is reflected in the ubiquitous teenager hunched over a video game; in the long line of commuting cars each carrying only one person; and in the condominium canyons filled with a warren of minute residences for one. In such a culture, it is not surprising to find so many stores like the Pink Pussy catering to the customer seeking quick, efficient, but solitary sexual enjoyment with no interpersonal fuss or bother.

Five

CHRONIC PELVIC LOCK
AND THE MODERN MAN

"The biggest problem with you gringos is that you do not know how to make love with the tongue," Evita, one of the Mexican women working the Girls Forever Massage Parlor, announced one afternoon.

"You mean they don't have a good technique?" I asked.

"Technique, technique, why you North American men always so worried about technique? 'Hey, honey, you like my technique?' That's what they all say to me. Or, 'Baby, I bet you don't have this kind of technique over in Vietnam or wherever you from.' They are all crazy about technique. They think you can learn how to make love from a book, like playing a computer or something. No, I don't mean technique. I mean what I said: American men do not know how to make love with the tongue." And she flicked her tongue between her bright orange lips. "I didn't say 'fucking with the tongue,' I said 'making love with the tongue.' Don't you know the difference? You make love with your tongue, with words; you fuck with your cock. You understand?"

Evita explained that a Latin man always says beautiful words to a woman, even to a prostitute. It makes her feel good, and it makes her enjoy making love to him, even though he may not otherwise be very attractive. The American man talks about himself. "Even when he comes, he always says, 'I am coming, I am coming, I am coming.' Why all the time this *I, I, I?* Why can't he say, 'You are beautiful,' 'You make me so happy,' 'You are wonderful in my arms'?"

"Because a woman would laugh at him?" I ventured hesitantly.

"That's probably true; the American woman doesn't even want to make love either. Everybody just wants to come all the time, and nobody here wants to make love. That's why when I get enough money, I am going to retire back to Mexico with my son and find a nice Mexican man to love me. No way I could ever marry a gringo, never."

Evita's criticisms were shared by a large number of foreign women working on the Strip. Americans don't talk as a part of sex, except to give an instant replay of the good parts. Americans talk mostly about themselves. Men and women talk about their careers, their investments, their exercise programs, their vacations, and the problems with their ex-spouses. If they are not speculating about the real-estate market, they are explaining how they "got things together" and changed from an uncaring, insensitive person to someone "in touch with personhood and personal feelings." This approaches what one American hooker called "playing in psychological vomit." Yet, to very many Americans, this is the ultimate intimacy.

In the recent past, women accepted this talk as part of the price of courtship; duty demanded that they listen and pretend interest in a man's sports, his job, his ideas, his car. The feminist consciousness-raising of the past two decades has changed this radically: Now both men and women demand equal time to discuss themselves.

The pragmatic side of American culture has always rejected the European tradition of "love talk," poetry, and baroque compliments. The whole thing seemed foppish, effeminate, and it reeked of silly aristocrats with too much leisure time. American lovemaking patterns rose in imitation of Clark Gable forcibly carrying Vivien Leigh up the stairs to the bedroom, of cowboys, swashbucklers, and men of adventure who were not good with words, but, when the time came, were able to move to satisfy those deep, unnamed stirrings within the heart and groin. With the steady dissemination of images like these, and with the triumph of America in two world wars, Europe abandoned much of its traditional lovemaking with words to follow the more taciturn style of the celluloid cowboys.

Evita was the only woman on the Strip to lecture me on the paucity of words in American lovemaking. The other women, both North American and foreign, were less concerned with what their partners said. But a consistent comment by the foreign women, whether from Thailand, Brazil, West Africa, or the Caribbean, was that North Americans were cold. Sometimes this was expanded to Anglo-Saxons in general and to Germans and Scandinavians. All of them were characterized as not smiling or laughing enough, and they were accused of not touching enough.

"Even American children are cold; you cannot grab one up in the store or rub his cheeks or his head, because he will cry and the mother will throw something at you." Violet's former roommate from Brazil explained, "In my country, everybody loves to touch and play with the children. I can kiss anybody's baby, even if I do not know them already. And the babies in my country like that very much. The babies here are so afraid that they cry if somebody touches them."

Another woman pointed out one day that only in America do people put bumper stickers on cars to tell other people to hug their children. According to her, everybody else in the world does that from instinct. Americans have to be told to do it, and still they forget it.

Anthropological research on child-rearing practices certainly supports the observation that Americans and northern Europeans do not touch as much as most other people in the world. Children in more primitive parts of the world spend most of their first few years in virtually constant contact with another body. They sleep in the mother's arms or cuddled next to her at night. They spend the day riding on her back or in a sling on her hip. Even in the harsh climate of the Arctic, the

Eskimo child touches warm skin by riding inside the mother's parka. If the mother is not holding the child, then it is in the arms of the father, or held by a neighbor, on the hip of an older sibling, or nursing from another woman. As the child gets older, it sleeps with brothers and sisters and helps to care for younger siblings, always touching them in the process.

By contrast, the northern European or American baby is wrapped in its own clothes and placed in its own bed, crib, cradle, or pen. For movement, the child is pushed in a stroller, carriage, or pram. As soon as possible, and sometimes from birth, the baby is fed by bottle rather than by breast. In America the bottle is frequently stuffed into a special holder so that the baby can feed alone in its crib. In northern Europe the baby is frequently left alone for hours with a rubber pacifier. By contrast, primitive women nurse their babies for years, and first start feeding them solid food by chewing it themselves and then gently spitting it into the baby's mouth.

Too much touching will presumably spoil the child and make it too dependent, according to the beliefs of Americans and northern Europeans. The child should be encouraged to do as much as possible on its own as soon as possible—dress itself, tie its own shoes, bathe itself, feed itself. The child stays at a proper distance from adults so that it cannot reach out and touch them. For fear that the child might pull someone's hair, snatch off his glasses, or drool on a new jacket, it stays confined in a playpen or crib, strapped into a carrying device or stroller, stuck in a high chair or a special seat in the car.

From time to time a movement arises to reform this trait in our society. Mothers organize to promote breastfeeding; parents urge one another to hug their children or tuck them in at night; some innovator adopts a tribal carrying device and suddenly mothers appear toting their children in special slings on their backs, draped from the side, or hanging in front of them. But such attempts to change the ingrained child-rearing habits of modern society rarely succeed with more than a small minority of conscientious parents.

People raised in the way that has now become normal in industrial society do not learn how to touch or enjoy being touched nearly as much as do people in traditional societies. Perhaps this is one reason why so many people in our culture turn their affection toward animals, which can be hugged, petted, held, snuggled with, slept with, kissed, bathed, combed, and played with in all the ways that other human beings cannot be. Parents leave their young children alone in the crib at night with a menagerie of stuffed animals, almost as if the adults were trying to train the infant to enjoy animal contact in lieu of human contact. Children receive puppies and kittens that will grow up with them and thereby give the child something to pet, stroke, cuddle, and hold.

This deep attachment to animals persists in adulthood. The lonely young woman or elderly widow in a city apartment has a small lapdog to love and lavish physical attention on. The man in the suburbs has his yard dog, which he thinks of as a great retriever and hunting dog even though he never goes hunting. The city professional keeps a large dog for jogging with in the park or along the river. The couple with no children keep Chihuahuas with names like Baby, Sugar, and Cupcake.

The people of the United States and northern Europe spend enough money on animal food to feed several underdeveloped nations. They spend more on meat for a single family dog than a whole family is likely to have in Bangladesh. They lavish additional money on medicines, toys, and grooming products. This attachment cannot be accounted for in any way except as an expression of the need for touching, for intimacy, and for a type of emotional attachment that people find difficult to make with one another in industrial society. They not only have had little training in responding to one another, but they often lead their adult lives isolated in small apartments or trailer parks scattered around the fringes of the community.

Given this background, it is hardly surprising that adults in these countries make such poor lovers. They do not understand how to enjoy giving or receiving the leisurely pleasure of touching. The focus of intercourse becomes the orgasm, the rubbing of genitals, and not the enjoyment of the body. Performance anxieties develop when there is too much focus on the genitals. Men may have trouble getting or maintaining an erection, or in preventing too quick ejaculation. Women may become nervous and unable to relax enough to enjoy sex. By the time a couple has worked out these problems, the copulatory act is likely to have settled into a dull routine. Without developing the tactile potential of the entire body, the adult is unlikely ever to become a proficient lover. Under such conditions, masturbation may seem an easier and more gratifying alternative.

The verbal clumsiness of American males and their lack of warmth and sensitivity were not the only criticisms leveled by Evita and some of the other women working the Strip. A very common complaint, particularly against white men, was their physical inflexibility and stiffness, their chronic pelvic lock.

In coitus, among almost all animals, the male penetrates the female from the rear. Even the gorillas and chimps, who spend much of their time on two feet rather than four, still assume the common mammalian coital position with the female bent over and the male entering her from behind. For these animals, copulation is not only brief but relatively easy. Both animals stand on their own feet, each bearing the load of its own body. Both animals also have their arms free to pull into or push away from each other. The male can steady himself with his arms against the female, or she can use her arms as extra support limbs. This position also allows the female to jerk away if she needs to.

With the transition to frontal coitus among humans, all of this changes. In the standard European-American position of female supine and male on top, the female is trapped beneath the male, who supports his body by constantly shifting his weight from legs to knees to elbows and back again. The male must thrust repeatedly from the pelvic area for several minutes with an accelerating rhythm and with no firm foundation on which to support his body without crushing some part of the female anatomy. In this position, cramps are fairly common, and even cardiac arrest among older men is possible, though rare.

These movements of the male body require more than simple instinctual motions and do not occur in any other normal human activity. The rotating, gyrating, and thrusting motions of coitus are not needed when a man runs in the hunt or flees from a predator. They are not needed in order to throw a spear, toss a rock, or shoot an arrow. They are not required for farming, fishing, and certainly not for working in an office or on an assembly line. They are unique to sexual encounters.

Because these motions never occur in any natural context, human societies invented ways to teach and practice them. Around the world, the most consistent way of teaching these skills has been through male dancing and male sports. These inculcate in the male a sense of rhythm and timing, and, most important of all, they provide opportunity for the exercise and practice of steady, consistent thrusting. Dancing in primitive and agricultural societies is often a primarily male affair, with the women watching and helping to keep time with chants or rhythmic clapping and stomping. Men have danced to gain power for battle and for success in the hunt. They have danced in gratitude for their kills and in gratitude for having survived. They have danced to bring rain or to bring sunshine or to celebrate the spring. They have danced in courtship and simply for pleasure and amusement. Dancing is an almost daily part of the lives of virtually all known primitive peoples, and it is a particularly important part of the male's normal routine when he is young and vigorous.

The pelvic activity in such dances, with men thrusting their genitals at one another and at the audience, was almost always denounced by the missionaries as lewd, licentious, and sinful. On those occasions when the two sexes danced together and thrust their genitals at one another, it often excited the bystanders as well as the dancers, and such evenings frequently led to what in the missionaries' eyes was unbridled carnality. Missionaries recognized the close connection between dancing and sexuality.

The public also easily recognized the sexuality of pelvic thrusting in Elvis Presley's early performances. "Elvis the Pelvis" gyrated his legs and thrust his hips every which way, creating a national sensation. When he first appeared on television, cameramen had to be careful to focus on the upper portion of his body in order not to show the too sensuous movements of his legs and hips. Television standards have eased, but the same sensuality of dance has continued from Presley through Mick Jagger, Michael Jackson, and other popular performers.

Elvis Presley caused a sensation because over the past 2,000 years European society had steadily de-eroticized dancing. From folk dancing to ballroom dancing, the form had been sanitized and made more wholesome in the eyes of an essentially antierotic society. The sense of rhythm remained, but the movements changed from acts of the whole body to acts of the legs and feet supplemented by the hands. From the stately minuet to the frenzied waltz, dance became a sequence of steps, rather than body motions.

Dance in the modern world has been further de-eroticized by being made into a spectator art, rather than a performing one. People watch, analyze, and critique dance, rather than participate in it. Even when the content of the dance is blatantly sexual and scandalous, as in Nijinsky's dance of the faun, the audience only observes. No one in the audience gains practice in pelvic thrusting or in sustained rhythmic activity; dance is a passive pastime for most. Most primitive societies also have people who watch the dancing, but these spectators are likely to become or to have been dancers themselves at another time, and during the course of a festival each individual may change repeatedly from watching to participating. In the West the distinction between performer and audience is much more rigid.

In addition to dance, cultures around the world invented diverse sports that required men to practice motions that made them better sex partners. The American Indians had numerous games using the rubber ball, which they invented. The Mayas had a game in which two teams vied with each other to pass a small ball through a very high hoop, but unlike contemporary basketball, the Mayan players were not allowed to use their hands; they hit the ball with their knees or hips, much as a modern soccer player does, developing great muscular control of the whole body and increasing its flexibility. The Muskogee Creek of the southeastern United States and other tribes in that area and in the Plains allowed players to use a long stick at the end of which was a small pouch for catching and tossing the ball. This game became a favorite of the European invaders and is still played today in modified form under the French name of lacrosse.

Around the world, games developed using not only rubber balls but pigskins, sheep bladders, a goat's head, or a clump of wax with feathers in it. These games were played mostly by males, giving them practice in a number of skills such as throwing, aiming, and working together, as well as the general attributes of strength and endurance. In most cases these were the same skills that made men better sex partners.

Like dancing, sports in American society, even more than in European society, have become spectator events rather than occasions for participation. The audience participates primarily by cheering on a favorite team or player. Tens of thousands pack the stadium, and millions more join in through television and radio, to watch a mere handful of men exert themselves. European men are also avid sports spectators, but they are also more likely to be players much farther into adulthood than are American men.

American sports have also been purged of some aspects that would have made them good training for sex. In the American trinity of baseball, basketball, and football, the players use the hands, arms, and legs, rather than the whole-body movement and coordination that characterize soccer. When the whole body *is* used, as in football, it functions as a solid wall in which mass surpasses agility. American sports have become increasingly games based on strategy and tactics, punctuated by sudden bursts of energy, rather than games of sustained and uninterrupted movement. Knowing exactly when to call a time-out or send in a substitute is often much more crucial than having an agile body.

Instead of providing good pelvic training for its males, modern Western society stresses this training for females. Females are expected to dance with a certain looseness at the hip that males must never show, and females are encouraged to walk with an exaggerated swaying of the hips, accentuated by the use of high-heeled shoes. Males, in contrast, are taught to walk as if they were clutching their life's savings between the cheeks of their buttocks. The pelvic area of the American male must not budge. When the Hula-Hoop became a fad in the 1950s, it was females who took it up and benefited most from the exercise.

Training females to be particularly agile in the pelvic area is a great help for couples who copulate lying on their sides or with the female on top. But when the standard European position is used, the agility of the female is virtually useless because she is pinned underneath the male.

The contemporary male, particularly in the United States, not only finds scant opportunity to develop the motions and skills most needed to become a good lover, but also has a tendency to become overweight very quickly after adolescence. A parallel situation in the nineteenth century characterized the wealthy and powerful men of the Middle East, who were accustomed to sitting around smoking hookahs, eating, and growing fat and lazy. They then turned to sex with women who were exceptionally good at gyrating their middles and thrusting during intercourse; the men reclined and the women did all the work. This skill developed into the art of belly dancing. European-American society may have to follow this example if the agility of its males continues to decline.

In a sense the troop of men descending daily on the women of the Strip are making the same choice as the nineteenth-century sultan: to be sexually serviced. They make no pretense of being good lovers. They are not there to make love but to find orgasm with as little effort as possible. One middle-aged government worker articulated this attitude when he said, "The only thing that counts is the climax, and the quicker I get there the better. Then I have it out of the way until the urge returns."

All societies get the kind of citizens that the societies themselves create. Our society seems to specialize in developing people who endure years of training to work complex machines, people who can fight long wars, and people who find pleasure in alcohol and other mood-altering drugs. But as women such as Evita, Violet, and the others working the Strip see in the harsh light of their experience, the society fails at producing people skilled in relating to one another verbally or sexually. Just as he-men have difficulty talking about love or even giving simple compliments with ease, so they lack the training to make love physically. As the Muria so well illustrate, making love is something that must be taught. Having sexual desires no more makes one a good lover than being hungry makes one a good cook. In both cases the natural drives are channeled through the culture; some cultures develop great cuisines, others rely on a few boiled staples. In the same way some cultures create great lovers, and others merely teach their members to reproduce.

Six

THE PRICE OF GOOD SEX

One evening during the after-work rush, Debbie dived into the midst of several customers around the cash register. "Jack, I need the key to the office fast," she said urgently.

Of course the Pink Pussy had no office, but whenever customers were around, that was the name we used for the large mirrored room that Violet had used as a dressing room. I pulled the key from behind the cash compartment in the register and handed it to her, and she disappeared quickly, closing the door behind her. She did not remain hidden long; as soon as the men around the counter dispersed, she opened the door halfway and called to me.

"Look over at McDonald's and tell me who's there," she asked.

I walked over to the front door to get a better look at McDonald's across the street. "How do I know who's there? Looks like the same people to me," I said, and began to list names of people as I spotted them at the tables by the large window.

"Look over at the far left," Debbie directed. "In about the second or third booth from the wall, do you see two men in coats and ties?"

"Talking with a girl in the booth?" I asked.

"With a girl? What girl?" Suddenly Debbie appeared at the door, hiding behind me and looking over my shoulder at the same time. Neither of us could recognize the girl from that distance, but I could tell that the two men were not regulars along the Strip. "Do me a *big* favor," Debbie pleaded with exaggerated pathos. "Watch them while I wait in the office, and if they come this way, let me know. Is the basement open?" Since I was not sure, she walked over to check it herself and found it unlocked. "All right, if they head this way, I'll dive into the basement. I know where they could never find me down there, plus I know how to get out of the coal chute."

I asked Debbie who the men were and what was going on, but she wouldn't say anything with so many people nearby. "I'll tell you later. Just keep an eye on them for now, and holler as soon as they do anything." As quickly as she closed the door, shutting herself into the office, she opened it again. "Oh, and tell me if anyone else goes over to talk with them." She closed and then opened the door once more. "Where's the damn radio, anyway? Did somebody steal it?"

I told her I did not know anything about a radio in the office, and I returned to the customers, wondering what was going on.

Debbie had shoulder-length blond hair that feathered back from her face and over her ears. She was always in the midst of one major crisis or another, and she dramatized everything. She was constantly fleeing from wild tricks, crazy pimps, lovesick boyfriends, various divisions of the local police, the FBI, the Montgomery County sheriff's office, the Virginia Highway Patrol, Treasury agents, angry landlords, jealous hookers, and social workers. Men fell in love with her after seeing her on the far side of the disco floor, and then chased her relentlessly. Club managers wanted her to dance for them and go off to Vegas or up to Atlantic City, where she could earn six times as much money as in D.C. Talent agents offered her movie contracts and Florida beach condominiums. Landlords, roommates, and lovers evicted her with great regularity, and always without reason. Debbie's stories never seemed to end, especially when she was taking cocaine or amphetamines.

The office, which was usually called the Red Room, had deep red carpeting that continued up the walls. A bench covered with the same carpet ran around three walls. Above the bench sparkled a long line of mirrors flecked with gold. The dusty room housed the vacuum cleaner, several cases of disinfectant, a crate of giant plastic garbage bags, some bent and discarded magazine racks, and assorted caps, umbrellas, raincoats, jackets, key rings, an introductory physics textbook, and other items left by customers over the past few months.

Debbie had once worked in the Pink Pussy. For several years the large room we called the office had supplied a handful of women known as hostesses. For $25, a customer could choose any hostess to go into the peep show with him. The money went to the house, but once inside the booth, the man could negotiate for a hand job or a blow job, and that money went to the hostess.

The Pink Pussy was a trick parlor when Debbie worked in it. Each day two shifts of girls rotated, so that at least two were always on duty in the Red Room, and on weekend nights as many as seven. The Pink Pussy's management maintained that it was not involved in prostitution, that it sold only the service of the woman's companionship with the man in the peep show; if the woman sold sexual services while in the booth, that had nothing to do with the management of the Pink Pussy. This rationale had served as an acceptable fiction until the last election and the accompanying crime-cleanup campaign. The Pink Pussy was targeted as one of the places due for a cleaning. Some of the women were arrested after going into the booths with undercover policemen. The local television news cameras arrived for an investigative journalism story showing the flashing marquee, suspicious women on the streets, and the manager backing into the shop while shielding his face with one hand and locking the door behind him with the other. Then everything quieted down and returned to normal—except for the women who had been arrested and for Debbie and the other women who escaped jail but became unemployed.

Several of the former Pussycats, as they had been called, still roamed the Strip, some of them working periodically in massage parlors, the Steak House, for one of the out-call prostitution services, or behind the bar at the Hadley. But such upward moves in the Strip's hierarchy of jobs was too difficult for most of them. They walked the streets, the lowest rung of prostitution. They would search out their own tricks and bring them into the Pink Pussy or to any place where they could service them easily, quickly, and safely.

Ever since then, Debbie had treated the Pink Pussy as her home, bringing over her problems to discuss with the night clerk, her luggage to store in the office, her dope to hide behind the counter, and her tricks to service in the peeps. She even expected the radio to be still waiting for her in the Red Room the night she came in to hide from the men at McDonald's.

The men finally left their booth and went out the front door. I called to Debbie, but getting no answer, I had to bang on the door. "They just left McDonald's and they seem to be heading this way," I told her when she finally opened the door.

I returned to the cash register and saw that the two men really did seem headed for the Pink Pussy. Trying to look very nonchalant, since they seemed to be watching me as they came, I told her out of the side of my mouth that the men were coming. Debbie bolted from the Red Room to the basement, and I heard the big bar on the basement door clunk down.

Only seconds after her disappearance, the two men strolled into the shop. I sat virtually motionless on the stool behind the counter and followed them with my eyes. They said nothing and I said nothing. One man was in his mid- to late thirties; the other in his forties. Both wore nondescript jackets with ties. The older one, who had a receding hairline, stationed himself across from me, directly in front of the hard-core magazines, with his back to the wall as if to guard the place. The younger man walked once around the front room, glancing at the books displayed and at the few customers browsing through them; then he walked into the back room. All the while, the guard stared at me, never moving his eyes. He just stood and stared. I could hear his partner rattling doors and pushing into various booths. Unable to look at the guard, I shifted my gaze out the front door and looked at the street, not even checking the mirrors to see what the man in the back was really doing, or if the guard had ever blinked.

I did not know who the men were or whether they were really looking for Debbie, but I was virtually certain they were law-enforcement officials. They seemed more like FBI agents than local vice-squad or homicide detectives; yet I thought it highly unlikely that the FBI had nothing better to do than bang around in the Pink Pussy searching for a hooker who could be easily arrested almost any night of the week. They also seemed much too old to be working the street. At their ages, they should have earned desk jobs.

After five or six minutes, the younger man came to the front again and pushed on the office door. It opened easily into the gaudy interior. He looked around the room without entering; then he strolled over to the basement door and gave it a push. It did not budge and he did not try to force it or to move the handle; instead, he continued on his casual stroll around the room. Neither one of them asked me anything or offered any explanation for what they were doing. I did not volunteer any information, nor did I ask them anything. I tried to ignore them as best as I could under the circumstances. Then the two men walked silently out the front door, leaving as calmly as they had entered.

I watched them stroll down the street, but they were out of my sight within a minute or two. No matter what they had wanted, they had interrupted my business and ended the evening rush. Only a few customers had left while the pair was in the shop, but as soon as the men walked out, all the rest filed out and headed up the street in the opposite direction.

Debbie must have known when everyone left, because I soon heard her tapping on the other side of the basement door. I shouted that all was clear, and she emerged. But she hid in the office for much of the night, waiting until the Strip grew quieter and much darker before she eased out the front door and went off to a new refuge for what remained of the night.

I do not recall first meeting Debbie; she was simply around

from the beginning of my work on the Strip. She seemed like dozens of other young women in the area, but she was slightly more noticeable because of her propensity for getting high on drugs and being very loud. She frequently came into the Pink Pussy to buy rolling papers and other types of drug paraphernalia.

She had quit school in the ninth grade and left Charleston, West Virginia, to move to Baltimore and live with a sister. She had trouble finding friends until she met and fell in love with Rick, who worked in one of the porno stores on the Strip. Because of him, she began coming into Washington frequently and hanging out with him and his friends. Her love affair withered, but her new circle of friends persisted, and she was soon having sex for money. At first it was only for special purposes —to visit the nearby amusement park; to buy some marijuana; to help Cindy raise bail; to buy Vance a Scorpio medallion for his birthday; or to buy train fare back to Baltimore or to Charleston to visit her mother. But soon it became a regular way of life, and she was living on the Strip, tricking to pay the rent, keep the car running, buy groceries, and still make all those other special purchases.

In many ways Debbie was unique. Because her younger sister was deaf, she knew enough sign language to communicate with the deaf kids who hung out on the Strip. She spent many hours playing video games with them and interpreting for them when one wanted to get into a summer job program, when others bought bad dope, or needed to borrow some money, or wanted her to make a phone call for them. When not wandering the streets, she preferred to hang out in Burger King because she was not permitted in McDonald's after squirting the assistant manager with ketchup; Wendy's had barred her when a customer reported that one of the clerks always gave her free food and drinks; the bus-station guard accused her of soliciting in the station and threatened to call the police if she ever returned; Kentucky Fried Chicken would not let her in because the manager there was a good friend of the one at McDonald's; and the Western Beef House would not admit her because when she worked there, she'd stolen money from the other women and allegedly from some of the customers, too.

According to Debbie, her favorite time on the Strip had been working at the Pink Pussy. She characterized the work as "dull but safe." Rather than standing around street corners or getting drunk in a bar waiting for a trick, she lounged around the Red Room all day. She tired of seeing "I Love Lucy" and "M*A*S*H" so many times that she knew most of the dialogue by heart, but she loved "All My Children" and "General Hospital." It was much better than standing on the corner at night alone with nothing to watch but the cars creeping by. In the Red Room, she had plenty of time to read magazines and tabloids, talk to the other girls and the clerk, as well as listen to the radio. But she complained that the manager had never allowed the girls to dance, because of some legal technicality that barred dancing in a bookstore. The manager had also told them that it was not very ladylike. Working in the Pink Pussy, Debbie drank less alcohol and did fewer drugs than any at other time, because the manager sent the girls home whenever they showed up for work high. Taking less dope kept her personality more stable and made her better liked. It also kept her out of trouble.

"You know how I am when I'm high—I just lose control altogether and do crazy things that I shouldn't. Like get in so many fights. Well, actually when I think of it, they are things I *should* do—like knock the shit out of Sara for screwing Mike or calling the cops on Buzz for selling heroin in my apartment. But even though I should do those things, they always get me in more trouble than the other person, and I wouldn't have done them at all if I hadn't been high."

In the Pink Pussy, she also earned substantially more money. The shop took its share and she took hers. In other places, she'd always had to split some of the money with the woman who set her up with the trick, with the bouncer at the bar where she found the trick, or with a boyfriend. At the Pink Pussy, she had more regular customers than when she worked the street. She was also safe there—safe from pimps, safe from weird tricks, safe from territorial fights with other hookers, safe from muggers, and (she thought) safe from the police. Like everyone else, she assumed that the Company had worked out a deal with the police chief, or the mayor, or somebody, not to harass the Pink Pussy. But that proved to be a myth when the police forced the girls back onto the street.

Less than a month after leaving the Pink Pussy, Debbie picked up a trick who took her to a motel across the river in Arlington, Virginia, and persuaded her to let him tie her with leather thongs. Once she was tied, he refused to let her go. He did not hit her or beat her, but he handled her roughly. He jerked her head around and made her fellate him. He pulled her hair and twisted it just enough to make her uncomfortable, but not to hurt so much that she would scream.

"I knew if I screamed, he would stuff something in my mouth really fast, and then he might get scared and kill me. The one thing you don't want to do is make a weirdo scared. Go along with them as long as you can, and hope that they get bored with the whole thing and give up before they cripple you."

When the man finished, he showered, dressed, and left $30 for her, but he did not untie her.

"I just rolled over to the foot of the bed and went to sleep. I could have kicked the telephone off the side and maybe dialed with my toe or something, but I was too tired. So I just waited until they came to clean the room. I didn't say a word until she was in the room, and then I got them to untie me. I just kept talking as fast as I could, jumped into my clothes, grabbed my money, and split before they had time to tell the manager."

After that, she took an indoor job again as a dancer, but was soon fired. She claims she did not steal the money but was accused of it because the other women disliked her and called her a street whore who had no business working in a club. The dancers considered themselves superior to her, she said, and when money was missing, naturally she was blamed. She went back to Baltimore for a while to live with her sister, but could not get along with her sister's husband and kids, so she and another woman went to Florida, where the other woman had contacts at a Miami club. They were hired and worked a few weeks, but Debbie left. She claimed she could not tolerate the

Cubans everywhere and the way they pinched so much. Soon she was back on the D.C. Strip, living with the pimp Tyrone and his three other "bitches," as the pimps call their women.

Debbie was in love with Tyrone. She told me that she never minded hanging out on the street, because it was for a special reason, not just for money but for Tyrone: It would make him happy and he would like her all the more. She was determined to be his "main woman" and make the others look like the "whores they really were." She and Tyrone talked about moving to California when he had enough money saved. Tyrone had friends everywhere, and they considered setting up a bar in San Francisco or maybe Seattle or Hollywood. To Debbie, all those cities seemed about the same—"way out there."

Even though she worked on the street, she felt safe because of Tyrone. Just as she thought the police protected her at the Pink Pussy, she thought Tyrone protected her on the Strip. He cared about her, and his notoriety was like a shield around her. Then one night, she drove with a fairly young man out to a cornfield in Virginia, just beyond Tyson's Mall. He pulled her blouse open and started biting her breasts. She did not wait around this time but jumped out of the car very quickly and started to run up the dirt road. He turned the car around and followed her, asking her to get back in and promising to take her back to the city without hurting her. She refused and kept walking. Then he started to speed away, but as he did so, Debbie pulled a paper and pencil from her pocket and wrote down his Maryland license number. She had already made a deliberate effort to remember every detail of his appearance and that of the car. Although it was very dark, Debbie says that the man must have seen her write down his number, because he turned around again and came down the road faster and faster, heading right for her. She jumped a small ditch and headed straight through the corn field.

A few minutes later, she made it back to the paved road and, walking very cautiously, arrived at a closed gas station with an outside public telephone. She called home, told one of the other women what had happened, and asked her to find

Tyrone. When Debbie called back ten minutes later, the woman said that Tyrone would come immediately to get her. An hour and several more frantic calls later, one of the women in the house drove out in Tyrone's car and picked Debbie up. Tyrone was tied up in some "negotiations," she said, and could not come himself. Later Debbie found out that he had been at the Blue Mouse with one of her other housemates. Despite all the information she gave him on the car and its license number, and her detailed description of "this maniac who tried to kill me," Tyrone told her to forget the whole thing. He accused her of overreacting, said she was a little high, wanted attention, was jealous because he did not come pick her up, was at fault herself for leaving the city with the man, and was stupid for not playing along and getting her money.

A couple of weeks later she saw the same man cruising down the Strip in the same car. She chased after him and beat on the door, but he sped away. The next time she saw him, she contented herself with screaming an insult from the sidewalk and not wasting energy in a futile chase. In time she learned to ignore him.

She broke up with Tyrone after he brought in a seventeen-year-old girl who he claimed was a relative. Tyrone was having an affair with her and, worse, wanted to use Debbie's bedroom. After a few days, Debbie and Tyrone had a stormy argument over the stereo he had given her, and finally she left him, leaving behind the furniture, stereo, and television he had given her. She assumes that he gave it all to the new girl.

One of Tyrone's prostitutes told me that Tyrone wanted to get rid of Debbie because of her heavy drug use. With the prevalence of AIDS among drug users, customers were more observant of needle marks on women's arms and more wary of odd behavior that might indicate the influence of drugs rather than alcohol. Debbie's income had been declining rapidly, and Tyrone thought it was because of both the needle marks on her arms and her erratic behavior in public.

It was only a few weeks after the end of her affair with Tyrone that Debbie ran into the Pink Pussy to hide from the two agents across the street. For several days afterward, I did not see her, but she finally telephoned me at work one night. She asked whether the men had been back.

"Yes, they've been up and down the Strip every day," I told her.

"Did they ask you anything—anything about me?" she wanted to know.

"No, they've never even spoken to me."

"Did they ask you about Tyrone? I guess you heard about him."

"No, I told you they haven't said a word to me. But I saw in the paper that he was arrested for narcotics in a sweep of U Street."

"Did anybody tell you about that girl? She turned out to be only thirteen years old, and he was pimping her. The cops have returned her to her parents in Richmond."

"I heard that, but some people say she's really older."

"That's a lie. I know for a fact she's thirteen and only in junior high school—I even know which school she went to. The FBI is going to get him for this one—pimping minors across state lines."

"They say that's why those men are hanging around so much lately—to clean up the minors from outside the District."

"That's why they were looking for me. They think I'm a minor, and they want to get me to testify against Tyrone for the dope and for the little-girl stuff. They'll bust me now for soliciting, or plant dope on me, or anything, and then they'll offer to let me off easy if I testify." Suddenly her voice shifted as though talking to someone else. "Hey, you fuckers, if you've bugged my phone, you may as well know that I'm nineteen years old, I was over eighteen when I met Tyrone, and you are violating my civil liberties by listening in on my private phone conversation. I know my rights. Oh, and one more thing—if you see Tyrone, tell him that I hope he rots."

Debbie stayed away a few weeks, and then she was back on the Strip again. The agents disappeared, and the crisis (whatever it had been) subsided. Tyrone's women raised bail and freed him from jail. One rumor on the street said that Debbie had started the whole thing by writing an anonymous letter to the FBI telling them how they could bust Tyrone for narcotics, and also telling them about the underage girl. Someone else said that the letter was written by another pimp. Others laughed at the idea of any letter at all. Tyrone, they said, was simply in the wrong place at the wrong time.

Such minidramas played regularly at the Pink Pussy and along the Strip. They arose with great furor, stirred up some excitement, and then faded out after a prostitute went to jail, a pimp was killed, a hustler turned informant, or a stripper moved on to try her luck in Miami. One heard so many explanations, excuses, stories, and eyewitness accounts that it was rarely possible to know what had really happened. Even what was published in the newspaper about happenings along the Strip seemed no more accurate than the rumors on the street. Pimps, prostitutes, and police all had their own perspectives and consequently their own explanations of everything that occurred, and rarely did the details of one coincide with the others.

Debbie's career on the Strip seemed typical of many. She circulated from one type of prostitution to another, and she rotated from being predator to being prey. One day she was subject to the demands of a new pimp in her life and the next day she was being turned out of a job because of a change in police policy or because of a manager's whim. As easy as it was for her to be victimized by managers, pimps, or police, Debbie just as easily became the exploiter, quick to make a few extra dollars if she detected a weakness in one of her customers, or if she saw the opportunity to finagle something even as trivial as a cigarette or a drink.

Debbie never ranked far from the bottom of the social order on the Strip. A few women even less successful than Debbie never managed at all to work any job other than streetwalker. At least Debbie had short stints in places such as the Pink Pussy or the strip bar, though she never managed to leave the street permanently for an indoor job.

Debbie was unusual in that she was slightly more independent than the average prostitute. George called her a "lone wolf," a term he sometimes used derogatorily and sometimes with a hint of respect. But George was less tolerant than I of her frequent appearances with tricks at the Pink Pussy. Usually I gave her greater freedom of action because she was one of the few prostitutes I got to know rather well over a long period of time.

There was a structural tension between the role of the porn clerk and that of the prostitute. By the code of the Strip, a prostitute talked to no male other than her pimp or a paying customer. Even though many women came and went in the store, my interactions with them were perfunctory. Lengthy conversations could be undertaken only with their men. Consequently, only special women—such as Violet, who worked as a dancer; Debbie, who was a lone wolf; and a few others who had no pimps—dared talk with me for long or maintain a long-term relationship of any kind.

Outside the store, many of the prostitutes I saw almost daily never spoke to me—not so much from fear of their pimps as from their enculturation into this system and their acceptance of its values. In truth, I probably stood in greater danger from their pimps than they did, for by the norms of this culture a man paid attention to a woman only because he wanted sex or money from her—both of them commodities that the pimp owned. I was trying to take either her sex or her money away from her pimp; for him, no other explanation was applicable. As in every other business culture in America, time is money, and to steal time from people is to steal money from them or from their bosses.

Seven

LEARNING TO PIMP

A frequently heard claim on the Strip was that Tyrone had been busted by the police because he had killed Jesse, another pimp. Jesse had been stabbed to death in front of his home the previous Christmas, and it was theorized that the police knew but could not prove that Tyrone was involved with the killing, so they arrested him on dope charges to make him talk or as a way to punish him. Like dozens of other rumors, stories, conjectures, and fantasies heard daily on the Strip, this one was hard to confirm or disprove and the best policy was simply to remember it.

I had never known Jesse—he died a few weeks before I took the job—but I did know his son, Jerry, who began coming into the Pink Pussy in February, almost as soon as he got out of prison. Jerry had been convicted of assault, robbery, and narcotics possession, all in one case, but he had served less than a single year in prison. Even though he had missed his father's funeral while in prison, he had cooked up a thousand schemes for continuing his father's work. He wanted to reassemble his father's women and pimp them himself. He wanted to have a call service so that his women did not have to stand on the streets, and he intended to make pornographic films. And then, of course, someday he would track down his father's killers and blow them off the face of the earth.

The first time I saw Jerry, he was wearing a black European-cut suit with a stark white shirt and thin black tie. He was twenty-one but looked older, a perception reinforced by his broad shoulders and solid build. He came into the store looking for Debbie or any of several other girls, some of whom I knew and some of whom I did not.

"I just came back from up north and I haven't seen any of them in a while. I just wanted to let them know I'm in town." I knew he was lying, since I already knew who he was and where he had been. I assumed that Debbie and the other women he asked for already knew that he was back on the Strip.

Over the next several days, Jerry stopped in each evening. He talked for a minute and then wandered to the back. He read each advertisement and looked at the picture posted on each door, but he never bothered to go into any of the booths. Instead he watched the people coming and going and exchanged a few words at most with them. Then he left.

One night he strolled in much as usual but had his stepbrother, Tex, with him. Tex's father had married Jerry's mother when the two boys were fairly young.

"Hold it," I said. "You're barred from here, Tex. George said you can't come in here at all." I stood up from the stool.

"It's all right, man," Jerry began. "We just want to pick up a pack of cigarettes. No hassle, okay? You're still my man now, aren't you, Jack?" He held out his hand and smiled a big television smile.

Somewhat reluctantly I shook hands with him. "Get your cigarettes and then take Tex on down the road."

"I don't mean to stall, but Tex needs some change." With that, Tex pulled a crumpled dollar bill from his pocket and handed it to me. He bought his cigarettes, Jerry bought a pack of rubber prophylactics, and the two of them left.

The next day Jerry returned alone. "I appreciate it—you letting Tex in yesterday. You're the only one on the Strip who will do it. You know it's hard for him, but now that I'm back, I'm going to keep him out of trouble. He'll do what I tell him, and if he gets out of line, I'll kick his ass all over the place. If he ever gives you any trouble, you just let me know." He spoke as though playing a role in a high-school play.

Actually I had no idea why Tex was barred from all the porno places. I just remembered George pointing him out to me on the street and swearing he was never to pass through the doors for any reason whatsoever. Yet Tex seemed to be the mildest, meekest guy on the block. He was about the same age and height as Jerry but even stockier. He always wore a wide leather belt with an agate and silver belt buckle holding up his denim jeans. He appeared harmless.

Curious, I asked Jerry why the other places would not let Tex in.

"Don't you know what the problem is? Tex tricked with that faggot son of John Henry's over at Washington Books. Then when the faggot boy wouldn't pay up, Tex got in a little scuffle with him. So the old man told everybody that if they let Tex in their stores, he would get back at them."

The explanation did not make complete sense to me, but it was obviously all I was going to get from Jerry now. "Anyway," he repeated, "I have now taken personal and complete responsibility for Tex. Any trouble, you call me!" He paused. "Meanwhile, I have to ask you about something. You weren't here when Alvin worked here with the women, were you?"

"No, that was long before me. I just came in January." I was not even sure exactly who Alvin was, but I did remember his name from a conversation with George or Debbie. He had worked in the Pink Pussy about the time that the police had turned all the Pussycats back out on the street.

"Well, you know all about the bitches Alvin worked in here and everything. You know how a person working in a quiet store like this could make some pretty good money if he wanted to do something like that a little more—a little more on the quiet, so to speak."

He paused to let this sink in, and I waited in confusion to see what he would say next.

"You don't seem too interested yourself. I can tell that. Well, I'm just going to leave that with you as a thought for the day, so to speak, and let you get back to your business." And Jerry strolled on out the door.

Later the same night, Tex returned alone. "Hey, man, you seen my brother?"

"Not since about two hours ago. He came in here and then headed up toward the Wide World of Sex."

"How about my cousin, Roger—you seen him?" Tex asked.

"Who is he?"

"You know, that tall, light-skinned dude I'm always walking up and down with. You know which one. He must be in the back because he told me to meet him here about now. Say, what time is it, anyway?"

"It's 10:07, but hold it, Tex, you can't go back there." I started around the corner.

"Hold on, hold on, I'm not going back there, I'm just looking for my cousin."

I grabbed Tex firmly with one hand on his shoulder and turned him around toward the front door. He did not resist, obeying like a good kid. "It's okay, man, I know you got your job, and rules is rules. I'm going—no hassle at all. Just let me pick up my smokes and I'll go. Got some change?"

To get him the change, I had to release his arm and return to the back of the counter. I handed him the coins, he bought the cigarettes from the machine, and asked me for matches. Then he opened the pack and lit up. "Would it maybe be all right if I just stood here by the door and watched for my cousin while I smoke this cigarette? He really did tell me to meet him here."

A bit exasperated, I agreed. "But only for one cigarette and then out."

"I sort of hoped that maybe Jerry could have cleared things up." He started this in the nonchalant manner of idle conversation as he stared out the glass door. "You know, Jerry is really getting in the business now. He's going down to the Boom Boom Room every night and the chicks are just flocking all over him. They want him to be their pimp and all. They want me to be a pimp, too, but I tell them all 'No, I love women too much to be your pimp.' I'm a lover, not a fighter. To be a pimp, you got to be mean and hate women. But anyway, now Jerry's got him some women and he's ready to work them, but he doesn't have a place, you know. He's staying with me and it's out New York Avenue too far for the girls to come, and we don't have a car."

I began to understand what Jerry had been hinting about earlier in the day. "What kind of place is he looking for?" I asked Tex.

"Oh, you know, a place where girls can make contacts with the right men. You know how it is on the streets. He doesn't want to set his women up there. He wants them to do inside work. That's why he wished old Alvin was back here. Alvin and him used to have a nice arrangement with the customers when Jerry was helping out his old man. Like the old man used to say, 'I've got the bitches and Alvin's got the stiffs. Together we got the money.' That was pretty good, wasn't it?" Tex laughed, slapping himself on the side of the leg. "Alvin always said that one way or another, women and men would be fucking and sucking in the back, and as long as everyone else was making money on it, he might as well get a little himself."

"So what happened?"

"Who knows? But I heard Alvin made a heck of a lot of money matching up dates for Jesse's women." Tex put out his cigarette and, just as he had promised, he left.

I fully expected that Jerry would show up the next day with several of his new women and ask me to let them start using the Red Room. I tried to run through the scenario in my head. How would I decline? If I accepted the deal, how much would I get per trick? Would I be legally liable for what the girls did in the back? Where would I keep the vacuum cleaner if the girls used the Red Room? Would they require more than the women who came in and out using the place now?

It was more than a week before Jerry showed up again. He was angry when he stomped in one afternoon while George and I were changing shifts. Directly behind him came Tex.

George stopped counting. "What the fuck do you want? Get your goddamn ass out of that door just as fast as you came in," he shouted at Tex.

"I'm just looking for somebody, man. I ain't going to cause no trouble at all," Tex answered.

"Damn right you're not going to cause no trouble, 'cause you're going to look somewhere else."

Tex looked over at Jerry as though waiting for him to say or do something, but Jerry's eyes were searching the front room. Then he went into the back. Tex slipped out the front door and stood just on the other side of the glass, watching for Jerry to emerge from the booths.

"Did you find what you were looking for?" George asked matter-of-factly when Jerry came to the front again.

"I'm looking for a bitch I'm gonna kill. You seen a short blond girl named Becky? She has this fur jacket on all the time, you know?"

"Sure, I know," answered George, holding a handful of dollar bills and looking up over his glasses. "She's down on the damn circle. Her and about twenty more just alike. How in the hell do you think I can keep track of all twenty thousand hookers in this town?"

"Thanks, you cocksucker, you're a fucking hell of a lot of help." Jerry stomped out the door and on down the street with Tex.

George resumed counting the money and filling out the change-of-shift papers. I pretended to be busy, not wanting him to ask me why Tex thought he could come back into the Pink Pussy. After he finished his work, he turned and asked me, "Do you know Mandy? She's a good-looking drag queen in the face, except that she's about six feet tall in heels and she has an Adam's apple the size of a cantaloupe."

I shook my head. "Why?"

"She's the one who found Tex and got him started down here. She's his 'mother,' as they say," he explained.

"Where did she find him?" I wondered.

George looked exasperated. "How the hell do I know where she found him? Somewhere here in D.C., I guess."

"Sorry, I thought maybe he came from Texas, with a name like that and all."

"Maybe he did come from Texas, maybe she found him at

the Alamo or something—that's not the point. The point is she found him somewhere one night and took him back to her room in the old Roma Hotel before they tore it down. Well, he was only fourteen or something and he had never been laid, so he thought she was the real thing and he was hot as all hell. Mandy yanks down his pants and she swears that his dick is so big it slapped her right in the face. She could hardly believe that a boy so short would have such a big dick. She was just sure that having a dick that big was what stunted his growth; it must of weighted him down or something, or maybe all the food went to make his dick grow instead of his body, or something, you know.

"Well, Mandy was so surprised that she wanted to measure the damn thing, but she couldn't find a tape measure. So she went next door and asked some other old drag queen if she had one, but she didn't. And soon she had half the hotel awake before she found a ruler, and everyone was so excited that they all poured into Mandy's room to see her measure it."

George was obviously enjoying his story. "I don't know how many there were, but this whore Charlene was there and her dyke girlfriend, Rover. They're the ones who still talk about it so much. Anyway, Charlene says that his dick was hard as rock but it wasn't over nine inches long. Mandy swears that it was longer than the ruler itself and it was so thick you couldn't get your hand around it. 'Takes two hands to hold a whopper,' as Mandy used to say. Well, anyway, that's how he got the name Tex, because Mandy said he was her urban cowboy and that only in Texas could God grow anything that big."

"Do you think he was embarrassed by all that?" I asked.

"Embarrassed? What in the hell would he be embarrassed for? Don't you understand anything? It's been his living ever since. You can get about two dollars an inch for that kind of meat, and that night at the Roma was the best advertisement he ever had. By the next night, everybody on the Strip knew about him and Mandy. In fact, he's so stupid he didn't even know that Mandy was a drag queen until somebody on the street told him, and then they had to explain to him what a drag queen was."

"What did he say to that?" I asked.

"How the hell do I know what he said? He probably didn't say anything at all. He probably just smiled that shit-eatin' grin of his the way he always does. But I'm telling you, watch out for him and don't let that smile fool you. He's Mr. Nice Guy, but in the last five years everybody who wants him has had him, and now he gets kind of pushy trying to hustle tricks. That's why no one will let him in the booths. He barges right in with guys and thinks that because he has the biggest dick on the Strip they will pay him to suck on it. He's so damn stupid he doesn't know that a lot of guys just aren't into that, no matter how long it is."

I assumed that George was trying nicely to tell me not to let Tex into the store again. I felt I had to defend myself. "I only let him come in for cigarettes. He's never set foot on the linoleum in the back."

"He's testing you. He may be stupid but he knows the Strip and you don't. He's just testing you, but I swear to you, he'll screw you over big. But it's your store and it's your tail if you get in trouble."

I nodded.

All evening I mulled over the things George had told me. I wanted to know more about Jesse, Jerry, and Tex for my research, but I certainly didn't want to get into any real trouble. Jesse was already dead. There was little doubt in my mind that Jerry was also capable of killing—and of just about anything else—but of the three, Tex seemed fairly harmless. Though he sometimes strutted about as cocky as a bantam rooster in a hen coop, he seemed easily pushed around and I had never seen him lose his temper.

I was still wondering about it all when Tex returned at midnight. He came in alone and stood silently by the door while I sold a package of pipe screens to Cheri, a dancer from the Royale. Tex stepped outside to talk to Cheri as she left, but I could not hear what they were saying. Then he came back inside and asked me again if I had seen Becky with the short blond hair and the fur jacket.

"Tex, I don't think I know her, and I don't think she's been in here today. Why would she come here?"

"I don't know. I just kept hoping she might. Jerry told me yesterday that she would."

"For what?" I knew the answer, of course.

"You know, to make a little money and all that. We have really been having a hard time lately. I've got this cold sore, and people don't relate to that too well, you know." He pointed to a large, thin raw spot running along the edge of his mouth like the trail left by a very long piece of spaghetti. "People don't understand that I've had these all my life. They're left over from chicken pox or something, but everybody is so paranoid about herpes. I tell them it's just a cold sore and not a sexual disease or anything. I ain't got AIDS. Maybe I would be better off if I did have AIDS; at least it wouldn't show up on my face. That girl Lucinda has it, but she works the streets just fine. As long as nobody can see it, then nobody worries about it." Tex's voice was whiny in contrast to his normal bravado.

"Maybe you should go to the health clinic?"

"No money and no time. What I need is some money. That's why Jerry put Becky out to work tonight." Tex sighed, leaning against the front doorframe.

"Who is she, anyway?" I asked.

"She's my girl. She gave me this gold chain," Tex said, pulling one of the three chains he wore from under the neck of his cowboy shirt. "I met her a while back at the Boom Boom Room. Her and a bunch of her friends really liked me. So we just kind of hit it off."

"Maybe she's up at the Boom Boom Room," I suggested.

"No, none of her friends up there have seen her. She's supposed to be here."

"Why here?" I asked again.

"Like I said, Jerry planned this out, not me. You see, last night when we all came in—Jerry's staying with me, you know —well, he and Becky wanted my bed. So I said okay and I went and slept on the couch. He was banging her so loud and she was groaning, so I turned the radio up pretty loud to go to sleep. The next thing I know I'm awake and hearing her hollering and carrying on again. And I thought to myself, Damn, he's banging her again, and she's *my* girlfriend and I'm in here alone. Well, then I realized he wasn't banging her—I mean, not with his dick and all. He was banging her with his fists. They were fighting. He kept saying to her, 'You're gonna sell that damn pussy, do you hear me? You're gonna sell it or I'm gonna kill you.' And she kept hollering that he could go ahead and kill her, she didn't care. Well, I had a hard time going back to sleep myself, but I finally did. Anyway, she was supposed to be here working, and Jerry's been looking everywhere for her. He just might kill her if he finds her."

"This isn't the first woman Jerry's tried to get to work for him, and she won't be the first to run away from him, either." I was guessing, but I believed it to be true.

"Yeah, but this isn't just anybody; this is my girlfriend and I don't want to lose her. I really like her. Anyway, you know me. I just like women. I couldn't do what Jerry does. I have never in my whole life hit a girl. I almost hit my mother with a bottle once and that's why I left. She asked me a lot of times to come home and I always go to visit, but I say I won't spend the night, because I know I might hit her. I don't mind fighting with men, you know, but if I ever hit my mother, I don't think I could live with myself. And I think that's true for all women. I just love them too much to hurt them. Could you beat up somebody you loved?"

"I hope not."

"You know, one of the tricks I do is with a woman in Georgetown. She's a nice lady, a really nice lady. She's over thirty or so and sort of chubby, you know, but real nice and wears good-looking clothes and all. Well, her husband comes down here sometimes and picks me up and drives me over there. We eat something like cake and coffee or something. They don't give me anything strong to drink, so usually I have to get a little high myself before I go.

"But anyway, I go over to her and we start having sex in the dining room or the living room and he watches through the doorway while he washes the dishes in the kitchen. She goes down on me and all. Well, she asks me to talk dirty to her and talk like I'm going to rape her and all that kind of stuff. Well, what do you do? How can you be making love and getting excited and all and then talk like you was going to fight or something? It's crazy. And especially because here she is this real nice lady who bakes cakes and wears this nice dress and stuff and lives in a nice house with lots of really expensive furniture.

"Well, she doesn't really mind that I don't do it. Sometimes I call her a couple of names and joke around a little like I'm playing hard, but I don't do anything, and I think she understands that because she likes me a lot."

Tex paused, staring out the window. "The man's the weird one, I think. I used to think he was really nice, picking me up and carrying me home all the time and giving me the money and washing the dishes and all that. But I don't know. He wanted to adopt me. They fixed me up a nice bedroom of my own and all. But I told them they couldn't adopt me because I already had a mother, a father, and a stepfather. The last thing I need is a couple more; I have enough problems with the ones I have. That was before Jerry's father died, or I'd of offered them him maybe." Tex laughed at the idea. "Can't you see Jerry living over there now? He'd sell everything they owned. And they're pretty rich, too. The man works in computers and his wife worked for the government, too. She was a pretty important secretary or something.

"Now, you see, I could make a lot of money with them and do a lot more, but I'm not that much into money, you know. I just like love. Anyway, I know how those people are, too. You give them everything and stay with them all the time and the next thing you know, they're tired of you and you're back on the street again. But you just go see them a couple times in a month and they'll keep coming for a long, long time. It's better to go slow like that and not get too greedy and ruin the whole trough by wallowing in it. You know what I mean?"

I nodded. "Yes, but a lot of people don't understand that."

"I understand it because I learned it the hard way. You know, even tricking with these guys all the time, I try to do them the same as the women. I figure I know how much I love women and that must be how much they love me, so why would

I want to mess them up? Most guys hate the gays and try to steal their wallets and beat 'em up and take all their money, but not me. I figure he'll give me a little this time and a little next time and in the long run I'll get a lot more than the ones who take all the money just one time."

Tex continued on a new theme. "You know, Jerry said I had to quit tricking with gays because it would make me queer. He said that there was a lot more money from women because Washington has so many women secretaries and managers and everything and not enough men. All the men are already married and the women are all coming here to Washington to find husbands—you know, like that woman judge Reagan appointed to Congress. Well, anyway, Jerry says that all these women are just horny as hell and I could make more money from them than from gays."

Tex opened the door abruptly and looked down the street as though he saw someone. For a moment it looked as though he were about to run, but then he came back in. "I thought that was Becky or one of her friends, but it must have been somebody else." He went on with his monologue.

"So now I got this woman who is a GS-thirteen and that's all right. Can you imagine? She gets all that money every month for the rest of her life. And it would be so nice to share it with her. And I have a couple others, and Jerry calls them up for me or gets me to do it, and we go out and then we eat something good—except for that woman from the Commerce Department. She took me to eat some of the strangest damn food, raw octopus or something—who even knows what that stuff was? So with her I choose the place to eat. But anyway, the others always go somewhere nice to eat and then we go screw. But the thing of it is, they won't pay. So Jerry makes me call them up and tell them that I need some new shoes and could I borrow the money. Or I say I have to buy my mother a present because she is in the hospital again, or I need some money to pay back a loan, and then I go get the money. They always give it to me. They're really nice women."

By this time I had begun filling out my evening reports and preparing to close. Only one customer was left in the back peeps, so I shouted for him to leave. Tex took that as the right time for him to leave as well, and he wandered on down the street.

Later that night as I walked over to headquarters to turn in my night deposit, I saw Jerry on the corner with Thelma and Warren. Jerry was shouting at them, but in a slow, exaggerated way as though he were talking to someone who was hard-of-hearing. Thelma and Warren, however, are both completely deaf. No matter how loudly he shouted, they would not hear him.

I walked on past the hopeless conversation, wondering why Jerry would show any interest in them. They were brother and sister and friends of Debbie's. They were sixteen or seventeen and some people said they were twins; others swore that they were not related and only pretended to be brother and sister. In any case, they stayed together. Both had black, smooth skin. Thelma wore the latest fashions and looked like a model, though to the best of my knowledge she was very poor. Warren often dressed like and fixed his hair like hers. When they both wore the same makeup and the same kind of dress, they did look like sisters.

They shared one bicycle. Warren pedaled, balancing Thelma on the back as they zoomed along the streets. He wore high-heeled shoes, and I was afraid his foot would slip off the pedal and cause an accident, or that they would be hit by one of the cement trucks that backed in and out of the construction pit all day. Since he was deaf, I thought he was taking a terrible chance. Still, he and Thelma managed to make it without apparent difficulty.

Sometimes people called them the Pointer Sisters because of their modish clothes, but at other times they were called the Prick Sisters. They often stayed in one of the abandoned rooms of the deserted hotel around the corner. Though it was boarded up, the building still had running water and I often heard it called the White House because of this luxury. People said that the two of them would take on all comers for sex parties as long as someone supplied them with dope. For a little dope, the Prick Sisters would do anything.

I never had the chance to talk with them. Unlike the other deaf people on the Strip, Warren and Thelma never tried to speak with their voices. They could write very little and depended on a form of generalized street signing to communicate with the hearing world. They came into the Pink Pussy occasionally, but I never let them stay longer than the time it took to buy cigarettes, rolling papers, lubricant, or other items. Thelma carried an identification card that listed her age as twenty-one, but I refused to accept it. I did not want to be arrested for allowing two deaf, underage kids into the pornography store.

Later Debbie told me that Jerry was trying to force Thelma and Warren to hustle as a pair of sisters. Jerry thought they were giving away too much free sex in the condemned hotel and that anyone who wanted to screw with them should pay first. "If they're old enough to fuck, they're old enough to get paid."

Several days passed before I saw Tex or Jerry. Then one night George stopped in to borrow $20 from the cash register. He often did this when he ran out of money during his drinking binges out on the Strip. While he was there, Jerry came charging into the store, followed by Tex. "You're a goddam dead motherfucker!" Jerry screamed, lunging straight at George.

George jumped out of his way and leaped behind the counter with me. For a minute there was silence. The two of us stared at the two of them. No one ever came behind the counter, because there was a persistent belief on the Strip that anyone who ventured behind a counter belonging to the Company would be shot on the spot. This myth (which I never discouraged) was said to be part of the unwritten law protecting porno clerks. We were also believed to have a gun behind the counter and a button that signaled for help from headquarters up the street. In fact, we did have a button, but no weapons other than the stick and my knife. George took the stick and I took the knife.

Jerry went ranting and raving around the room. He was not completely out of control, but all the customers cleared out of the peeps and left the store quickly. "You old motherfucker,

94

you got the cops after me!" he bellowed. "They tried to bust me in the bus station for soliciting. They said they had a signed complaint from a gray-haired man in the Pink Pussy."

George yelled back just as loudly. "That's a crock of shit! You've fucking made a mistake or somebody's lying to you!"

"If somebody signs a warrant for me, my probation goes, and I'll kill the son of a bitch that puts me back in prison. I mean I'll cut your damn yellow heart right out of your body and stuff it right up your ass. You hear me?"

Tex watched silently, his entire body bobbing up and down to the accompaniment of Jerry's screaming. He seemed mesmerized.

By now George had calmed down. "Now listen to me, you failed pimp," he said. "You better get your facts straight before you come after me, otherwise you're going to wish you *were* in jail. I suggest you get back on the street right now and find out if there really is a warrant out for you and if so for what and by whom. Then come talk to me."

For a moment Jerry did not seem to know what to do. Then he whirled around suddenly as though he were a karate expert, let loose with a yell, and kicked in the side of the large standing ashtray next to the counter. The base tumbled along the floor, and the tray sailed across the book rack and landed on the hard-core shelf, tearing the cover of a doctor-nurse book and scattering cigarette butts and a cup of half-melted ice all around the room.

After this flamboyant gesture, Jerry charged from the store, followed by Tex. We saw Tex kick the parking meter in front and then pretend to karate-chop the next one. George locked the door behind them and helped me clean up the mess. We made a few joking comments about the incident, but I was feeling guilty. I knew that if I had never allowed either of them to come into the store, this episode would not have happened. I also thought that Jerry was crazy enough to kill anyone he thought had wronged him. I vowed silently never to let them back.

Later that very night, however, Tex showed up again as though nothing had happened, and I was too curious to kick him out.

He stood silently by the door, staring at the street. Finally, I spoke. "Did you ever find Becky?" I immediately thought it was a stupid question in light of all the other events of the night.

"Yeah, we found her. She came back to the place to pick up her other shoes. She thought nobody was home, but I was there. I grabbed my belt and beat the shit out of her. I told her she was a goddamn whore and she had to sell that pussy, sell that pussy. I kept saying that to her. You know, you can't trust women. Jerry's right. You really can't trust 'em. No matter how much you love them, you just have to beat 'em. I always believed that, you just have to."

The trouble with Tex and Jerry ended as quickly as it began. It was true that the police were after him. Among the charges was pimping Warren and Thelma, who, it was said, were only thirteen and fourteen respectively. Jerry's probation was revoked and he was taken off to jail a few days later.

The pimp is king of the Strip. He not only controls the money and therefore the power of this subculture, but he carries the most prestige and respect with in the system of the Strip. The term *pimp* is not usually one of odium as outsiders often assume; it is what most young males on the Strip want to be. As with so many high-prestige jobs, from movie star to president, many feel called but few are chosen. The stereotypic image of the pimp in his fur jacket driving his outlandish purple Cadillac is an accurate one, even though today they are just as apt to drive Mercedes, BMWs, and Volvos, too. But these are only the most successful of the pimps. Just as Hollywood is full of unknown actors and Washington houses numerous would-be politicians who will never become household names, the Strip teems with young men trying to hustle one or two women to work for them. In his failures Jerry is more typical of the average pimp than is the fur-clad pimp in the purple Cadillac.

Eight

THE GIFT OF SEX

A male roadrunner seeking to copulate with a female brings her a lizard or other delicacy to excite her attention. The male, however, does not release the food to the female until after she has copulated with him. Male finches and cuckoos feed their partners during the actual act of copulation as a way to hold the females' interest. The male tern simply tosses the female a small fish, which she consumes during copulation. Throughout the animal kingdom, and particularly among birds, the male commonly gives the female a gift of food as part of the sex act.

Chimpanzees and baboons frequently share fruit or even meat with females who are in estrus. Sometimes a female who is not in estrus solicits such a gift merely by presenting her genitals to the male as though she were ready to be mounted and penetrated. Something like this was probably common among our own humanoid ancestors.

Evidence of this same tendency appears in Malinowski's account of sexual life among the Trobriand Islanders.

> In the course of every love affair the man has constantly to
> give small presents to the woman. To the natives the need
> of one-sided payment is self-evident. This custom implies

97

that sexual intercourse, even where there is mutual attachment, is a service rendered by the female to the male. . . . This rule is by no means logical or self-evident. Considering the great freedom of women and their equality with men in all matters, especially that of sex, considering also that the natives fully realize that women are as inclined to intercourse as men, one would expect the sexual relation to be regarded as an exchange of services itself reciprocal. But custom, arbitrary and inconsequent here as elsewhere, decrees that it is a service from women to men, and men have to pay.

This custom, however, may not be quite as "arbitrary" as Malinowski states. Even though the reasons may not be clear, the evidence is that in most societies such gifts usually flow from male to female. It has puzzled a number of observers in societies scattered throughout the world. Writing of the South American Sharanahua people, Janet Siskin, too, observes that sex is always accompanied by a gift of food to the female.

Whenever men prove their virility by hunting and thus gain wives or offer meat to seduce a woman, the theme is an exchange of meat for sex. This theme is not unusual, but it cannot be understood by a direct appeal either to biology or psychology. That is, I know of no evidence that women are naturally or universally less interested in sex or more interested in meat than are men.

The gift need not always be food. Tobacco is particularly popular among the aborigines of Australia, and women frequently demand it at each meeting with a lover. In many instances money or any other valuable serves the same purpose. Even within marriage, a Thonga man is advised to give his wife a sixpence or a shilling and she will allow him to make sexual advances toward her. In a sampling of world societies, Donald Symons reports that even where women sometimes give gifts to men as a part of coitus, the man always gives a gift of at least equal and usually much greater value. In no cases reported did women customarily make gifts to the male greater in value than those he presented to her. The most common of all patterns is that in which the man gives a valuable gift and the woman gives nothing. Symons found this to be true among groups as diverse as the Easter Islanders, the Hausa, the Delaware, the Kapauki, the Samoans, the Navajo, the Nootka, and the Wogeo.

In the book *Gifts and Poison,* F. G. Bailey observes that any gift puts the recipient in a relationship of debt to the giver. Ever since the publication of *The Gift* by Marcel Mauss, anthropologists have worked with this idea to untangle the complex web of human gift giving and reciprocation. The English word *gift* means poison in German, and this irony underscores the negative aspect of gift giving: the debt of reciprocation. In yet another twist of words, the German word *revanchieren* means both to get revenge and to repay a gift; it is related to the English word *revenge* and the French *revancher.* This interplay of gift, poison, and revenge in the Indo-European languages shows to what extent these concepts are intertwined in European culture.

A young man sending his girlfriend a dozen roses, the businessman buying a fur coat for his secretary, and the teenage boy taking the girl next door out for tacos are all operating in a cultural pattern that is not necessarily altruistic. On the Strip, narcotics, particularly cocaine, take the role of the gift of choice for any man courting any woman, but even buying her a drink or merely offering her a cigarette can serve the same function. All these males place the females in debt to them, and by the standards of Western culture, sex should be the appropriate payment. To say that these males are operating out of "love" sidesteps the issue, and to call it altruism would be appropriate only if the men were acting anonymously. Such behavior is usually lumped under the rubric of *courtship.* But the distinction between courtship and prostitution is cultural and completely arbitrary.

When an American teenage boy borrows the family car to take the girl next door out for a taco, and the two of them then park by the river, where the young girl gives him a hand job as he rubs her breasts, that is all part of courtship. Our term for this is *petting,* and though it is perceived as not entirely proper, it is certainly not seen as prostitution, even if the two of them never date again. Yet when a man picks up a woman on a street corner and she gives him a hand job in return for $40, it is prostitution even if their relationship has been ongoing for years. If the act is performed by poorer people, performed in a bad part of town, or performed by people in another culture, then it is even more likely to be labeled prostitution.

In much the same way that the dominant group in modern society defines as prostitution, the behaviors of people in classes it deems "lower" than itself, it also defines similar behaviors in exotic cultures. A starving Ik woman in the north of drought-ridden Uganda who has sex in exchange for a bowl of milk from a herdsman is prostituting herself. When an Indian woman on the Amazon demands food before she will have sex, she is called a prostitute. In the views of outsiders such as missionaries or government officials, the aborigine accepting tobacco for sex is prostituting herself,

This is not a judgment that the scientific community extends to animals. Thus when the female roadrunner copulates for a frog, or the tern for a fish, it is called bird courtship, not bird prostitution.

When a secretary sleeps with her boss and receives a promotion, a trip to Las Vegas, money to help buy a new car, or jewelry, it is called dating or courtship unless one of them is married, in which case the different category of an "affair" is brought to bear. But in neither case is it called prostitution.

When a husband and wife are divorced, the wife may be awarded large sums of money and large pieces of property for the services she has rendered him, but it is not labeled prostitution. Similarly the dowry arrangements and the marriage arrangements of the wealthy and the aristocratic in Western history are never thought of as prostitution.

In many respects the institution of marriage itself, as feminists pointed out clearly in the 1970s, is not very different from prostitution. Prostitutes, however, do not have to clean the house and cook. In contemporary society with its disposable spouses, the distinctions among prostitutes, mistresses, and a succession of wives are often fine and arbitrary, based more on social status than on sexual labor.

In many societies prostitutes are not as clearly separated out from normal society as the Strip separates them from the remainder of the city. Until the 1920s, a specialized form of prostitution existed on Guadalcanal, in the Solomon Island chain of Melanesia just off the New Guinea coast. The senior man in a matrilineage acquired a woman by capture in war, or took his own niece and made her into a *rembi*, who was rubbed with special magic potions to make her attractive to men and yet barren at the same time. Her owner then offered her sexual services for the standard price of two porpoise teeth to islanders and five porpoise teeth to outsiders. To advertise her status, the *rembi* wore a skirt shorter than that of most women and a large number of ornaments. Every day she bathed and oiled herself very carefully in order to stay constantly ready for sexual relations with any paying male. In exchange for these services, she was freed from normal domestic duties in her manager's household; she did not cook, clean, gather food, garden, or care for children. When her sexual career ended, magic was again applied, this time to make her fertile once again and to make her ready for marriage. Through magic she became modest and faithful. Then her manager arranged a good marriage for her at roughly a quarter of the normal bride-price.

In the southern New Hebrides Islands, all the unmarried males live in a bachelor hut to which is attached a woman called a *iowahanan*. She services the sexual needs of all the men who do not have other partners. This is similar to the *mespil* women of the Caroline Islands. The *mespil* keeps all the men of a single clan sexually satisfied. Both the *iowahanan* and the *mespil* are also responsible for teaching the younger men about sex. No woman would consider marrying a man who had not had sufficient practice with one of these special sex teachers. Such women receive respect for performing an important social service for the community. In time they also marry; and when they do, they are considered prize women for their knowledge of sex and because so many men found them desirable. Even other women respect these sex specialists who help to make the males better lovers and who keep them satisfied. They are repositories of valued knowledge.

This attitude of respect and appreciation for prostitutes held sway in the Western world in ancient times. Prostitutes often worked in sacred temples in the Mediterranean and were esteemed as sacred, religious women. A temple harlot plays a key role in *The Epic of Gilgamesh*, making her the first woman to appear in literature. In this Sumerian-Babylonian tale of 5,000 years ago, a goddess is spurned by King Gilgamesh, and in revenge she creates a wild man named Enkidu to lure the king into a fight. Rather than challenging the newcomer, Gilgamesh sends a harlot, who makes love to Enkidu, changing him from a beast to a man. She then proceeds to teach him the arts of civilization, such as pastoralism and the use of wine and religion, before bringing him into the city, where he becomes the bosom companion of Gilgamesh. Thus the harlot first appeared as missionary and priestess as well as prostitute.

Even in the earlier writings of the Bible, harlots are not treated with scorn. Tamar, the same woman with whom Onan would not sleep, is rewarded by bearing twins after sitting by the city gates and prostituting herself to her father-in-law. Genesis develops the complex relationship of sex and its sale in the account of Abram, who married his half sister Sarai. As the head of his nomadic patrilineage, Abram led his followers to Egypt, where Sarai caught the attention of the pharaoh. "And he entreated A'bram well for her sake; and he had sheep, and oxen, and he asses and menservants, and maidservants, and she asses and camels" (Gen. 12. 16). This large payment by the pharaoh for the use of Abram's wife could be construed as a form of purchase or bride-price, but later, when the pharaoh returned Sarai to Abram, Abram kept all the goods. Had this been a marriage and divorce, he would have had to return them. "And A'bram went up out of Egypt, he and his wife, and all that he had, and Lot with him, into the south. And A'bram was very rich in cattle, in silver, and in gold" (Gen. 13. 1, 2).

Abram carried so much loot that he and his nephew Lot quarreled, eventually dividing the goods between them. Lot then marched on to Sodom while Abram and Sarai headed for Canaan. Lot later offered his daughters to the men of Sodom to protect the men in his household, much as his aunt, Sarai, had been given to the pharaoh. After Sodom was destroyed and his wife turned to a pillar of salt, Lot copulated with each of his daughters, impregnated each one, and thus made sure that his branch of the family did not die out.

Meanwhile, Abram and Sarai negotiated a new pact with the Lord and changed their names to Abraham and Sarah; but the two were up to the same old tricks. Traveling to the land of Gerar, Sarah lived with King Abimelech, who knew she was Abraham's sister but did not know that she was also his wife. When Abimelech returned her to Abraham, he too gave "sheep and oxen, and menservants, and womenservants" (Gen. 20. 14) and even a thousand pieces of silver (Gen. 20. 16). With all this buying and selling of his sister/wife, it's no wonder that Abraham was a hundred years old before he finally had a son by her.

While biblical exegesis is rarely an easy task and is never incontrovertible, this sequence does present a fairly consistent picture of a nomadic group wandering through the Near East selling the sexual services of its womenfolk to men in the cities. And God, who quickly killed Onan for spilling his seed on the ground and slew other men for lesser sexual crimes, does not bat an eye at the buying and selling of Sarah, at Abraham's fathering children by his wife/sister's maids, or at incest between Abraham and his sister and between Lot and his daughters. Instead God chooses Abraham as the founder of Israel and ultimately of Christianity as well.

In ancient Greece, the hetaerae were respected prostitutes well educated in music, philosophy, and politics; they often attained positions of great influence in government and commerce. In training, education, and skill, they resembled the more recent geishas of Japan. Greece also had temple prostitutes, as did Egypt, Babylon, and Cyprus. Prostitution was not frowned upon nor persecuted in the earlier centuries of the Christian era. Saint Augustine certainly did not view prostitution as a sacred art, but the women who practiced it had their practical place in society. According to Saint Augustine, if you remove prostitutes "you will pollute all things with lust" (Augustine *De Ordine* 2. 4[12]). Prostitutes drained the more sinful inclinations of the males away from proper society. Saint Thomas Aquinas had the same attitude: "Take away the sewer and you will fill the palace with pollution. . . . Take away the prostitutes from the world, and you will fill it with sodomy" (Aquinas *Summa Theologica* II-II 10, 11).

Except in sporadic instances, attitudes toward prostitutes have declined steadily since classical times, as have the conditions under which they work. The United States and Europe witnessed a revival of elaborate houses of prostitution during the Victorian era, but by World War I this phase had passed. Prostitutes returned to the streets, to sleazy bars, and to a closer alliance with other forms of crime. Contemporary society seems much more comfortable with the form of prostitution practiced by Debbie and Tex, by massage-parlor employees, and by much more expensive call girls and mistresses servicing a smaller, wealthy group.

Legalizing prostitution, however, does not suddenly elevate the prostitute, free her from the pimps, or separate her from the other criminal activities, involving drugs, fencing, and robbery, with which prostitution is so closely allied. The state of Nevada and several European countries have legalized prostitution. The women are licensed and restricted to working in certain places. They are inspected regularly for disease, and the government taxes them substantially. These legal businesses produce tremendous revenues for the state, and they help protect the customer against disease and the more egregious forms of abuse. The women themselves receive some workers' benefits, such as the right to sue their employers, health-insurance coverage, and social-security rights. By and large, however, legalization benefits the government and management more than it does the women.

Legal or not, prostitution is always pushed into special areas of town. Authorities create a sex ghetto, whether in the tightly confined Combat Zone of Boston, the Strip in Washington, or the Forty-second Street/Times Square area in New York

City. And whether the sex ghetto is legal, as in Berlin, Amsterdam, and Frankfurt, or illegal, as in Chicago, Los Angeles, Boston, and Washington, organized crime and the pimp system control it.

This idea of crowding the sinners together to protect the virtuous was clearly presaged in the writings of Saint Augustine and Saint Thomas Aquinas. European society quickly translated it into public policy.

On June 3, 1358, for example, the Greater Council of the city of Venice passed a resolution asking the captains of the city wards to help in "providing some place in Venice proper for the habitation of sinful women." Later these sinful women were all confined to an area known as the Castalleto. Once assembled, and with so many eager customers, the women were more easily organized by pimps. The problem of the pimps became so bad that in 1423 the Council of Forty banned them "in order that they may not continue to live on and appropriate the earnings of said wretched girls, but that the said girls be left free to go on living in the Castalleto if they so please, and without molestation." This relationship between pimp and streetwalker appears to have been much the same as on the Strip of Washington today. In this same resolution, the council concluded from its study of the problem that

> many corrupted youths, who might rather be termed pimps, not caring to live by the sweat of their own brows, are in the habit of daily following after prostitutes, living off the property and evil doing of the latter, taking from them their money and other goods, threatening them and frequently beating them, when the said prostitutes do not wish to give up their money.

These words describe men such as Tyrone, Jerry, and Jesse in contemporary Washington as accurately as they did the pimps of Venice over 500 years ago. The business of prostitution has been remarkably consistent throughout Western history since it changed from being a sacred activity controlled by religion to a strictly economic one controlled by pimps and procurers. It is in sharp contrast to the equally secular forms of prostitution in the Orient practiced in the traditional Chinese teahouses or Japanese geisha houses. Prostitution was organized as a business much like any other legitimate commercial undertaking. Organized crime was not a major element of prostitution in these countries until they, too, began to Westernize.

There appear to be no easy solutions to the myriad problems associated with prostitution today. Those who claim that legalization would solve the problems have only to look at prostitution in places where it is legal to see that many of the same problems persist. On the other hand, those who claim that making it illegal and arresting all the prostitutes and their customers would diminish or end the practice cannot point to any society in the world, except possibly for mainland China and the Soviet Union, where this has effectively lowered prostitution rates.

Nine

TRADE

"It was better before the sexual revolution. I have always prided myself on being the ugliest and fattest man on the street, and yet I could always get ten good-looking ones a night." Frank may have exaggerated slightly in claiming to be the fattest and ugliest, but he came very close to taking top honors. He was not so much ugly as slovenly. His clothes always looked as if he had slept in them.

Frank worked as a general flunky for the Company. Several nights a week when I was too busy to walk up to headquarters for change, I telephoned and Frank would bring me a bag filled with plastic tubes, each containing eighty quarters. Of all the people on the Strip, I probably trusted Frank most. I did not need to count the tubes when he delivered them; I knew they would total exactly what they should. Frank was the only person in whom I had enough trust to leave him in charge of the cash register and store while I took a break or ran a quick errand.

Frank had retired from the marines a decade or so before coming to work for the Company. He had a wife or a former wife—I was never sure which—somewhere out west, as well as three grown children scattered around the country, but that part of his life seemed dead. He rarely mentioned it, and I do not think that any of his family were in contact with him. He lived in a small apartment just off the Strip, within easy walking distance from the Pink Pussy and Company headquarters.

Frank loved to hear jokes about sex, religion, politics, ethnic groups, and homosexuals. The topic never mattered so long as the joke was funny. Each night when he came into the store, he had two or three new jokes to tell, but usually he forgot the punch line of one, or placed it at the wrong time in another. Even the one joke he remembered usually emerged so laboriously that its humor was quashed. Still, he never gave up trying, and that was part of the reason so many people on the Strip liked him. When he entered the Western Beef House or Sabina's, the dancers all waved and winked at him. As soon as he sat down, one of them would dance from table to table to get to him and give him a kiss. Sometimes she kissed him on the forehead and tickled his chin. She enjoyed flirting with him and throughout these little comic scenes, Frank smiled, bantered with the bartender, and enjoyed being the star. He never tired of such episodes or grew irritated with the girls who initiated them.

Only two things bothered Frank—"pimps and fags"—but even they did not cause him to lose his temper. "I can't stand to be around either one, because neither one is a man. Both of them dress too frilly and they strut around like they're better than everyone else. But the worst is that they both abuse people so much. That's why I always let any girl who needs it use my place as a way to escape from the pimps." Frank frequently displayed a protective interest in some of the women he knew on the Strip. I never saw him get into an actual fight with a pimp over a woman, but he often came very close to it.

Despite his expressed dislike of homosexuals, Frank fellated another male almost every day. Sometimes he strolled into the Pink Pussy with a young soldier or a disheveled youth. Without pausing to talk, Frank led the man directly to a booth in the back, and somehow fat Frank and the guy managed to squeeze in together. Frank then fellated the guy, who watched the film. Frank knew enough to take these men to the booth into which I had the most difficulty seeing; and from a sense of propriety, I rarely watched, knowing that he would provoke no trouble. My only concern was that some of the partners he brought in might harm him or otherwise cause a disturbance.

One night Frank spent over three hours in the store with me watching a police stakeout. Some undercover agents, said to be from the city police department, had chained a moped to the parking sign in front of the Pink Pussy and were watching it from inside an abandoned building next door. I had not noticed the agents until Frank arrived and explained that someone had phoned headquarters to say that the police were staking out the Pink Pussy again. He came down to help me out, he told me.

A hooker who followed Frank into the shop said the bike was no more than a robbery decoy. She reported that the same agents had left a bicycle chained for three days in front of the Kentucky Fried Chicken place and no one had touched it because they knew it was a stakeout. She claimed the police were merely repeating that effort with better bait.

Whatever the reason for the stakeout, we had virtually no business. A few solitary men wandered unsuspectingly into the shop, but even they quickly felt the unease and moved on to another store.

Frank and I sat watching the window through which the police alternately stared at the moped, stared at us, and surveyed the street. Frank handed me his pistol to put on the counter under some night report forms. He wanted it close if we needed it, but he did not want it concealed on his body in violation of the law.

As we sat around that night, Frank talked a great deal and covered a lot of subjects. He said that life on the Strip was getting worse. His favorite time had been around the end of the Vietnam War. "There used to be a lot more horny soldiers around in those days. I could walk up to them on the street and ask them if they wanted to go see a dirty movie, take them in, and do them. If that didn't work, I asked them if they wanted to smoke. They always wanted to get high back then, but today everyone gets high with no trouble. That's why I'm glad the government is raising the drinking age back to twenty-one again. That will bring a lot more boys back into the city looking for ways to get high. It makes the young guys nicer to old ones like me. They know I can get them something to drink. And then I can also get them into my apartment a little easier. If they can't get into the clubs and bars until they are twenty-one, then they'll need places to go to drink. That way I have something to offer them again. Then my sex life will improve."

Frank also felt that his sex life had been changed by the sexual revolution, which made guys more interested in masturbation. "The trouble with these kids today is that they all like their hands too much. I haven't seen anything like it before. Ten years ago a boy would hardly touch himself if he had any other possible way of getting off. But now young boys would rather go into the peeps, watch a couple of lesbians, and get themselves off. They would rather do that than have a BJ. And it doesn't matter if they have a boyfriend, a girlfriend, or a sugar daddy, they would rather get off by themselves watching those damn movies. You see 'em walk in here, go to the booth, and slam that motherfucking door behind them just daring anyone to touch it. Boys used to think it was really bad to be gay, but they would still rather have a BJ from another guy than bring themselves off. It was harder for them to get girls back then. Then came the sexual revolution, and they all decided it wasn't so bad to be doing each other. Now the pendulum is swinging back the other way, and they have all decided that they can do it to themselves and don't need guys *or* girls to help them with it.

"Everyone's moved out to the suburbs now, too. For a while I worked out there in the suburbs. I worked at a sandwich shop and I used to keep good sex books around, and these guys would come in and look at the books and then let me do them. But then one by one they all got married. I was up to six steady guys for a while, but then it dropped down to only one and he got married, too. So I quit and moved back into the city and decided that I would just have to pick up what I could on the side.

"I first started tricking with guys when I was in my early

110

thirties. At first I was just 'trade'; I would occasionally let some fairy blow me. I was living in California then, at the marine base. It really scared me to death, and afterward I hated it and hated myself for doing it. That's why even now I try not to ever push a guy. I know how strange he might feel about it, because even when he likes it, he hates it. Eventually I got over it when I read a column in a newspaper that said what was normal was whatever brought someone pleasure and what was abnormal was just whatever brought people discomfort in sex. Even though the article was talking about regular, straight sex, I interpreted it for my own case. And then I began to feel better about the whole thing."

The agents next door were still watching the moped. Frank was certain that this was what the police wanted everyone on the Strip to think, when actually they were staking out the Pink Pussy for some reason.

Frank decided to go out front for a while to see if he could lure the cops out of the building they were hiding in. At first he stood leaning against the moped to talk with a woman friend who passed by. Then he began pacing back and forth. Finally he disappeared for twenty minutes. When he returned, he brought a cup of coffee for himself, a container of iced tea for me, and a large bag of fried onion rings for us to share.

"One of them is wearing one of those hearing-aid radios in his ear," Frank reported. "It's just like the ones the Secret Service always wears around the president, but I don't think the local robbery detectives would be wearing them down here on the Strip. I couldn't get any action out of them at all. We'll just have to wait."

I felt fairly secure with Frank there, calm and sensible. As long as I did not have to shoot a policeman, I was prepared to follow his advice in the whole matter and let him keep control.

Soon Frank was rambling on again about his likes and dislikes. "Right now, with so few good soldiers around, I mostly like hillbilly types—real ridge runners. They come to town in those damn beat-up old cars and sometimes live in them for weeks looking for work and friends. They never cause any trouble, but a lot of people are afraid of them. I like to do whatever makes them feel really good. I can tell when they get into something, and I would rather do that than ask them what they want. What they say they want and what they really respond to are not the same. But I don't like to kiss a guy unless he is really special to me and I know that he likes it."

On another occasion Frank had explained that he liked to have sex only with "straight guys" because he does not want to catch AIDS, or "gay cancer," as he usually calls it. According to his explanation, as long as he is having sex with supposedly heterosexual men, he will not catch AIDS. Following the same precaution, he said he had stopped tricking with guys who were heavy drug users, or when he thought they were using drugs, he would not swallow the sperm. He figured that as long as he spit the sperm out, he could not catch AIDS.

For Frank the spread of AIDS was just one more justification of his dislike for the openly gay men on the Strip. But this dislike did not begin with the AIDS epidemic and had much more diverse causes.

"Generally, I don't care for gay people as friends or as people to have sex with. Gay guys are insulted if I try to approach them. They wouldn't think of going to bed with someone like me. Anyway, gay guys are much more likely to abuse you. In the gay world, the younger always prey upon the older. The younger gay guys are out to get everything they can from the older gays. And the straight guys, they just like to get their rocks off. Most straights will let you do them just so they can get off. And the straight guys who do want the money will be up front about it. They tell you that they charge this much or whatever. Then if you don't want them, you don't have to take them. But gays will take you for all the money they can get, and they lead you on like they really like you and are not after the money.

"A straight guy doesn't pretend that he is in love with you, but he will treat you fair. The only straight men to watch out for are the ones in their thirties. They are past the time in life when their looks can attract men, women, or money, so they are likely to rob you if they can. Younger guys know that if you don't want to pay them, then somebody else will, so they don't waste the time trying to rob you. But the older guy may think that you are his last chance and he will go with you just to get your money.

"For a while I went out with this straight guy who was heavily into drugs. One day I had worked for sixteen hours without a break and I came home dead tired. As soon as I hit the bed, this guy rolled over and told me to fix him some eggs and bacon. I told him I was too tired, but he pulled my pistol out and pointed it right at me. So I got up and cooked the meal, but I told him I was not doing it because I wanted to but only because of the gun. He then fired my gun into the address book beside the bed.

"A few days later he came in really high one night. He was acting mean and pulled out the gun and pointed it at me again. 'You don't think I'll shoot you, do you?' he asked me. I told him that, yes, I did think he would. So he did. He shot me in the leg. I had this other, really old guy living there with me then. So the boy grabbed the old man up and pointed the gun to his head and told him that he was next. I took all of my money and tried to give it to him. I told him to leave and that nothing would happen. I told him to throw the gun in the laundry room downstairs and then to get out.

"The guy came to his senses and left. Then I called the police and told them I had been attacked in the laundry room. When they went down to look, they found the gun, but the guy was still there, too. The guy told them that he lived in the building. So the police let him and the old man ride with me in the ambulance, and the guy held my hand the whole way.

"Later the police came into the emergency room and questioned me about it again. They told me they'd seen gay magazines and asked if we were gay. I told them that the boy and the old man were not but I was. They then said that if they spent a lot of effort searching for this attacker I'd told them about and he turned out not to be true, they would throw me in prison. I'd been in prison and I sure didn't want to go back. Meanwhile one of the cops said he heard the boy on the telephone sobbing and confessing everything to his mother—she knew all about our relationship. So the next day, the boy and I went down to the police station and signed papers saying that he had done it but no charges would be pressed.

"That boy is married now and lives out of state. He still calls me and sometimes comes to visit. He wanted me to come up when he got married. He tried to send me the money, but I couldn't go."

As I listened to Frank's story, I forgot to watch the stakeout. When Frank wandered back over to the door to look out again, he saw that the agents were no longer in their hiding place, but the moped was still chained up out front. Frank went to look for the policemen.

Half an hour later, one of the agents came into the store. He nodded at me, asked perfunctorily, "How you doing tonight?" and wandered around. The store was empty, but in front of me on the counter was Frank's pistol. I suddenly wondered if it was the same one that the boy had used to shoot Frank in the leg. I made a note on my pad to ask him, but I never did. Somewhere in the course of either Frank's exit or the agent's entry, the wind had blown part of the paper covering off the pistol, exposing the grip. Gradually, I reached across the counter to cover it without arousing the policeman's suspicion.

"How is it out there tonight?" I asked him, unsure whether to act as though he were just another customer or acknowledge that I knew what he was doing.

"About like usual for this time of year."

"So what are you up to out there then?" I risked getting a little closer to the subject.

"I ask myself the same thing when I could be home watching 'Dallas.'"

Already I was stuck. I did not know what to say next, but he resolved this by walking out. "See you before long," he called as he left.

The statement perplexed me. Was that a standard "see you around" comment or was there a hidden meaning in it? At the same time his partner came walking up the street carrying two boxes of Church's fried chicken and some drinks. The two of them ducked back inside the building, and in the dark I could no longer tell what they were doing.

A few minutes later Frank came waddling back down the street also carrying two boxes of Church's fried chicken and some drinks. "I picked us up some supper. I hope you like corn on the cob. If not, I'll eat yours."

"Did you see the cop in there?" I asked.

"Yeah, that's why I went in. He was drinking a cup of coffee with another plainclothes type with a hearing aid. I sat down in the booth next to them, but they were just shooting the crap. One must be going on vacation to Czechoslovakia because he talked about that. The one guy wanted to quit for the night, but the other one told him to hang on another hour or two and relief would take over for him." As he talked, Frank covered the counter with fried chicken, corn, french fries, cole slaw, and napkins. "I brought something to show you after dinner," he said, pointing to a crumpled grocery bag he had also brought. "I stopped by my house to pick it up, but I don't want you to get grease all over it, so wait until you finish eating."

We continued speculating about the guards outside as we ate. When everything was cleared away, Frank lifted up the bag. "These are my prize pictures," he said, pulling out a stack of Polaroid photographs. Each picture showed a naked or nearly naked young man. The standard poses showed him standing in front of a television set with an erection or seated on the couch with an erection. Some of the men in the pictures covered their faces with their hands or with a pillow; others turned their faces away from the camera. Most of them, however, stared straight into the lens with a broad grin as though proud of their bodies. The bodies varied from adolescent-thin to fully mature men with moustaches and paunches.

Like a box of pictures waiting to be cataloged in the family album, each photograph had a name and date inscribed on the bottom, some with additional comment noting the hometown, the meeting place, or the number of orgasms. There were probably more than 200 photographs in all. "There would have been a lot more, but the cops confiscated the rest when they raided the apartment the time of the shooting," Frank explained.

"Here's a picture of Ray, the guy who shot me in the leg." Frank handed me a picture of a redheaded guy of about twenty with his blue jeans pulled down around his knees and his penis pointed like a gun. "And this is another marine. Doesn't he look like a real man with this short hair and that big hunk? Well, look at this picture of him two years later. It's the same guy." He handed me a picture of a guy with much longer hair and several new tattoos on his body.

"Look at this one. He went home with me and then asked me to fuck him. He said that he always wanted to be treated like a woman and I could do it for him. I told him he was crazy, that my dick was too small to fuck him. He lives with two lesbians now and he's found himself some kind of lover. He was a weird one."

Going through the stack of pictures—and we went through the entire stack—Frank showed me guys who had robbed him, beaten him, and stabbed him. He also showed me scars on his chest and arms from knife blades, a screwdriver, and a thrown beer bottle. He showed me pictures of guys who were later killed in automobile accidents, who had married and divorced, who had gone to prison, and mostly guys who had appeared in his life for one night and a few pictures and then disappeared forever.

Frank seemed genuinely to cherish the pictures. Though he kept them in a crumpled old bag, he wiped my fingerprints off each one with his sleeve as I handed it back to him, and placed it in the bag with the care of a bride washing and putting away treasured pieces of china. He could have talked about them all through the night if we had not been interrupted by the departure of the agents. They walked out of their hiding spot, unlocked the moped, and placed it inside a waiting truck.

The next week I read an article in the newspaper about the police raiding a series of call-girl and call-boy businesses. The businesses were not connected with the Company, but they had been selling their client lists and files to members of the Czechoslovakian secret police. American government agencies joined forces to investigate Communist infiltration of the sex industry in the Washington vicinity. Frank later told me that this was what the agents had been investigating on the Strip that night. They did a series of stakeouts on all kinds of businesses

116

over a period of several weeks. They photographed the license plates of cars cruising the area, hookers and hustlers working, and customers coming and going. Some people said they were investigating government workers and military men to see which ones came into the area. Others speculated that they were just searching for Communist diplomats and spies.

Frank's life-style appeared abnormal by Strip standards in that he took so many unknown men home with him. Most men seeking quick sexual contact with other males found their opportunities in one of the pornography stores. The Pink Pussy attracted a daily round of men seeking sexual encounters with other men. Usually these were quick blow jobs initiated, performed, and terminated in the silent culture of the back room.

Richard, a thirty-five-year-old clerk in a Connecticut Avenue men's store, came into the Pink Pussy almost every afternoon toward the end of the rush hour, when the young lawyers finally crawl out of their offices. Young lawyers in three-piece suits were Richard's type. He met them, fellated them, and went on with his evening.

Maurice came in a little later than Richard. Despite being over six feet tall and quite black, Maurice referred to himself as "strictly a white lady, honey, strictly a white lady." This was always said with a slightly effeminate wave of the wrist, but Maurice was not a transvestite; on the contrary, he was often mistaken for a pimp. He liked to fellate younger men in their twenties. "But I never do the same one twice. I believe in sharing with the less fortunate. If I've had him once, I leave him for someone else and I look for some new thing upon which to bestow my blessing. Especially white boys you should never do twice, because once they've seen black, they never want to go back, and it's so hard to get rid of them after that."

A steady stream of men, usually younger men, came into the Pink Pussy for blow jobs. A few came in as regularly as Richard and Maurice. Every Thursday night a Trailways bus driver would walk in just after eight o'clock. He would hand me his briefcase to hold behind the counter while he went into a booth and watched a film with the door cracked open. Soon another man would slip in and fellate him. On the way out again, he would tip me a couple of quarters for watching his bag.

On weekend nights a sporadic stream of solitary young men from all branches of the military came through late in the evening. As long as they were alone, someone would approach them and usually score. Only once did I have a soldier storm out telling me that I should call the police because of "the goddamn faggots in the back." Most soldiers seem to know that they can get blow jobs in the back of porno stores, and occasionally one asked me directly if it was true that he could get a blow job there.

Young office men, whom we collectively referred to as the "young lawyers"—the kind Richard preferred—seemed the commonest candidates for blow jobs, but they were also the hardest for me to know anything about. They rushed into the place, often looked at the front rows of magazines for a while, then darted into the back and into a booth. Then they were gone. Whether they preferred this type of sexual activity because they were overworked and did not have time to date, or because they were underpaid and could not afford dates, I never really knew.

The most difficult customers for me were the younger men, since it was difficult to ascertain whether they were in the store to make contact with a prostitute, to look for a man to give them a blow job, or to earn money by letting some man fellate them. I knew most of the regular male hustlers on the Strip by sight and they knew not to do business in the back. I usually trusted them to use a booth if they wanted to watch a film or hide for a short time, but I seldom let them go back with their customers. Sometimes students, construction workers, or young unemployed men hung around the back and appeared to be cruising for sex without knowing exactly what to do. I kept a watchful eye on them to ensure that they caused no trouble with the wrong customers, did not disrupt other forms of business, and did not panic and do anything violent. Such neophytes were the most likely to disturb the normal pattern of social interaction or to panic. By watching them carefully and very openly, I discouraged them from lingering in the Pink Pussy and they often moved on, presumably to another store. In time some of them learned how the system operated and then became regular customers.

According to the explanation commonly given on the Strip, men often begin this practice in the younger years as "trade," which means they let other men blow them but do not touch the other men's genitals. This changes over the course of a few years as the novice becomes more sexually active, until finally he is giving blow jobs to anonymous and usually younger men. As the men often say, "Today's trade is tomorrow's competition."

The Pink Pussy attracted much of this so-called trade after the nearby Stallion was razed in preparation for the parking lot of the new D.C. Convention Center. The Stallion supposedly had nothing but booths in the back with no films in them. The booths resembled toilet stalls and there were holes in the partitions between them. Men paid a cover charge to go in and they cruised until they found someone with whom to have sex. This business was a commercial version of the "tearoom trade" in public bathrooms analyzed by the sociologist Laud Humphreys. Because so many public bathrooms in parks and subways have been closed, much of the sex business from them has moved into pornography stores and into businesses such as the French Tearoom and the Stallion.

Anonymous sex remains available all over the city of Washington. From the men's room on the top floor of the House of Representatives Office Building to a particular toilet in the Library of Congress or Woodward & Lothrop's department store, men hang around waiting to have sex with other men or to masturbate while watching other men. Similar meeting grounds for impersonal sex can be found in a number of public parks and areas such as Capitol Hill in Denver, Loring Park in Minneapolis, Balboa Park in San Diego, and Golden Gate Park in San Francisco. These places are so well known throughout the United States and Europe that guidebooks listing them are sold in many of the porno stores, although the Pink Pussy did not carry them. The guides also list the appropriate toilets on most college campuses, the right highway rest-stop areas in

119

rural states, the best truck stops, and the better-used pornography stores in red-light districts.

According to Humphreys's study of such places in one midwestern city, the men who have sex in such places are usually married and living with their families, and have above-average educations (fourteen years) and above-median incomes. They have 1.9 children, have an average age of thirty-four, and lead lives that in almost all aspects appear normal. Often they feel socially or psychologically threatened by gay bars in the gay community and do not identify with them. They do not want to risk going into gay bars and businesses, but they are neither hypocrites nor "closet queens." Because they have heterosexual bonds, they do not look for relationships in these anonymous encounters; they merely seek a quick, easy, and impersonal sexual outlet.

The sudden arrival of AIDS at the start of the 1980s had a major impact on the anonymous sex in stores such as the Pink Pussy: It increased. The Company owned one gay bookstore and a gay bathhouse, both of them long popular as places where homosexual men could meet for easy and quick sex. Business declined markedly in both these places as the fear of AIDS increased and homosexual men became more afraid of each other as sexual partners. Many of these customers began frequenting the Pink Pussy and other heterosexual stores more often than in the past. Like Frank, they were searching for sexual encounters with so-called straight men, presumably less likely to be carrying AIDS than were gay men. Men who led ostensibly heterosexual lives but were accustomed to occasional forays into the gay baths or some other gay locale in search of a quick sexual encounter now stayed away from such places. Instead they sought the same kind of sexual encounters in "safe" places, including the Pink Pussy. This, too, was beginning to create more opportunities for men like Frank. AIDS did not bring back the numbers of tricks that the Vietnam War era had provided him, but life was improving.

When Captain William Bligh sailed the *Bounty* into Tahiti 200 years ago, he found a type of man he thought disgusting:

one raised to live "solely for the caresses of the men," as he wrote. The good captain was interested enough in these people to question one of them at great length and to have him strip down so that the captain could make sure that the man had a penis and testicles and was not some form of eunuch. The *mahu*, as such a man is called, is frequently effeminate in actions, speech, and dress, but he is not a transvestite. He leads the life of a man, even though he has sexual relations with other men.

Traditionally, the *mahu* performed fellatio or "ate the penis" of men. Captain Bligh reported that men had interfemural intercourse with the *mahu* by sticking the penis between his legs, but Bligh and most subsequent reporters denied that the Tahitians practiced sodomy. That practice was reportedly learned much later from the French and is still viewed as nontraditional activity. Unlike the transvestites of the American Plains Indians and Siberia, the *mahu* does not live as a woman or marry men. Instead he is something of a sexual resource for the entire male population of a community. *The Tahitians*, a study by psychiatrist/anthropologist Robert I. Levy, reports that each community has a single *mahu*. When that one dies, the people say, God arranges for another one to take his place.

The *mahu* is supposedly self-selected in that he is a boy who does not want to grow up following the traditional male routines; he may prefer doing girls' tasks or having girls for friends, for instance. But Levy also points out that there is often pressure on the boy from family or neighbors to become a *mahu*. One boy, for example, lived alone with his grandfather and in caring for him had to perform many of the female household tasks. His grandfather had neighbors make female items of clothing for him, and when the boy was in school, older boys approached him to solicit sexual acts. At the age of fourteen, he began fellating sixteen-year-old boys. Later he gave up the feminine articles of clothing, but by then he was firmly established in his role as mahu and continued having sexual relations with males. Given these circumstances, it was not clear how much of the boy's development as a *mahu* was genuinely "self-selected" and how much was due to the influence of his grandfather, neighbors, and schoolmates.

The mahu from one community does not have sexual relations with the mahus of other communities—that is, with other homosexuals like himself. His only sex partners are "normal" males. The men using the *mahu* for sexual pleasure do not consider the act shameful and they are open about having gone to a *mahu*. They allow themselves to be fellated, but disclaim any active sexual role on their part. Men typically use the *mahu* when they do not have another sexual outlet. Any man needing sexual contact but not having access to a female can turn to the mahu. This probably lessens pressures on the female population, which might otherwise be in greater demand for sexual services to unattached or temporarily alone males. The men do not see the sexual act with the *mahu* as being inferior to intercourse, and in some ways it is regarded as much better, as one informant explained to Levy:

> It's just like doing it with a woman, but his way of doing it is better than with a woman, as you just take it easy while he does it to you. . . . He doesn't let go quickly and it makes you very limp. When you go to a woman, it's not always satisfactory. When you go to the mahu, it's more satisfactory. The sexual pleasure is great. You can't stand it any more, and because of that you try to push his head away.

Frank's life closely resembles a *mahu*'s in many respects, as do the lives of a large number of men who frequent tearooms and cruising areas waiting to service other males sexually. Whether completely homosexual or actively bisexual, these men are not wholly part of either the homosexual or the heterosexual world. They live a life in each community, a circumstance that often causes them to be called hypocrites. It is not a valid charge. Having become fond of a male society, they have developed a sexual preference for other males but for primarily heterosexual ones.

There are many such men in the United States and, to a lesser but substantial extent, in Germany, France, and other

European nations. They are an example of a common form of the quick sex produced and consumed in contemporary society. It is a strange society indeed that creates a sociosexual structure like this for erotic gratification.

Ten

THE NEW SERVANT CLASS

As Frank's case indicates, homosexuals and homosexual activities were a significant part of the commerce in the Pink Pussy and all along the Strip. Many of the businesses catered mainly to them: Homosexuals had their own pornography stores, theaters, bars, private clubs, baths, and cruising ground. Despite this, they were financially significant customers of nearly every other business on the Strip as well, except for the massage parlors and other forms of female prostitution. They were also a major segment of the work force in both heterosexual and homosexual businesses. Some gay men, such as Frank, preferred the bars where nude women danced; some worked as bouncers and cooks; others went to straight pornographic films as well as gay ones; and a few even hustled on the streets as prostitutes. They were an integral part of life on the Strip.

A culture can build as many different social institutions based on homosexuality as it can build on heterosexuality. Historically, cultures have also found ways to use homosexual relations to build something of practical value to the society as a whole. The Spartans, who were very concerned about the need for defense and a strong army, used the erotic tie between older and younger males to build a tightly integrated military force, acting on the assumption that two lovers will fight harder in battle for each other when they are side by side. This benefited the whole army and thereby helped all of Spartan society. In a much different way, the Plains Indians utilized homosexual males as highly esteemed medicine men and shamans who often married chiefs and other respected men. Because these berdaches, as they were called, had the strength of men, they were excellent at such jobs as curing the large bison pelts, making tepees from skins, and other strenuous jobs usually done by the women.

The Azande people live in the eastern part of the Sudan and are today a part of that nation, but in the past they were divided into a number of rival kingdoms often at war with one another. Each king maintained a large standing army at the seat of his royal court. The army lived in a series of barracks that protected the seat of royal power. The presence of so many young men together, as with any army anywhere in the world, created tremendous sexual tension. In the case of the Azande, the tension was greatly intensified by strictly enforced laws against adultery and rape. Women were married very young, and any man not her husband who was caught with a woman would have his lips, nose, genitals, and hands cut off. If he survived this ordeal, he paid a fine and lived the remainder of his life as a virtually worthless person, unable to work or do anything of value.

Few men risked such severe punishment. One alternative open to them was masturbation, which was tolerated by the society so long as it was done discreetly and not flaunted. Another acceptable sexual outlet for the young warrior was to take a boy as a temporary wife during his military service. The warrior approached the boy's family through the proper channels and, if accepted, paid a bride-price of about five spears, less than half the price of a girl bride. Once negotiated and agreed upon, this marriage was legal in every sense of the term. The boy bride, or *kumba gude,* lived with his warrior husband and performed most of the services a wife would perform. The *kumba gude* gathered wood for the fire, drew water, arranged the warrior's toilet, and fetched the warrior's food each day. At night they slept together, the warrior satisfying his sexual desires by rubbing against the body of his lover.

For the *kumba gude,* the marriage served as a military apprenticeship. From his warrior lover he learned how to be a soldier. Whenever the warrior marched off to battle, the *kumba gude* marched with him carrying the warrior's shield. Even though the young boy was not permitted on the battlefield, he gradually acquired the skills he would need when he himself became a warrior in his early twenties. In this way the institution of boy marriage among the Azande filled two major needs simultaneously: Soldiers were kept sexually satisfied without disrupting the lives of women, and a new generation of soldiers was trained.

Throughout this process, the boy's family kept careful watch on the warrior who was husband to their son. If he was good to the boy and proved a decent husband, the family would be willing to negotiate the marriage of one of their daughters to him when he finished his military service. If the warrior proved unsatisfactory, the family would not risk uniting itself with him permanently through a daughter and grandchildren. In this way the boy marriage served also as a training ground and testing ground for real marriage. It was a form of trial marriage without the risk of children or the messy issues of inheritance.

Azande kings often acquired boys whom they married to their sons when the sons reached puberty. The boy kept the young prince sexually satisfied for a few years, and thereby out of the king's harem or out of the danger of an adulterous relationship that might bring havoc to the royal household. Sometimes the princes became so fond of these early lovers that they kept them as part of their households even after acquiring female wives. Though this was not considered proper for an older man and indicated immaturity, it was nevertheless tolerated as neither strange nor wrong. Thus, though Azande society placed limits on homosexuality, it was an important practice used to fulfill many social as well as sexual needs.

From time to time in Western history, parallels to this system of the Azande developed in European and American society. In traditional British boys' boarding schools, younger boys served as "fags" to the older boys, performing domestic chores, tending the fire, and serving food. Often the younger boys also served as sexual partners for the older boys. In time the fags themselves became upperclassmen and acquired fags of their own. In a similar process, ships' officers often carried cabin boys on board to provide, much as the name implies, very intimate services. Meanwhile older sailors satisfied themselves with younger sailors. The contemporary prison system in the West rests on a social basis of younger inmates serving as both sexual partners and servants of the older, larger males.

All these examples differ from the Azande system in that the Western world formally disapproves of them and makes periodic efforts to eradicate them. Such practices are relatively covert, remaining outside the "normal" lives of most people in the culture. Sailors, boarding-school boys, and prisoners may all institutionalize these relationships, but they do not bring them into conventional society as did the Azande or the ancient Greeks, who bragged about such affiliations and wrote poems lauding them.

For the most part such sex practices never served a useful social purpose in the West. Consequently, homosexual behavior was at best tolerated and ignored; and at worst, those who practiced it were burned at the stake by the church, herded into concentration camps and killed by the Nazis, and imprisoned in nearly all Western societies over the course of their history. Society rarely tolerates what it does not need or cannot use.

During the twentieth century a gradual though *very* tentative and restrictive social and legal acceptance of homosexuality has been developing. Even in countries such as the United States, where homosexual acts are still illegal in most states, attitudes toward such acts have eased slightly. This immediately raises the question of why. Unless one believes the highly dubious notion that modern people are more enlightened or more tolerant than their forebears, one must assume that there is a practical reason for the gradual acceptance of a "gay" population. A possible explanation arose in observing gay men in and out of the Pink Pussy. Some were open about their sexuality, and this openness spread throughout their lives to their families and landlords as well as employers and colleagues. In contrast, many of the men kept it as much a secret as possible. Even within the porno store, they would not look at any of the homosexual books, magazines, or films, or give any outward sign of being interested in homosexuality until they made contact with a specific other male.

By months of talking with these different sets of men produced one consistent observation: The two sets belonged to different occupational groups. The secretive men most often worked for the government, or in construction, or in office jobs. The men who were open worked in service occupations or retail sales. Rarely would a hair stylist, florist, or male nurse seek to hide his gay activities and pretend to be interested in straight pornography. On the other hand, only rarely did a lawyer from the Commerce Department, a schoolteacher, a bus driver, or a doctor act openly gay in the store, even when he had sex with other males in the booths.

Openly gay men worked as waiters; as clerks in clothing, jewelry, or department stores; as caterers; and sometimes as secretaries, nurses, or street vendors. They were very heavily represented in the lower ranks of the retail and service professions, which required only moderate training. They also tended to work in those services or sales that served more affluent patrons. They worked in the more expensive department stores, restaurants, and hair styling salons, and of course such services such as catering, decorating, and housecleaning were oriented toward affluent customers.

In earlier decades many of these jobs had been performed by house servants, usually members of ethnic or racial minorities, particularly blacks. As other employment opportunities opened up for the servant population in America, the services they performed moved outside the home and into private businesses. Rather than keep a cook and other servants, people dine out more often or have catered parties at home. Rather than hire a permanent yardman, they use a landscaping service on a scheduled basis and buy flowers from a florist as needed. Rather than have a nurse or maid stay up all night with a sick family member, they will put the ailing person in a hospital or nursing home. Rather than have a seamstress or tailor make the family clothes, they buy them ready-made.

Wealthier members of society have always preferred that these tasks be performed by males. As Thorstein Veblen pointed out very clearly in *The Theory of the Leisure Class* in 1899, the use of male servants always carries much more prestige than the use of female servants. Dinner served by a man with a silver tray is more impressive than the same dinner served on the same tray by a female servant. Today restaurants that use male waiters rather than female ones rank as more exclusive, a distinction usually underscored by the menu prices and the tips of the employees. Richer women go to male hair stylists, particularly to ones trained in Europe, while less affluent women make do with female hair stylists. Exclusive men's clothing stores are more likely to hire male clerks, while discount stores have female clerks or adolescent boys. The clerk in the elegant jewelry store is likely to be male, but the clerk behind the jewelry counter at Sears or K-Mart is much more likely to be female.

This propensity for demonstrating social status by using males to perform services creates a special problem. Many of these services are intimate—touching the head, adjusting the clothing, choosing new bedroom wallpaper, applying makeup, giving massages, fitting shoes—and are often performed in secluded places such as dressing rooms, private booths, or the home. The more exclusive and private the service, the more likely it is to be performed by a male, and this opens up the possibility of sexual contact.

Throughout history many different solutions to this problem were tried. In classical Mediterranean and Asian societies, male servants were frequently castrated, and in northern Europe prepubescent boys were frequently used as pages and servants for aristocratic women. A vestige of this persists today in the young male ringbearers so often used in formal weddings; this is a plebeian imitation of a formerly aristocratic practice. Similar male and female pages flourish in the American Congress.

In the nineteenth century, when all European and American men wore beards, male servants were clean-shaven. According to Veblen, this sociological form of emasculation made the servants look more like women or young boys and thus be less sexually appealing to the women they served. In the southern states and South America, the men were not only clean-shaven but had a different color skin, whether slaves or servants. A strong ideology and a very firmly instilled caste system further minimized any expression of sexual interest between the women being served and the men doing the serving. In Latin-American countries the differences between serving-class men and aristocratic men was further heightened by the use of Indian servants, who have very little facial hair. This distinction continues today, with Indians and mestizos working as servants.

The twentieth century brought new job opportunities for many of the servant-class males and females of various ethnic groups. At the same time, changing technology and changing life-styles required fewer services to be performed at home. It was in precisely these service-oriented jobs, usually of a very intimate or domestic nature, that openly homosexual men grouped. When a woman in Beverly Hills drives down to her favorite boutique on Rodeo Drive, a man will park her car for her and a male clerk will help her try on a new French dress or the latest Italian shoes. She may have her hair fixed by a French male hairdresser after going to the spa for her aerobics class, given by a would-be Hollywood male star, and a quick massage from the masseur. At noon she meets another woman and her male makeup specialist for an intimate meal served by flossy waiters with cute first names and the ability to recite a long list of house specials after taking memory training in acting class. After lunch she dashes home to meet her decorator —he suggests changing the color of her dressing room—and she gives orders to a bevy of delivery men and caterers preparing for her evening dinner party with candles floating in the pool.

Affluent women are in constant intimate contact with men, often very attractive young men, which gives them great prestige. Yet they are entirely safe from the possibility of sexual contact. This keeps their reputations clean and their husbands at ease.

Few people live that kind of life, of course. Most women are out working at jobs of their own and have more important concerns. Still, the same status system operates. The female lawyer or business executive wants to take her clients to lunch at an exclusive restaurant, and that means one with male waiters, but she does not want to be embarrassed by a waiter's flirting with her or with her guest. She wants the added prestige of a male hairdresser or clerk, but she does not want one who fondles her breast while adjusting her clothes. She wants males around, but she wants them as asexual as possible.

The economic demand for males to perform high-status services, and yet be sexually neutral, has created a job niche for openly gay males. Rather than being penalized for their sexual orientation, they are employed for it. Men in professions that are not oriented toward personal services are not encouraged to be gay or show signs of homosexuality.

This twentieth-century utilization of homosexuals has brought with it small gay communities nestled in urban areas having a high concentration of personal-service businesses. Trendy restaurants, interior-design shops, hair salons, antique stores, boutiques, florists, and gift shops group together, and the gay men who run and own them often live in the adjoining community. A host of secondary businesses open to provide the gay men with bars and professional services such as doctors, lawyers, accountants, dentists, and ministers. This then becomes a gay community. Such communities are found in every metropolitan area of the United States today, although much less frequently in Europe, and they are as similar to one another, and distinctive from other ethnic communities, as possible. They have as standardized a set of services as did the original restaurants, gift shops, and laundries of Chinatowns; the jewelers, clothing stores, and delicatessens of Jewish districts; and the record stores, coffee shops, and restaurants of Hispanic neighborhoods.

Now that a part of society—and mostly the more affluent

part—has found a use for homosexual males, homosexuality is somewhat better tolerated. Whether this is a major departure from past attitudes or merely a passing fad for a few generations is difficult to determine. This tenuous acceptance of a small part of the homosexual population could be easily overthrown by the emergence of a new ethnic group who performs the tasks of the gay males more efficiently or cheaply. It could also be easily threatened by one of those periodic political movements of the working classes. Often couched in religious terms, these movements lash out at symbols of upper-class privilege and decadence that are not supposed to exist in egalitarian society. The gay men who serve the upper and the upper middle class might make very convenient and highly emotionally charged targets for such outbursts.

Compared with the industries that provide personal services, other professions and occupations show little tolerance for homosexuals. Even where the laws may prohibit discrimination, only a few doctors, lawyers, construction workers, truck drivers, elected officials, clerics, teachers, and factory workers live openly as homosexuals. The same social system that rewards homosexuals who take service jobs catering to the professional classes acts much more harshly against members of these professional classes for being openly homosexual. Openly gay professionals seem to work only where there is enough business to support them from the gay community itself, so that they need not depend on the larger society for a livelihood. Obviously, the gay community can support only a limited number of doctors, lawyers, dentists, plumbers, and masons.

The tenuousness of the acceptance of a gay ghetto and of homosexual men in service jobs became evident with the AIDS epidemic. Suddenly, obviously homosexual men working in jobs involving intimate services or food handling became the object of fear and discrimination once again. Thus even gay men who were working in jobs that had opened up to homosexuals felt tremendous pressure to return to the "closet," or at least to be much more discreet in exhibiting behaviors commonly stereotyped as homosexual.

The jobs in which pressures were evident in downtown Washington in the 1980s seem to parallel, though not precisely, the occupational categories found by Laud Humphreys in his study of St. Louis in the 1960s. The men who were having homosexual relations in public bathrooms and who were working as teachers and government workers, as well as truck drivers, soldiers, and other blue-collar workers, were much more secretive about their sex lives than were self-employed men such as beauticians, decorators, artists, and students.

Although Western society has at least currently found the male homosexual useful and thus rewarded a segment of this population with money and jobs, no such use has been found for the homosexual female. No profession rewards the women who practice it for being lesbians. Financially, they remain one of the poorest groups in contemporary society. Some have gained marginal acceptance, living on the fringes of the male homosexual community and occasionally working in that community, but there are no lesbian districts anywhere comparable to those of males found in all major cities. While the affluence of the male homosexual community has led to the renovation of large sections of towns and the building of elaborate meeting places for them, such as discos, bars, restaurants, and bathhouses, homosexual females still congregate in small, simple bars much like the taverns and pubs that cater to working-class people everywhere.

Lesbians tend to conceal their sex lives in order to work in a wide range of conventional occupations that might otherwise look askance at them. There are very few occupations in which they are perceived to have special assets, and even in those occupations they cannot flaunt their sexual preference. One of these is the military, which knowingly recruits and utilizes lesbians because they make very good soldiers without the risk of pregnancy or the conflicting demands of a home and a mobile career. (Officially, any woman found to be a lesbian would be ousted as unworthy.) Aside from the military, lesbians seem to be scattered among various occupations rather than concentrated in certain ones as are openly gay males.

For different reasons, lesbian relationships are accepted

among a minority of prostitutes. Many of the women who worked in massage parlors and other businesses of prostitution but did not have pimps or boyfriends lived instead in lesbian relationships. These women were not penalized in the red-light district, and in fact employers and managers of such establishments often seemed glad to have them as employees since they would not bring with them the hassles caused by pimps and boyfriends. Even among clients, there was a small but steady demand for women who would make love to each other while the man watched or joined in. Although many women who are not lesbians are able and willing to perform in such tricks, the lesbians have a slight advantage. It is ironic that prostitution is the only profession in Western society where lesbians may have a slight edge over heterosexual women.

Unlike male homosexuals, the female homosexual has no haven. She has neither an occupational group nor a residential neighborhood in which she can live openly as a lesbian or to which she can retreat for periodic revitalization. She has far fewer opportunities to emerge from her closet if she wants to survive economically in modern society. Not only must the lesbians of the professional classes keep their sexual identities secret, but also women of the working class, who risk numerous reprisals such as losing their jobs, custody of their children, or their place of residence. One of the few places where a lesbian can live openly is in a section of a red-light district, such as the Strip, and then only if she is willing to live by prostitution or a related means.

In many ironic twists like this, the Strip rendered useless the traditional distinctions between homosexual and heterosexual. It was virtually meaningless to refer to a lesbian who worked as a prostitute as either homosexual or heterosexual. Similarly, these terms did not help in understanding the male customer who enjoyed oral sex performed by a transvestite prostitute as much as that performed by a female prostitute; or the young man who performed daily in a heterosexual show but preferred male involvements off stage. It was equally difficult to categorize the male hustler who lived by having sex with men but was married to a prostitute; and most difficult of all was the transsexual who had been a male soldier but after his sex-change operation entered a lesbian relationship with a woman.

The Strip accommodated all these people with a rough equality and judged them by its own norms rather than by those of the larger culture. A customer looking for sex was an equal target for robbery whether he was straight or gay, but by the same token a woman could find work as a dancer regardless of her sexual preference.

In the final analysis, the only reason for the existence of the Strip was to serve the sexual desires of the greater society. That society was just as willing to accept this service from women and men who were homosexual as from those who were hetero-sexual. The sexual preferences of the servant are of little interest to the master, so long as the servant is available when needed.

Eleven

THE SENSUOUS APE

Tuesdays were usually very quiet in the Pink Pussy, and that was the day we always received our delivery of new magazines and other materials from the Company. The delivery man dropped them off early in the day, and they would be piled in a box waiting for me when I arrived. During the course of the evening I had to "check" all the goods. That meant I had to examine each picture in each magazine, advertisement, and playing card, looking for any of the forbidden five—blood, urine, feces, animals, and children. Any items that violated this standard I dropped back into the box, and they were returned the following week.

Within a few months I had learned how to flip through a whole box of new magazines in less than an hour. The material was so monotonous that I quickly spotted any deviation. The picture stories tended to repeat one another closely within each category we used in our shelving scheme. The soft-core magazines were likely to choose a young woman in some quite ordinary role, such as secretary, tennis player, nurse, sunbather, waitress, or grocery shopper. Very quickly, when she is alone, she reveals herself to be a sex-starved creature who slowly takes off her clothes, begins to masturbate, and works herself into a couple of frenzied orgasms, at least one of which requires that a phallus-shaped object be inserted into the vagina.

The hard-core pornography followed much the same scenario, except that the woman did all this with a man, someone she met at work, in the laundromat, delivering pizza, working in the garden, or at the airport. The magazines never built exotic stories of princes and princesses in medieval Europe, of migrant workers in the vineyards or castaways on a windswept island. Instead, they featured ordinary women and men in ordinary situations. Very quickly, however, the familiar situation would change into a frenzied sexual encounter. The couple would perform oral sex on each other, use a variety of copulatory positions, and manage to bring other women into the act, or occasionally other men. In the process the male star would ejaculate several times, each time outside the female's body for full visual impact.

Because of the requirements of the cameras, the poses used by both the females and the males in such pictures differ from virtually all positions people normally use during coitus. The primary objective in all the pictures is to display the genitals, an act that is normally taboo in all human societies. One of the myths of modern society is that in primitive societies where people go naked, they do not mind exposing their genitals, being as casual about their genitals as their ears. That notion does not reflect the reality of life anywhere in the world. In societies such as the Yanomamo of Venezuela, the women are almost always naked, but they learn to walk, sit, and lie decorously so that their vulvas never show. Men keep the penis foreskin tied so that the head never protrudes in public. Even the classical Greek athletes who performed naked tied a small string around the foreskin, concealing the penis head much as men do in many primitive societies today. The less clothing a people wears, usually the more modest it is about exposing the inner labia of the females or the head of the penis of the males. Nudity makes people more modest.

But though other cultures do not offer a parallel to the poses adopted by the models in the Pink Pussy magazines, many of these poses, especially those appearing in soft porn without male partners, resemble the classic presenting stance of female baboons. The woman often presents her buttocks to the camera, but she bends over far enough that, with a tug from one of her hands, the inner labia also face the camera. The woman then twists her head around so that her full face and, if possible, one breast also appear in the picture. The sexuality of the picture is increased by the application of makeup to moisten and redden the interior portions of the genitals, and by shaving back the pubic hair so that it does not hide the genitals. When one of the model's fingers intrudes slightly between the labia, the fingernail appears in bright red to further emphasize that spot on the photograph.

Among our primate cousins, such as the chimpanzees and baboons, the female's genital area swells and reddens when she is ready for copulation. This accenting of the genitals closely parallels what is used in pornography, making the woman seem to be in a form of artificial estrus. She appears to be in heat, something that has long since disappeared in human evolution.

Females in the animal kingdom show no interest in copulation unless they are in estrus, which pushes them inexorably toward male contact and usually pregnancy. Estrus is the driving force behind animal sex. Without it, the females seem content to eat, sleep, play, rest, and groom one another with little interest in sex. The males seem content to do the same, until they become excited by the sight and smell of a female in heat. Estrus is the sex drive for most mammals, especially for our fellow primates.

When estrus vanished during the evolutionary process, however, the human female developed a response that no other female in the animal world has. The human female has orgasms. No other female animal in the world has ever been observed in the wild undergoing anything related to an orgasm. On the contrary, coitus often appears to be very painful to the female animal; at best she seems merely bored or indifferent. Yet the human female undergoes a physiological process very close to the physiological transformation of the human male during orgasm, but without ejaculation. With sustained stimulation, she can produce a whole sequence of orgasms, unlike the human male.

This loss of estrus and the development of the orgasm in human females is far more than a minor aspect of female sensuality. In some respects it represents the very keystone that holds together human society. As amply demonstrated in the work of anthropologists such as Helen Fisher, once women had orgasmic capabilities, they were potentially available and interested in sex at all times of the year, not merely during estrus. A woman enjoyed sex as much when she menstruated as when she ovulated. She could have sex even while pregnant or nursing. Her sexual pleasure diverged radically from her reproductive cycle. The fact that women were capable of copulation all the time kept males around all the time. By and large, in the primate world males show interest in females only when they are in estrus and therefore ready to copulate; at other times males ignore them.

The changes provoked by the female orgasm may also have caused evolutionary changes in male sexual anatomy. One of the most striking differences between the anatomy of the human male and that of other male primates is the relatively enormous size of the human penis. The huge, half-ton gorilla, for example, makes do with a penis whose small size is a joke in comparison to the human's. The chimpanzee, which has very large testicles, also has a penis much smaller than that of his cousin, the human. This large human penis serves no practical purpose in urination or any other bodily function necessary to the male. A small penis can produce an ejaculation and orgasm as efficiently as a large one. A small one can discharge as many sperm as a large one. Thus, the large penis does not benefit the male directly. It therefore seems probable that with the evolution of the female orgasm, women began selecting as their sexual partners men with larger penises.

The human penis differs from that of other animals in another important respect. Whereas most animals keep the penis safely retracted inside the body until needed, the human penis dangles precariously exposed at all times, protected only by a thin sheath of very flimsy foreskin. Again, there is no practical reason for this. The testicles hang outside the main part of the body because this keeps the delicate sperm from overheating and being killed, but it would certainly seem safer to keep the penis inside as other animals do. The exposed penis, however, waves as a virtual flag in front of a man, and thus serves as an advertisement for its length. It seems probable it made the protohuman male more attractive to the protohuman female.

But despite—or perhaps because of—this larger and more exposed penis, the human male did not become more efficient in copulation. The male chimpanzee, with his very small penis, can penetrate and ejaculate in a mere ten seconds. The tiny macaque needs only eleven seconds. Even the comparatively slow howler monkey finishes in twenty seconds. By comparison, the human male takes a full two to three *minutes* after erection and penetration before he ejaculates—a rate about fifteen times slower than the chimpanzee. Moreover, the human male becomes even slower, rather than faster, with age and experience. Again, there is no practical reason for this slow pace and the great expenditure of time and energy the male requires in coitus, except that it gives pleasure to the female, making orgasm possible for her, and extends the pleasure of the male. Female chimpanzees, baboons, and monkeys do not have orgasms and show no interest in prolonging coitus. Once the human female developed the orgasm, she became interested in partners who could bring her to orgasm.

The tremendous exertion the human male expends to sustain an erection and copulate for several minutes tires him and depletes his energy. Even very young and healthy males usually take an hour or so before repeating the act. By comparison, a male chimpanzee copulates easily a dozen times in a day with little effort or expenditure of energy, and he can repeat this indefinitely, day after day, as long as he is presented with fresh females in estrus.

All these evolutionary changes in human sexuality are related to the transition to upright posture and bipedal locomotion. This gradual change was accompanied by a chain reaction of other alterations. In comparison to other primates, the human breast protrudes very prominently. Even on human males, the dark areola around the nipple highlights it on the chest. In men with hairy chests, the hair often grows in a swirling pattern that further highlights the nipple. In the female, the breasts are large and swollen, but the most logical explanation for this is not sexual: The fatty tissue of the breast keeps the mother's milk warm in the absence of fur. In both males and females, however, the nipple is comprised of erectile tissues much like those of the penis and clitoris and stiffens when stimulated. In the female, this produces a practical result: When nursing is more pleasurable to the mother, she is more likely to do it. No practical reason exists for the erect male nipple and its sensitivity, but it does make sex a more pleasurable experience.

Many societies ignore the nipple as an erogenous zone. Western societies acknowledge the female nipple as erotic but ignore the male nipple. Humans in other cultures rub the breasts with the hand, and kiss and suck on the nipples. Even without those conscious efforts, the rubbing motion of one body against another during face-to-face coitus stimulates the nipple.

Other parts of the human body also took on potentially sexual significance in the course of evolution. After the genitals, the lips are among the most sensitive parts of the human anatomy. By comparison, most primates have virtually no lips at all, the mouth being a slit in the face with a fair amount of flexibility but virtually no fat deposits. Human lips, like the genitals and nipples, engorge with blood when the person becomes sexually excited, and are sensitive to all forms of tactile stimulation. Most cultures exploit this sensitivity in sexual encounters, although not necessarily through kissing. Biting of the lips is widespread in the South Pacific, as is rubbing of the lips on the cheeks or other parts of the partner's body.

From earlobes to feet, erogenous zones dot the human body. Depending on the culture, almost any part of the body can be made into a sexually exciting area that becomes supersensitive to the touch and gives pleasure to the partner who touches it. On the other hand, no society could exploit completely all the body's erogenous areas, so it chooses only a few for special concentration. Still, the anatomical potential is there, for in a sense the entire human skin acts as a single sexual organ: It flushes with blood and grows warmer during sexual stimulation, lubricating itself with perspiration for the easy rubbing of the two bodies together. Humans everywhere in the world show a preference for coital positions that maximize the amount of body touching. By contrast, most other mammals, including the other primates, use positions that bring only the genitals into contact, not their entire bodies.

Having evolved into a hairless ape, the human developed a whole-body sensuality unlike any other animal. Paradoxically, at the same time that humans evolved into highly sexual creatures, they also developed a deep-seated modesty. Most animals, including the other primates, do not hesitate to copulate in full view of others. Humans throughout the world, however, show a great reluctance to do this. Rules vary from society to society, and some are more rigid than others, but all societies, including those in which people go naked during the day and sleep in large communal huts or around communal fires at night, still enforce elaborate rules and taboos to minimize displays of sexual activity. People copulate in the bush away from other people, quietly in the dark of night, or beneath blankets and furs.

This modesty probably developed as one element among the many other changes in sexual evolution. The prolonged coital act, performed in a reclining rather than a standing position, and with the total involvement of the female as well as the male, made copulating humans vulnerable to hungry predators. In contrast, most animals that stand to copulate can easily break into a quick run if danger approaches. By seeking out private places or private times of night for the long, reclining act of copulation, human partners protected themselves from predators and from other humans.

Human males are sexually excited by the sight of acts of copulation. Among primates in general, the sight of a couple copulating, as well as the sight of solitary females in estrus, sexually excites the male, who may then attack the copulating couple and take the female for himself. This danger was probably another reason humans sought privacy for their sex acts.

Daily, men in the Pink Pussy had the opportunity to view sights that were inherently stimulating and attractive to them, and rarely available in other settings. Deep in the male psyche there seems to lurk some residue of the ancient primate propensity for sexual excitement at the sight of other couples copulating, or at the sight of exposed female genitals. In contrast, women, even though they may have selected partners based on penis size, probably did not become sexually excited at the sight of the male genitals. When monkeys and apes display their penises, the females do not become excited at the spectacle; they usually move away.

Though researchers must be wary in formulating theories regarding the biological basis of culturally specific forms of behavior, the physical limitations of the human body do establish the range of human behavior. Within this range different societies, and even different groups within a society, set up conditions that elicit behaviors from one part of that range while suppressing or ignoring behaviors from another part. It is by no means certain that something inherent within the human male drives him toward pornography. However, it appears that something in pornography does play on and exploit a very deep and gender-specific trait found in the males of many species: to become sexually stimulated by the sight of sexual acts. Thus among human beings, pictures, films, and performances of sexual acts have a greater potential to excite males than females, and males today spend billions of dollars annually to see and to buy such materials from thousands of stores like the Pink Pussy. Females may respond to the emotional component of "soft porn" available on midnight cable TV, but anatomical displays are not likely to stimulate them.

Twelve

HOW MUCH SEX IS "NORMAL"?

To live and work on the Strip was to be surrounded by myriad permutations of sexuality. The businesses on the Strip all made their profits from selling sex, whether in celluloid, flesh, video, fantasy, or paper. From this segment of contemporary life, it might appear that people today are much more sexually oriented than were people in the past. The culture bombards modern man with sexual stimuli and pushes him more deeply into novel sexual activities and interests than could ever happen in a "natural" condition. Certainly the experiences of the Strip would support such a theory. Only a highly sexual people would need special parts of town set aside wholly for the continuous enactment of sexual fantasies and novelties. Only a very erotic culture would support stores devoted to pictures of nothing but copulating couples. Only very sexually active people would patronize theaters showing nothing but sex movies twenty-four hours a day, seven days a week.

By virtually every measure available, however, Americans and Europeans on the whole have less sex than the rest of the world. From the first systematic data collection in the 1930s through the celebrated Kinsey studies of the 1940s and 1950s and on to the numerous magazine surveys of the 1970s and

144

1980s, the same pattern persists: Couples copulate an average of two to three times a week. Yet anthropological research shows consistently that daily coitus seems to be the norm for humans elsewhere. According to John Gagnon, the Western rate is only one-third the Polynesian rate. As reported by Ford and Beach, "in most societies on which information is available, every adult normally engages in heterosexual intercourse once daily or nightly during the periods when coitus is permitted." This is a rate that only 15 percent of American couples follow.

Their coital rate places Americans in the bottom quadrant of the lusty sexual societies in the world. Modern Americans rank just above the Jivaro of Ecuador, the Yapese of Micronesia, the Dugum Dani of New Guinea, and the Irish. Except for this handful of primitive societies, and the Europeans and Americans, most people start sex much earlier in life and do it more frequently, with a greater diversity of partners, and until a later age. Some societies strive to push the rate of coitus up close to the biological limit. Contemporary Western societies, despite such places as the Strip and all the apparent emphasis on sex, have very low rates. In some cases, such as the two Germanys and other northern European nations, populations are no longer able to maintain themselves through natural reproduction and are actually declining. Though this decline must be partly credited to improved birth control, much of it is due to comparatively low rates of sexual frequency. Westerners begin sex later, do it less often with fewer partners, and stop it sooner.

According to extensive interviews by Marc Swartz, the Bena of Tanzania claim that they have sex six times a night, each night of the week. Any man who cannot meet this standard of marital duty has no grounds for complaint if his wife commits adultery. Only men who are quite old slack off.

Though the claims of the Bena may be exaggerated, scientific evidence indicates persistently high rates of coitus in a number of African societies. In a study of the Kgatla, for example, Isaac Schapera reported that "normally two or at the most three acts of coitus take place during the night; once before sleeping, and once on waking at dawn seem to be the common practice." The total number of copulations may be as high as six or seven on the first day and night following a special period of required abstinence. The men try to keep it below that figure, however, for fear that too much sex during the daytime will cause them to lose weight and tire them.

A Kgtala man who cannot impregnate his wife should allow her to be impregnated by another man. And if a husband is absent for long periods of time, he must not complain if his wife seeks sex with other men. The Kgtala perceive sex as a need that demands fulfillment. In addition to this daily sex, Kgtala men frequently start affairs with other women and even keep mistresses. Wives often encourage their husbands to have affairs as a way to keep them from bringing home another wife.

A study of a group of Bala men provided detailed records of their sexual activity over a three-week period. Of the ten men studied, the least sexually active copulated once a day while the most active copulated twice each day. Most of the men copulated once on most days and occasionally two or more times in a single day. Even though these men copulated mostly with their wives, 11.6 percent of the copulations were with other women.

Most societies with higher rates of coitus recognize a sliding scale of sexual expectations based on age, with younger couples expected to copulate much more than older couples. Among the Santals of India, for example, a newlywed couple must copulate four to five times a day every day until the wife is pregnant. Research among the Mangains of the Marshall Islands in the South Pacific indicates that a married man of eighteen has coitus three times a night, each night of the week. This declines to twice a night for five or six nights of the week by age twenty-eight, and to one time a night three or four nights a week by age thirty-eight. By age forty-eight it is down to only two or three times a week.

Similarly, among the Lepcha young couples may copulate from five to nine times in a night, but "they would then be tired the next day." By age thirty, however, the rate drops to only once a night each night. In old age, couples may go three to four

146

nights without copulating. In Australia, aborigines have much higher coital rates than Westerners. The Aranda, for example, have sex intermittently three to five times during the night.

Even allowing for exaggeration, and though in all cases evidence proves hard to document, the general pattern emerges clearly. Multiple acts of copulation each night in succession occur frequently in societies as varied as those found in India, Africa, Australia, and throughout the South Pacific. This high frequency derives from the diversity of sexual institutions encouraged in many of these societies, while Westerners have only two real alternatives: courtship and marriage, or prostitution zones such as the Strip.

Other societies have invented new institutions. The Turu of Tanzania fall in love. According to Harold K. Schneider, who lived among them and studied them, the Turu have a concept of romantic love similar to that of Europeans and Americans. Lovers spend as much time together as practical, exchange small gifts as tokens of their affection, and help each other with their daily tasks. They copulate using varied positions and techniques. They are also frequently jealous and thus prone to lovers' quarrels; but these relationships tend to be fairly stable and, after the heated passion of the initial years, they turn into deeper emotional bonds built on permanent love.

The lovers never marry each other, however, because they are already married to other spouses. Marriage for the Turu is a relationship based on economic and familial considerations rather than on mere love and emotion. A husband and wife are very dependent upon one another for sustenance and for the prosperity of their family. Their relationship tends to be formalized: The wife can never look her husband in the eye, nor can she ever mention his name, for to do so would be a sign of disrespect; in all ways she should be subservient to him. Their sexual union lacks spontaneity and serves to produce children, not pleasure. Coitus is performed with each spouse lying on his or her side facing the other and lacks the variations of coitus between lovers. Romance is channeled into the much more pleasurable but less practical relationship called the *mbuya*. In this way each person uses a spouse for security and economic cooperation and a lover for romance and good sex.

The Turu spouse should never flaunt this *mbuya* in front of his or her mate. To do so would be distasteful, for as the Turu say, "Our eyes refuse to accept what our minds accept." Under these rules, the woman should never visit the home of her lover, since that would be an invasion of the domain of his wife and children. Instead, the man visits the home of his lover when her husband is away. An unexpected return of the woman's husband, however, can provoke a quarrel, and in some cases the husband may demand payment of a fine from the wife's lover.

When in due time the *mbuya* relationship stabilizes, the husband drops his resistance to his wife's lover and, in turn, the wife drops her resistance to her husband's lover. The husband can then expect certain forms of assistance from his wife's lover, and has to provide the same forms of assistance to the husband of his lover. The two men help each other in cultivating the fields, caring for the animals, house building, and other male tasks. They also undertake ritual exchanges of beer. Meanwhile, women who share the same man through marriage and a *mbuya* also begin to help each other with the care of their children, food preparation, and other domestic work.

On the other side of the world, in the Marquesas Islands of the Pacific, another sexual institution evolved. According to the research of Ralph Linton, Marquesan households vied with one another to attract the strongest and best-looking men into a polyandrous marriage. In such a household, the wife tried to be as attractive as possible and as good a lover as possible in order to attract and hold the better men of the village as husbands. The wife and her husbands then lived together in a large home atop a huge stone platform. The larger the platform, the more prestige it conferred on the family, indicating a household of strong and viral men. If the family acquired too many husbands or if the wife began to tire of her sexual labors for so many husbands, the family chose a secondary wife. Thus in the larger households, up to a dozen different males might be living with two or three commonly shared wives.

The Kaingang Indians of Brazil form even more complicated marital systems. For them marriage does not exist in a very formal sense; people drift into sexual relationships and drift out again. But some of these relationships may be of long duration and thus come close to what we call marriage. A man or a woman may live with one spouse and yet have a long-term lover, much like the Turu. Or a set of households may merge when one of the spouses brings home a new lover to join the family. Fathers may share their younger wives with their sons as a way of keeping the sons and their hunting prowess in their own household instead of another's.

One woman in the tribe ended up with two unrelated men as her husbands, but since both of them had adolescent sons, she also became the wife of the two boys. She bore her four husbands a total of nine children, some of whom, of course, were the uncles and aunts of their own half siblings. With four husbands and nine children to care for, she persuaded one of her nieces to come join them as a second wife. The new wife then went on to bear the four men ten more children for a family total of twenty-five people. During a series of bloody raids by Brazilian mestizos, all four of the husbands and a handful of the children were killed; the original wife then married a son-in-law. Throughout this long life of varied sexual relations, the woman had a series of temporary lovers who never came to live in the household as husbands.

The Brazilian Mehinaku studied by Thomas Gregor practice a form of adultery called "alligatoring," named for the lustful life of that animal. Men clear out small pieces of land somewhere at the back of their lovers' huts. Here the lovers meet and copulate, using a peculiar position in which the woman stands on one leg and wraps the other around the man's waist. In this position they can copulate and still watch the house in case the husband emerges. Sex is something of a sport, and people delight in taking chances at being exposed or caught. Men sometimes sneak into the hut itself to have sex with the wife while the husband is asleep. The younger the couple, the more danger such activities provoke, because younger husbands tend to be very jealous of their wives' lovers. As they grow older, they become more tolerant, though they never like direct confrontation with the spouse's lover.

149

At one time Gregor studied a village of only thirty-seven adults and discovered that there were eighty-eight known love affairs in progress in addition to all the marriages. One woman named Kuyalu, the most popular in the village, had a total of fourteen lovers. Indeed, because of her popularity, she did not have or need a husband; she received enough presents from her lovers to support herself and her children without a permanent male in the household.

Under special circumstances in some societies, husbands make the arrangements for their wives' lovers. These deputed lovers are usually used when the husband and wife are unable to bear children. Among the Tallensi, a husband who has not fathered a child recognizes that something may be wrong with him, and that the lack of children is not necessarily his wife's fault. To remedy this he may discuss the situation with his lineage elders, and they may decide to let the wife find a lover or they may search one out within his group of friends or relatives. In order for the deputed lover to be officially accepted, he is first presented to the elders of the clan in a ceremony. The elders sacrifice a chicken and present the deputed lover to the spirits of the ancestors. After this official recognition of his status and his temporary acceptance in the clan, he can have sex with the woman as often as the two of them desire until she is pregnant. The lover, however, has no claim on any ensuing children. Aside from this one practice, adultery is severely condemned among the Tallensi.

According to Fustel de Coulanges, this practice was also common in the classical world. In both Sparta and Athens, a man who did not have children would use a brother or other relative as a deputed lover for his wife. As among the Tallensi, any children born from such a union belonged to the woman's husband and not to the genitor of the child. Such a system also seems to have been operant in biblical times, as illustrated by the story of Tamar and Onan.

In many societies throughout the world, a husband or wife automatically has sexual access to the spouse's siblings. The Siriono of eastern Bolivia are typical in that any man can have sexual relations with his wife's sisters, and any wife can have sexual relations with her husband's brothers. These include not merely full siblings but also a large number of other men and women whom the Siriono classify as brothers and sisters, thus providing each person with a large number of potential sex partners at any given time. Similar customs are found among groups as widespread as the aborigines of Australia and the Yanomamo of Venezuela.

In addition to these long-term sexual unions outside of marriage, some societies have devised spouse exchange and customs of sexual hospitality. This is perhaps best known among the Eskimo, where visiting men often expect to have sex with the wife or one of the wives of the host. In addition, Eskimo men may sometimes exchange wives permanently, not necessarily for the sake of sexual variety but to confuse any malevolent spirits. Women, who traditionally rank very low in Eskimo society, have little to say about the transaction.

Masai warriors of Kenya and Tanzania customarily have sex with the wives of their peers. Young men of the same age belong to an age grade that links them closely. During this time all the young men and women of the same age are permitted to have sex with each other. Most of this stops at marriage, but some sexual intimacy continues through a form of sexual hospitality in which any visiting age peer of the husband may be allowed to sleep with the wife, whom he probably already knows.

Among the Gadagas, a group of Hindu peasants in the western corner of Tamil Nadu, India, the men frequently share their wives with their Toda trading partners whenever the partner visits. In such cases the intent is at least partially mercenary, not merely hospitable, because the Gadagas husband hopes that by doing this he will make a better deal. A Gadagas woman may take as her lover any man of a higher caste than her husband. Husbands approve of this practice, believing it brings greater purity to their own caste. Women are punished, however, for polluting themselves by having relations with lower-caste males. This means that low-caste women have a diversity of potential lovers, whereas higher-caste women have a dearth of lovers. For males the opposite holds: High-caste men can have many different lovers, and lower-caste men very few. In some respects the Indian system parallels the traditional sexual caste system in the American South and parts of Latin America.

Another version of sexual hospitality and the exchange of spouses developed among the Ulithi people of the northern Caroline archipelago in Micronesia. The people of Ulithi also have a special holiday feast called *pi suphui,* which loosely translates as the feast of a hundred pettings. The feast occurs at set intervals and everyone participates except for young children and the elderly. During this celebration couples go off into the woods to picnic, relax, and have fun, including sex. The only stipulation is that a person cannot go with his or her own spouse or a close relative; otherwise, free choice reigns for females and males alike. During the evening each one changes partners several times through a tag system that allows a person to break in on another couple. The *pi suphui* also gives young people a chance to explore each other's body, even if they are still too immature to copulate.

Studies by Ronald and Catherine Berndt show that Australian aborigines had provided a similar period of ritual license. During these times women usually took the initiative in choosing lovers, or their husbands might recruit lovers for them. The Canela and other Indians of Brazil practice similar customs. One of the most extensive sex rituals, however, is that reported for the Marquesan wedding. According to the study by Bengt Danielson, all the male guests at a wedding line up afterward to copulate with the bride. All the while the bride rests her head on the knee of her husband. The first guest in line is always the lowest-status male present, and the ceremony slowly works its way through all the men up to the chief. The husband comes last. Even though the wife may have to spend several days in bed to recuperate from the ceremony, everyone considers it a great honor for her to have entertained so large a number of men.

All such ceremonies and practices were lumped together by Western missionaries as pagan orgies and were severely condemned. In many societies they have been wiped out completely, and in others they continue in what is at best a secretive form and more often as a misshapen sexual parody of a former tradition.

In Western society a reasonable amount of evidence indicates that such sexual patterns are well within the normal capacity even of young men. Male homosexuals living in areas of great opportunity for contact with other homosexuals show high rates of sexual activity. This is particularly so for men who frequent places designed for quick, anonymous sex, such as bathhouses, the back rooms and basements of certain gay bars, and designated public toilets and secluded parks. Frank and others like him seem less interested in the pleasure of any single encounter than in the triumph of accruing large numbers. The fun is in the score, not in the act. Frank bragged of having sex with three guys in one day, without much concern for the quality of any individual episode.

One private homosexual club in Washington, D.C., featured a constant flow of homosexual films interspersed with a live show of teenage boys in sexual acts. The boys performed five times a day and demonstrated erections for each show. Each boy appeared twice in each of the five daily sets, and unless he maintained his erection for a half-hour backstage, this meant that he had to produce a second erection in the show. Thus, each boy appeared ten times with ten different erections during a twelve-hour period. The boys did this for seven consecutive days before having a day off. Between shows, they often prostituted themselves with customers, and in addition they frequently had sexual affairs with one another or with other lovers. Even though these boys rarely had orgasms during stage performances, they did have a dozen or more erections per day interspersed with episodic orgasms off stage. After a week of this, some boys moved directly on to other clubs in the circuit, and thus may not have had a single day off for as many as six weeks. Because of these taxing demands, the theaters use a guy known as a "fluffer," whose job it is to help the boys achieve an erection for each stage appearance.

Situations like these make extraordinary demands on the male's ability to engage in sex, but such demands—or opportunities—are comparatively rare. Some heterosexual men in

Western society have the opportunity to engage in coitus virtually at will, but they are usually elite males who have access to
diverse female partners. The memoirs of various people associated with Charlie Chaplin, for example, claim that he was
capable of six copulations a night with only a five-minute pause
in between. This active sex life had him frequently in court for
paternity suits, and he married several times.

The sex reputations of such men as Gary Cooper, Errol
Flynn, Clark Gable, and John Barrymore may be exaggerated,
but there are enough eyewitness accounts, court testimonies,
and legal affidavits to attest to the prodigious sex lives they led.
Their sex partners reportedly numbered in the hundreds, and
they frequently had multiple sexual encounters in a single
night. Such sexual athleticism resembles the anonymous sex in
the gay bathhouses and massage parlors along the Strip. Men
seek lists of conquests; prostitutes seek to turn as many tricks
and earn as much money as possible.

Whatever the reasons for this degree of sexual activity, it
does give us an idea of the upper limits of human sexual capacity. It appears that, given full opportunity and a diversity of
partners, men even in our own society are perfectly capable of
approaching the high frequency observed among the Aranda,
the Bena, and other groups. But this still does not give us a clear
picture of the range of what might be considered normal rates
of sexual activity in humans. For this, we also need to mention
those cultures that have unusually low rates of coitus.

Among the traditional Cheyenne Indians of the American
Plains in the nineteenth century, parents were encouraged to
abstain from sex up to fourteen years after the birth of a child,
because sexual acts depleted the parents' energy. According to
Cheyenne belief, if all energies, efforts, thoughts, and emotions
focused on the rearing of the child, the child would make a
much better adult in the end. At the birth of the child, the
parents made a vow to remain celibate for seven to fourteen
years, depending on their level of dedication to the child; and
once made, the vow could not be broken. The spacing of births
tended to show that the vows were being observed.

This exceptionally long postpartum sexual taboo accorded

154

with other antisexual aspects of Cheyenne society. Premarital intercourse was virtually unknown, and rape and adultery seldom occurred. The Cheyenne followed the strictest codes of sexual behavior known for a whole society anywhere in the world, and from all available evidence they were meticulous in upholding this code. Men drew shame and opprobrium for sexual exploits. Adulterous women had their faces mutilated or were placed alone on the prairie, abandoned to anyone who wanted them. Men acquired honor and prestige for renouncing sex and living celibate lives. Even the normal flow of life was punctuated by long periods of celibacy for the entire tribe in preparation for war or for lengthy annual religious rites. In all such instances the renunciation of sex served as a way to collect and save energy, which could then be directed toward activities beneficial to the whole group, rather than being wasted on the frivolous pleasure of two individuals.

The postpartum-sex taboo is one of the commonest ways of reducing the sexual activity of married couples. The Cheyenne were an extreme, though even for them the taboo was voluntary. Among many other people it is less voluntary but also less lengthy. The Dugum Dani are one example. Inhabiting the highland valley of Irian in the Indonesian sector of the island of New Guinea, they live by growing sweet potatoes and other vegetables and by keeping herds of pigs. The Dugum Dani impose a sex ban of up to five years after the birth of each child, depending on how long it takes the child to be weaned and to "get around on its own." In some cases this may be a mere three or four years, but in many cases it is longer.

Some people also observe a prepartum sex taboo either with or without the postpartum taboo. Among the Pilago of Argentina, intercourse is prohibited after the sixth month of pregnancy. As with the Dugum Dani, it may not be resumed until the child is able to get around on its own, but Pilago children are encouraged to become independent more quickly than Dugum Dani children.

In numerous societies the notion that sexual abstinence makes one a better person helps to lower the rates of copulation. The people of Yap, for example, believe that intercourse saps health and vitality. They were so concerned with this that the Yap population had a very low rate of intercourse, probably around twice per month, and eventually they were threatened with extinction.

Abstinence is sometimes elaborated into a theory of the need for sperm retention. Gandhi did much to popularize this doctrine in modern India and thus changed many very liberal sexual attitudes into much more puritanical ones. Following *bramahcharya,* he taught that the retention of sperm increased a man's holiness. Gandhi went so far as to sleep in the same bed with attractive women as a way of testing and affirming his control of his sexual impulses. Something of this same idea seems evident in the writings of Plato, who describes in awe how Socrates slept in the same bed with his favorite student without having sexual relations, as a way of testing and affirming his own virtue.

This same idea permeates Western history. Monks, nuns, and priests in the Catholic church are deemed more sacred for adhering to a vow of lifelong chastity. Even married people are encouraged to abstain from sex during times of sacred religious rites such as Lent or Advent, and on certain holy days.

The idea that the loss of sperm is a detriment to men has persisted in both official and folk belief through the centuries and continues into the present. Athletes are still taught to abstain from sex for as long as possible before competition so as not to deplete their energy, concentration, and drive. Even though some athletes, such as Joe Namath, tried deliberately to shatter the myth, it survives.

In our society it is assumed that sex interferes even with the physically much less demanding activity of learning—that even thinking about sex is debilitating. From grammar school through college, teachers complain that their students think about sex, have sex, or play sexual games so constantly that they are not able to learn. Sex is seen as a constant hindrance, while other physical activities, such as sports, are seen as good and as actually enhancing learning if done in moderation. Moderate sports activity is thought to drain excess energy and thus allow students to concentrate better.

156

Anthropologist Weston LaBarre reports that in many parts of the world semen is equated with bone marrow and the brain. This means that each time a man ejaculates he loses some of this vital essence and then has not only less semen but less bone marrow and brain as well. This view makes semen a precious commodity that is expended only at great cost, so society must work to prevent its young men from squandering their valuable inheritance. This is a set of beliefs so old in human history that LaBarre calls it the "stone age superstition."

The low coital rates in contemporary Western societies may be airily dismissed as a mere artifact of the Christian religion that has dominated Europe for nearly 2,000 years. In the case of America, sexual conservatism seems to be even stronger because of the strong puritanism of its founding settlers. But none of these religious explanations adequately explains the antisex sentiment. Long before Europe embraced Christianity, the continent's essentially antisexual ethos seemed well established. The ancient Germans executed adulterous women well before they had heard the gospel of Jesus Christ, and Roman fathers killed their nonvirgin daughters. Despite the lax morality of higher-ranking citizens of the Roman Empire, restrictive sexual standards were imposed on the common people.

It is not necessary to scour the past, however, to find a major clue to the antierotic nature of many contemporary societies. If exceptionally prosexual societies and their very high rates of coitus are compared with antisexual societies and their correspondingly low rates, a pattern springs forth. There is a correlation between antisexual attitudes and the prevalence of warfare. When war and violence are frequent in a society, that society is hostile or restrictive toward sex.

The Dugum Dani of New Guinea are an example. According to a study that Karl Heider made while living among them, they are divided into alliances that raid one another frequently. To protect against this, all the able-bodied men spend most of each day on border patrol, watching for an attack, while the women do the horticultural work and the children tend the pigs. When not actually on the battlefield fighting, the men

157

mend their watchtowers, make equipment, prepare for battle, or organize a raid into enemy territory. Warfare is a full-time occupation for the males. About 28 percent of the men and about 2.5 percent of the women will die in warfare.

The violence of the Dani is further evidenced by the practice of chopping off the fingers of small girls whenever a male relative dies. In a society in which so many men die in battle or from wounds incurred in battle, very few females survive childhood with more than two fingers on each hand. These two, the thumb and index finger, are deemed essential and sufficient to perform women's work.

The Jivaro of lowland Ecuador have long been warriors. For centuries they resisted the conquering Incas and the invading Spanish. Much of their success came not only from their fierceness in battle but also from the notoriety of their practice of shrinking the heads of their defeated rivals. (Upon slaying an enemy, the Jivaro removed the skull and by alternately boiling and drying the facial skin and scalp, shrank them to one-quarter their original size.) Much of a Jivaro male's time was spent digging traps to defend his homestead, raiding other groups, and hunting. Because of the high death rates of males, men were permitted to have several wives, but despite this they copulated only once every six to eight days. They claimed that they preferred spending their time hunting.

As a migratory people following the buffalo and constantly harried by European settlers and other Indians, the Cheyenne also lived in a state of steady warfare. The men were organized into war societies and were constantly prepared to fight either the whites or bands of competing Indians. The lives of the males centered around the twin constellation of hunting and fighting and the ancillary acts of preparing their equipment, riding, raiding other groups' horses, practicing archery, and performing magic to help them in their fights. They, too, had their own set of blood rituals; theirs involved self-torture and mutilation. In some of their ceremonies, the young warriors put large hooks through their pectoral muscles and then attached these to ropes by which they could suspend themselves from trees or poles until the hooks ripped through the flesh. Other men attached such hooks to their backs, hung buffalo skulls from them, and then ran through the village until the weight of the skulls finally pulled the hooks out of their backs.

One finds the same correlation of high levels of violence with low sexual activity among some of the great civilizations of history. During its rise, Islam fostered a civilization of great militancy in which many lives were spent in conquest. Despite the later creation of books such as *The Perfumed Garden*, Islam's sexual code prescribed rigid male and female separation and extreme punishment, often death, for the female who violated her chastity and thus besmirched the family honor. In the late twentieth century, we see the same combination of sexual rigidity and violence among Moslems fighting incessant holy wars and returning women to the veil.

Throughout much of its history, Europe and its fledgling offspring cultures in America, South Africa, Australia, and New Zealand spent much time and effort at war, preparing for war, or recovering from war. The kingdom, empire, city-state, or principality was constantly expanding into new territory. Indians, Maoris, Asians, Africans, and Australian aborigines had to be exterminated. Civil wars and revolutions as well as wars of independence had to be waged. Crusades were undertaken to free people from the yoke of Islam, the yoke of the Turks, the yoke of paganism, the yoke of catholicism, the yoke of fascism, or the yoke of communism. Each new century brought with it new types of war and violence.

American and European societies have resembled the Dani, Cheyenne, and Jivaro in their concentration on warfare and violence rather than on sexuality. Men who must spend much of their youth in military training have little time for erotic training. By contrast, the men in Polynesia, parts of Africa, and much of Amazonia, though willing to fight when necessary, still devoted considerably more time to learning the techniques of lovemaking. For them, pride was based on attracting and keeping the sexual attention of as many women as possible. They had little time for chasing after scalps, raiding for horses, avenging feuds, conquering new lands, or serving in armies away from home. The more time and energy a society or an individual expends on fighting and violence, the less time and energy remain for sex and eroticism.

Thirteen

KIDDY SEX

During my third month in the Pink Pussy, a group of people turned the building next door to us into a video-game arcade. Either the building belonged to the Company or the long-term lease did; I was never certain which. The room held a number of rickety old beds left from when it served the Company as a bordello under the guises of a massage parlor, a modeling studio, and a counseling center. The new tenants tossed out the beds, ripped out the partitions separating the cubicles, and moved in twenty different video games and a couple of pinball machines, all within a day. The next day they hung out a sign and opened for business.

Like so many businesses on the Strip, it was unclear who owned the place versus who managed it and who worked in it, but a large number of people seemed to be associated with the arcade. Many of the men wore long hair, beards, tattoos, and lots of leather, and rode motorcycles. But collectively the group also traveled in dilapidated old cars, rusted station wagons, and one nearly new, red Cadillac. Our orders from headquarters specified that we should be helpful. Apparently the Company had cultivated some interest in the business, though why was unclear at the time. All I knew was that the arcade had been

161

expelled from one of the Maryland suburbs because of new legislation regulating commercial uses of video games.

The Strip had always teemed with teenage kids, but with the arrival of the video arcade they congregated more densely around the Pink Pussy. They hung out in clumps along the sidewalk, boys punching girls, girls slapping boys. They tossed Frisbees at each other, drink cans at passing cars, ice cubes on pedestrians, and rocks at stray dogs. They borrowed and exchanged cigarettes, sticks of gum, change, drinks, dope, combs, makeup, hats, identification cards, jewelry, and car keys. They sat on the curb, stood in the middle of the sidewalk, lounged in doorways, leaned on parking meters, and draped themselves over one another.

They filtered into the store all day long wanting change, cigarettes, matches, screens for their hashish pipes, imitation cocaine, rolling papers, and dozens of other items. Unless they were over eighteen, they had to buy what they needed and leave quickly, but the younger ones tried constantly to stay. They came in with false or altered identification. They came in with no identification but stalled and looked around as they searched their pockets and shoes for the card they swore they had. They had notes from home saying that their parents gave them permission to go into the store, and they had phone numbers with which I could verify the notes. Daily, small groups pushed into the shop to look around or steal things as I yelled and thrashed out at them with a stick, herding them back out the door.

Frequently, a small band of boys dashed in and headed straight back for the peep booths. They scattered into different booths while I grabbed a slower-moving boy. As soon as I tossed him out, I went to the other booths and dragged the teenagers away one by one. I could shout at them all I wanted, but none would leave the booth until I opened the door and grabbed him; even then kids would hold on to the coatrack, the door handle, or even the seat, trying to watch one more minute and hoping that the machine would click off before I managed to break their hold. Even after I had hauled them out of the booths, they scuffled and pulled as a stalling technique to give their buddies more time. Though they resisted doggedly, they were usually not violent. Violent people did not undertake such juvenile pranks. Still, I was careful not to hurt the boys and provoke a real fight. I had heard too many tales of the damage a handful of kids could do to a store when they became enraged or vindictive. Though I was not fond of this game, I played by their rules.

The kids on the Strip seemed to be there for much the same reason that they might loiter around a roller rink, a shopping mall, or a football stadium. They came in from the suburbs after school, or they lived in the center city and used the Strip for a playground. They drifted around, spending some nights with friends in abandoned buildings, other nights back home with their families. Some were true runaways from out of town. During the time I worked on the Strip, the surrounding suburbs were tightening laws not only on the video arcades but also on the sale of drug paraphernalia and alcohol. This drove the high-school kids from the suburbs into the Strip to do or buy that which had previously been legal for them in their own communities. Even the movie theaters in the shopping malls grew less willing to show martial arts and other, more violent films, sending them instead to movie houses scattered along the Strip and in the surrounding area. The teenagers also came for the myriad fast-food places, which they used as private clubs, meeting one another, wasting time, and eating. The fast-food places also had jobs for them. For those who did not want or could not get legitimate jobs, there were plenty of illegal ways to earn money in the vicinity by dealing in drugs, alcohol, or stolen goods.

In some respects the kids on the Strip constituted their own separate subculture. They spent a great deal of energy on cultivating boyfriends and girlfriends, relating who said what to whom, sharing whiskey, finding a little marijuana to smoke, and cruising around in the family car on weekends. They were much like young people gathered together almost anywhere, but because this was the Strip, their activities connected with and became a part of its larger culture. Boys buying and selling a little dope for their friends easily became involved in larger-scale buying and selling. Small-time shoplifters learned to cooperate in bigger scams. Simple vandalism turned into car stripping, or breaking and entering. Even the innocent dating games of the teenagers sometimes matured into full prostitution. The social system of the Strip was already there, making it easy for some very young people to become caught up in it.

A girl who one month chased a boyfriend might the next month work for a pimp, selling sex nightly on the Strip. Pimps quickly exploited young girls willing to sell themselves, but there were always more than enough girls who made themselves available without pimps. Greed is a powerful motive in our society. Many young boys and girls faced with the chance to have more spending money, to afford a new stereo, to buy the latest shoes or record album in exchange for a few moments of sex are glad to do it. Even if they do not want the money for themselves, they may want it for the people they love, since the giving of money and material goods is a sure sign of love in modern society. These young people are not freaks, with a totally different value system from the society at large. They are quite typical kids in search of money, companionship, and fun.

Sandy regularly patrolled the streets with some of her girlfriends or her latest boyfriend. When she was sixteen, one of the eighteen-year-old boys persuaded her to make a set of nude photographs. She was promised $500 for the day's sitting. The process took a week, after a number of botched appointments, bad weather, and much confused communication. At the time she signed her model release, the photographer paid her $60 as a down payment, the rest to be delivered when the magazine accepted the photographs. Of this she had to give $25 to the guy who arranged to have the portfolio made. Her net pay came to $35, and the photographer never gave her any more money. All the pictures were simple nude shots—she sat around a small brick courtyard as though sunning herself. A few pictures showed her with her legs open to reveal the inner vaginal area, but she did not pretend to masturbate or perform sexual acts. She does not know what happened to the pictures or whether they were ever published.

Regina also posed for a series of photographs, at age fifteen, but she was partially clothed and she paid the photographer for the shots, which she wanted to use in a portfolio for modeling. Although she brought clothes along with her, the photographer gave her some very revealing bathing suits and lingerie to model. He persuaded her to expose her breasts in some of the pictures, to reveal part of her pubic hair in others, and to wear bikini bottoms so tight that they outlined her genitals. Later her friends showed her these same pictures in a soft-core pornographic magazine.

Larry was a fifteen-year-old who described himself as "an amateur panhandler." According to him, "You really have to earn more than ten dollars every day to be a professional, and I don't have quite enough interest to stick with it that long. I get eight bucks and I am tired of standing on the streets." Larry shared a room with another guy in the abandoned hotel called the White House. They had a kerosene lantern for light and built a fire when the weather was cold. Once a week Larry went to the Mission, where he bathed, listened to a sermon, and had a good dinner. Other food he gathered from the trash dumpsters behind the various restaurants, sometimes carrying some of it back to the White House, where he sold or bartered it to the other residents.

Seventeen-year-old Donna worked afternoons in a hamburger restaurant; even though she spent much of her day on the Strip, she was not allowed to work during school hours. Donna had a very round face that made her look even younger than she was. She smoked a lot, but claimed she had "passed the drinking stage—I just outgrew it." She explained that "when I was younger we always had to have a bottle to pass around every day, but now when I see other kids doing that, I tell them they are just crazy. Some of them are already alcoholics, and I guess I could have been one, too, but I was lucky."

Sixteen-year-old Dino used a fake identification card to get a job as a nude dancer in the private men's club. He was tall and thin and had enough of a moustache to make him look close to eighteen. Card or not, I never let him in the Pink Pussy, but I did see him perform in one of the clubs. He had a long foreskin that made his penis appear fairly large. After dancing a few minutes on the stage, he came to the edge of the stage and let several men standing in line fellate him, one after the other. Dino was arrested once in a raid, but he said that the police let him go when he showed his card and spoke only in Spanish, pretending not to understand English.

Dino's girlfriend, Cathy, lived with her sister, who was a stripper on the night shift at the Blue Mouse. Cathy had a baby at fifteen, before she met Dino. She tried to raise it alone, but her sister, her sister's boyfriend, and Dino all objected to the baby so much that she gave it up for adoption. When the government stopped her welfare allotment for mothers with dependent children, she demanded her baby back again. The baby was returned and she gave it to another sister to raise, while she continued to collect the welfare money.

Willis and his sixteen-year-old wife, Denise, came to the District of Columbia from North Carolina. At age twenty Willis worked in the Wild World of Sex porn store, where he sent customers over to his apartment for sex with Denise. Denise only gave blow jobs and hand jobs. "I save real sex for my husband. He is the only man I have ever slept with or ever plan to. I was raised a Baptist, you know." At least once a week they had a big fight and she ran away to stay with one of her other friends, but she invariably went back to Willis after only a day. She frequently threatened to tell her father what Willis made her do. "My daddy almost killed him once in North Carolina. I know that if he ever heard about this, he would kill us both."

Tracy was the daughter of a professor at the University of Maryland and rode the subway down to the Strip several times a week to visit Mike. He worked in the theater that shows martial-arts films, and the two of them planned to marry as soon as she was old enough.

Tim was a seventeen-year-old boy who frequented the Strip but claimed to be "married" to a male lawyer with whom he lived in nearby Fairfax. Tim had fake identification and he and his "husband" sometimes went to clubs with nude dancing women, but they never went into homosexual bars. The "husband" had a fourteen-year-old son who also came to the Strip. According to Tim, "The boy is no good; he's a damn hustler. I try to be a mother to him and teach him to go to school, but he won't listen to me. He told his own father to throw me out; he said he could be his dad's son, friend, and lover and do everything for him that I could do. The boy is sick and ought to live with his real mother." Later Tim broke up with his "husband," claiming the son had caused it and was now sleeping with the father. Tim reported it to the welfare department, provoking an investigation.

Suzy and Brad were high-school sophomores who drove into the Strip regularly from a middle-class neighborhood in Annandale, Maryland. On the Strip, Brad bought dope for himself and to resell at his school. He swore that he would never use anything addictive, but he also used cocaine. Suzy occasionally tried the cocaine, but Brad did not deal enough to support a habit for two people.

The full scope of child prostitution in porn rows such as the Strip is difficult to measure. Some girls try it once or twice and flee. Some return to it periodically to earn extra cash but otherwise live a somewhat normal life at home. Other girls stay on and do it as a permanent career. The police work diligently to find the underage girls and boys prostituting themselves on the streets. This seems to be a top priority for them, but it is an unending pursuit. The list of runaways and thrill seekers grows and grows, and it is difficult for anyone, including the police, to tell which girl may turn one or two tricks and then decide that this is not the right life for her, and which is the girl likely to become a full-time prostitute.

The popularity of young girls as prostitutes seems to be increasing—partly because of their increased availability on the streets, and partly because of the spread of AIDS among prostitutes. Business became harder for older prostitutes in their twenties. According to the folk explanations current on the Strip, men began turning to younger girls because the girls were less likely to be infected with AIDS than were the women who had been working the Strip for a few years. Even if the young girl was a drug user, she was unlikely to have been one for very long, so would not have had long-term exposure to

AIDS. Pimps like Tyrone were kicking out older prostitutes, such as Debbie, and taking in teenage girls despite the increased potential for legal problems.

The AIDS scare also made men more conscious of selecting healthy-looking prostitutes as sexual partners. Women who had lived and worked on the Strip for five or six years were more likely to appear worn or even haggard and to depend on more makeup to cover sagging skin, growing wrinkles, and a multitude of skin ailments. By contrast, the young girls appeared more robust and healthy and relied much less, if at all, on makeup. Thus, the increased health-consciousness of the general public was creating a greater demand for child prostitutes.

Although sexual business for minors was increasing on the Strip, the Pink Pussy did not have a corresponding increase in the demand for photographs of minors. We received periodic requests from customers who genuinely seemed to want them, but more often such requests came from men we assumed were undercover police searching for forbidden pornography. The store did, however, carry material that catered to the same tastes. Whole lines of magazines specialize in young women who look much younger than they supposedly are. They have underdeveloped breasts and hips; they usually shave off all pubic hair; and their hair and clothing, together with the props in the pictures, evoke a childlike image. They pose as teenage cheerleaders, as little girls in their rooms listening to records, and as baby-sitters. One issue had a series showing a teenage girl alone in a locker room after a ball game. While showering she begins to masturbate, whereupon the men's coach comes in unexpectedly. He stuffs his quickly erected penis into her mouth; at first she tries to push it out but then begins to enjoy it. After she pulls him down on top of her, he licks her shaved genitals before copulating with her.

Many films and magazines repeat this situation of an older man with a young girl and only the details vary. The little girl is sucking a lollipop and a large black man forces her to suck him instead. A man is taking a nap and his daughter plays with his genitals while he sleeps, causing him to wake up just as she is inserting his penis into her vagina. As long as the models in such magazines and films are eighteen years of age or older, the material is legal.

In all cases, the models pose as teenagers or preteens. It is very difficult for them to imitate a child of only six or seven years of age. Child pornography exists, but it was not available in the Pink Pussy, nor to my knowledge in any of the other stores on the Strip. It obviously is sold through other networks, but it does not pass through the Strip. People who work for the Company told me such materials pass through the mails or through personal exchange networks in much the way dope or any other illegal goods are sold. Most of it is produced by individual entrepreneurs who have no affiliation with the larger pornography companies such as the Company. The volume and profit in these areas is much too small for the big companies to bother with it.

A number of our paperback books featured sexual adventures involving children in their early teens. Incest stories were particularly popular, in virtually every possible combination: mothers seducing sons; fathers seducing daughters; mothers with daughters; and fathers with sons. Almost always, the sex was intergenerational; stories about siblings or cousins were rare. Other books featured similar intergenerational themes without the incest: teachers having sex with students; doctors with teenage patients; guidance counselors and parole officers with their wards; policemen with delinquents. Scout leaders, Sunday school teachers, bosses, and ministers were all common subjects. The stories were heterosexual and homosexual, often combined into a book that offered some of everything.

Almost all of this pornography is bought by older adult males, men of about the same age as the fathers and teachers in the stories. I never sold such a book to a female. It was also rare for a young male in his twenties or teens to buy them. Younger men who bought such books usually chose ones that were homosexual in theme.

Sexual interactions between adults and children can be found in other societies as well as ours, but they usually lack the exploitative component. The Kaingang in Santa Catarina State in the highlands of southeastern Brazil were studied from

1932 to 1934 by Jules Henry, a student of Ruth Benedict and Franz Boas. The Kaingang are forest nomads confined to an Indian reservation by the Brazilian government and forced to combine hunting with farming for subsistence. Like many of the technologically very primitive peoples in the world, they are rather open about bodily functions, including sex. Children are taught from infancy that sex is fun and funny. Like many mothers around the world, the Kaingang mother frequently masturbates her children as a way of soothing them when they have an upset stomach or are teething. Masturbation of the child serves as a way of playing with it and making it feel good, or simply as a warm and loving form of intimate contact, much as a European mother might stick a small piece of candy into her child's mouth.

Children are also the objects of much cuddling and fondling. On cool nights everyone likes to huddle with someone else for warmth. An adult will frequently call to a child to come join him or her and sleep together. Adults also try to entice the children into sexual activities of all kinds, but never through force. If the adult does anything that the child finds unpleasant, the child leaves that adult and joins one of many others who are eager for the company and the new body to cuddle and fondle. Full intercourse between parent and child or between two full siblings is not permitted, but most other forms of contact, and relationships with virtually any other person, are accepted as normal.

Henry studied another group of Indians on the Pilcomayo River in the Gran Chaco of Argentina. These Indians, called Pilago, are also open and frank about sexual matters, but adults do not initiate very much sexual activity with children. Mothers masturbate their sons, and some mothers were observed becoming sexually excited in doing so. They then used the foot of the infant to rub against their vulvas and masturbate themselves.

Aside from such acts, the children are left on their own to get their sexual pleasures wherever and as best they can. This is not too difficult a quest. When being carried, the child rides on the mother's or some other person's hip. This contact is all

170

the more intimate if the mother and child are both naked. The mother's walking rubs the child's exposed genitals against her exposed flesh in a rhythmic manner much like horseback riding, and the mother thus becomes a source of frequent sexual pleasure as well as of the many other kinds of pleasures that mothers routinely provide. Having learned the pleasures of this kind of body contact, young boys in particular quickly learn to use the technique on other people. Boys frequently rub their bodies against their sisters or against their male companions as a form of sexual stimulation. Sometimes a number of children will pile on top of one another and have an orgy of genital rubbing against one another's bodies.

The Pilago child is much more responsible for his or her own sexual satisfaction than the Kaingang. The Kaingang child always has someone who wants to play sexual games and therefore never has to take the initiative or bother playing at sex with other children. Among the Pilago, after the early years of the mother's masturbating the infant, the child is dependent on its own initiative and motivation for finding sexual outlets and partners.

The giving and receiving of sexual pleasure with children is common in many societies and in many ways. Among the Cayapa of Esmeraldas Province in Ecuador, parents often play with their sons by holding them up in the air and sucking on their penises. Such an act is never seen as wrong or immoral since it brings obvious pleasure to the child. The parents enjoy it in the same way that an American parent might enjoy kissing a child on the neck or taking a baby's fingers in the mouth and sucking or chewing playfully on them.

The Siriono of northern and eastern Bolivia enjoy tickling their small children. They particularly like to tickle their necks and genitals. Mothers masturbate their children, particularly while nursing them, and thereby double the child's pleasure in maternal contact. According to Allan Holmberg, who studied them, the mothers also show signs of sexual arousal when they do this. The child learns to fondle its mother's nipple even when not sucking on it and thereby make it erect. The mother may then take the young boy and rub his erect penis over her genitals. A boy's sexual precocity is something to be proud of. Parents like to show off their son's erections. Fathers frequently masturbate their small sons, too, but though the father may get a partial erection from playing with his son's penis, he does not perform a sexual act that is similar to the mother's rubbing the son's genitals over hers.

Although such practices may seem bizarre to Westerners, similar behaviors were common in the Western world until fairly recently. When the future king Louis XIII of France was still an infant, his mother and other adults would frequently play with his penis and make jokes about it. We are told that he particularly enjoyed having people kiss his penis, and his parents often took him to bed with them for sexual play. This was done openly before the whole court. As Phillipe Aries points out, the concept of childhood did not exist in the Middle Ages and the child was seen as having and giving much the same kinds of pleasures as adults. Children were considered to be and treated as miniature adults. They were dressed in the same styles, ate the same foods, and, to the extent practical, enjoyed the same pleasures as adults.

With the invention of childhood as a prolonged phase of life in which children were kept dependent and were seen as "pure" and sexless, it was assumed that children needed shielding from the pernicious sexual influence of wicked maids and devious older children. The child was to remain sexually pure and innocent as long as possible. In the early part of this century, Sigmund Freud spent much of his career trying to convince people that children have a sexual life, both physically and mentally, from virtually the time they are born. Even though Freud has been embraced in the United States, although not much elsewhere in the world, Americans still ignore this sexual aspect of childhood. The myth persists that so long as no one interferes in any way, the child will grow up to be "naturally" untroubled by sexual "hang-ups" or problems.

Many primitive tribes acknowledge the inherent sexuality of children with the same ease with which they acknowledge children's other biological needs and desires. Usually this is a perfunctory recognition. In some cases, however, sexual activity by and with children can be elaborated into very complex forms of social organization.

In studying the Sambia, Gilbert Herdt recorded highly elaborate patterns of sexual relations between men and boys. The Sambia believe that a male's supply of sperm is limited and that the only way for a male to get it is by obtaining it from another male. Sperm is viewed as necessary for a boy's growth as well as for his later procreation. The sperm is what goes into the mother to make a child and it must also go into a child to make him grow and mature. Thus young boys learn to fellate older males in their tribe to obtain their sperm. Older males are obligated to give sperm to the younger males but often do so reluctantly, because they do not like to give up their life essence. Later in life these boys will marry and have families of their own with the sperm they accumulated while young.

Variations on this behavior are common among many different New Guinea groups. Sometimes the sperm is transferred anally through sodomy as well as orally through fellatio. As convoluted as this rationale for sex with young boys may be, it may contain a core of rationality, inasmuch as such practices may keep the birthrates down in an already strained environment. In addition, sperm is high in protein, and in a primitive tribe even small amounts of protein could make a difference in the maturation and development of young men at just that time in life when they need extra protein for muscle and bone development. All of this is very important in a society that lives in a harsh environment and is trying to train its males to be particularly fierce warriors. These sex behaviors can have the practical effect of conserving energy and protein and not wasting what would otherwise serve only to create more children to feed.

In all these societies, children are encouraged to be sexual beings from the time they first feel any sexual stirrings or sensations at all. Children in these societies, however, are not sexually abused. Because adults are always close at hand, a child can easily escape the clutches of an older sex partner by crying for help. Forcing sex on children is not a part of this culture, but the adults do not inhibit other forms of sexual contact.

The children of contemporary Western society stand in sharp contrast to those children. Modern children live largely in a segregated world, a "child's world." They attend school or day-care centers with other children. They join the Scouts and church programs with other children. They play on ball teams and take swimming or dancing lessons with other children. Western society segregates youngsters from the adult world as much as possible. The children are left in the care of a few adults who teach them, train them, supervise their play, and provide them with day care. Since the average child thus receives daily attention from a minimum number of adults, children compete constantly with one another for recognition from the teacher, the coach, the troop leader, and any other adult in their world. Clumped together and away from adults, the children make easy targets for those people supposedly caring for them who choose to take sexual advantage of them.

The children have been primed for such encounters by a culture that has denied their sexuality and starved them of touching. As Evita observed, a society that must make bumper stickers to remind parents to hug children is obviously an odd society. One convicted child molester said, "Remember, if you don't hug your children, I will." Understandably, these children respond favorably when a teacher or any adult around them rubs their cheeks, pats them on the head, sits next to them, or allows them to curl up in his or her lap. These shared intimacies make the child feel special and are easily extended into other kinds of special touching. The child may even take the initiative in such relationships. She may feel curious and also comfortable enough with Uncle Charley to squeeze the big bulge in his pants. She may enjoy playing with his "fire hose" and ask him to let her do it again.

Western society creates children so deprived of attention and of touching, sensual experiences that they are eager and willing partners for exploitative sexual encounters with adults. As soon as they are old enough, thousands of them flock into red-light districts or more innocuous places and willingly go along with the sexual schemes of people far older than themselves. They are still too young to understand fully what the

174

sexual act is, but they do it because it is intimate and warm. Young girls sleep with older boys and then quickly allow themselves to be prostituted by these older boys to even older men.

Some of the same lures that attract some children to the Strip and the Pink Pussy attract other, less adventurous children to sexual experiments with adults in their community. The two worlds differ only slightly. Modern culture creates children who actively seek out or willingly respond to the sexual advances of adults. In return they are rewarded with adult attention and caresses, as well as with tangible goods that vary from money in the case of child prostitutes to ice cream cones and quarters for the video machines for children in the suburbs.

Though sexual activities with children are found in societies as various as the Kaingang or Cayapa as well as in the modern United States, Canada, Germany, and other Western nations, only our contemporary societies create massive and very real child abuse. Cayapa men do not penetrate three-year-old girls or sodomize seven-year-old boys, but Americans do so at an extremely high rate. Societies that at first appear to be very permissive regarding child sexuality in the end have far less sexual exploitation of their children.

Fourteen

OLDER WOMEN MAKE BETTER LOVERS

"Did I tell you about this new one I'm working on?" Gary asked on a Saturday afternoon, as he waited for a co-worker who was to drive him out to the Ladies Club in the Maryland suburbs. "She's married to this really top colonel at the Pentagon, but she looks about thirty-five—in really good shape. She belongs to this snazzy health club where she goes every day, but her husband is a real boozer. And he's all the time in South America or somewhere, anyway, because he's one of the top traveling guys for his outfit. So she usually drives his black Seville. She has this little Ford Escort, but she never drives it."

As he talked, Gary strutted around the room and played with the zipper on his leather jacket, which glistened as black as his hair and eyebrows. Gary presented an ominous yet nervous image, looking more like a hoodlum on the street corner than a New Jersey boy who made the dean's list for one semester at American University and then took a job stripping and dancing at the Ladies Club. His "tough kid" persona combined bits of the younger versions of John Travolta, Matt Dillon, Marlon Brando, and James Dean into a readily recognizable American stereotype that fit in appropriately with the rest of the troupe. His routine was usually the second act of each set, just

176

behind Monsieur Marcel, the suave, continental romantic, and just before John, the Hairy Hulk Weight Lifter, also known as "John the Bod." Brad, the all-American young professional next door, rounded out the group, but sometimes they added a few novelty numbers, such as Abdul El Qocq, who would light his special fire-resistant G-string at the climax of his act.

"How did you meet this new one? At the club?" I asked.

"She was in there with a big group, but I picked her out right away for being class. I sat down and talked with her for a long time after the act, but of course it's kind of hard when all the other women are watching. I asked her back behind the stage, but I think she was too worried about the wrong impression in front of her friends. So I gave her my card and told her I had an answering service so she could call any time."

"Did she call?"

"Well, you see, I called her. I think she was pretty surprised, but I found her number real easy and called to tell her what a pleasure it was getting to know her, and any time she wanted to come back to see my act just let me know and I would have a comp ticket waiting in her name at the box office. She said she would definitely be back. Of course, a lot of times these women chicken out. They want to go through with it, but they just can't make that move."

A lot of Gary's women seem to chicken out. Every couple of weeks he had a new one he was seeing, was about to see, or who was dying to get a hold on him. The big one was the congresswoman, who tipped him $5 for his act and invited him to have a drink with her and the women in her office out celebrating the conclusion of a hearing. She did send him an autographed picture of herself after he sent her one of himself, but aside from that I never saw any tangible evidence of an affair, torrid or otherwise. It was the same with the New York model who wanted him to move up and be closer to her; the GS-14 in the Energy Department who took him up to La Brasserie on Capitol Hill for dinner with all the "political hotshots"; the business executive from Dallas who wanted to rent him an apartment at the Watergate; and the presidential aide who let him use her car while she was with the president in California.

Every Friday and Saturday afternoon Gary came to the Pink Pussy with a new story or an update on an old story, which he recited while he waited for his ride. Gary didn't like waiting on the street, because people might think he was waiting for a bus or trying to hustle, so he always stayed inside the store, smoking the short, thin cigars to which he was addicted.

In addition to his job at the Ladies Club, Gary worked private parties whenever he could and sometimes did assignments for Surprise-Strip, a fledgling business that sent male or female strippers out to homes, offices, and restaurants to strip. He mostly received assignments to strip for secretaries in honor of heir birthdays or promotions, but sometimes he was called upon to help college girls celebrate the end of exams, to liven up a bridal shower, and to embarrass old maids at dinner in quiet restaurants with lace napkins on blue tablecloths. Like everyone else in his business, Gary also passed for a model and loved to wave his portfolio of pictures, which was, of course, under perpetual consideration at *Playgirl* headquarters. He wanted to do clothing advertisements locally, but his plans never seemed to work out. Gary liked the idea of modeling, yet he always wanted it clearly understood that he was not gay. He claimed not to have prejudices against gays, but he did not want to be mistaken for one simply because he modeled and danced.

Though Gary's "class" types—such as the colonel's wife, the congresswoman, and the business executive—never came down to the Strip, he often arrived with Myra, a reservations clerk working for one of the airlines on K Street. Myra appeared to be in her middle to late thirties. She bleached her hair blond, wore very high heels that made her thick hips less conspicuous, and plucked her eyebrows bare, leaving only a single pencil line over her lizard-cold eyes. She appeared in the neighborhood regularly with certain kinds of guys called "popcorn pimps."

These young men in their late teens and early twenties dated slightly older women with steady jobs and a few minor physical defects. Such men usually wanted to be pimps, but because of the competition for prostitutes, they were having to play gigolo instead, depending on the women to pay for drinks and dinner. The woman bought the movie tickets and supplied the popcorn. She supplied the car and the gas, and sometimes she might lend him a little money, help him pay the rent, buy him some new shoes, or keep his record and video collection current. In the terminology of the street, however, these men were pimps rather than gigolos because the word *pimp* implied control over the woman rather than just serving her. According to this distinction, the man who took a woman's money was "pimping" her, and it did not matter whether she earned that money from prostitution or from office work.

Despite his involvement with Myra, Gary did not consider himself a popcorn pimp since he had professional status as a dancer. To him, popcorn pimps weren't much better than male street hustlers, except they happened to hustle women instead of men. Having a steady job, even if only a weekend job, kept him one notch above the guys who lived on the gratuities of women who lacked many physical charms but had an income of their own. He did take occasional offerings from some of these same women, but for him these were truly extras in life and not his financial support. He did not pawn their gifts to buy food or use the "gas money" to take out his own dates. For Gary, going out with doting women seemed more of an ego boost than a financial aid. He enjoyed being admired, sought after, and having numerous messages left on his answering machine.

Myra is one of those women who enjoys the macho and rebellious persona surrounding guys like Gary. "I like the act," says Myra. "I figure that a guy should be clever enough to entertain a woman, to make a good show. Some of my friends think I'm crazy for going out with guys like these. They sit at home waiting for a call from some young lawyer or pilot or congressional aide. I tell you I've already been out with them all, and I was married to one of them for seven years. You make them feel like God and they make you feel like God's doormat. And they control your life. I never knew where my own money was going. He invested in this and he invested in that and took it out of here to stick it there. When we finally split, I figured that I must have held all the losing investments and he had the winning ones, because he walked away looking pretty good.

179

"That would all be okay if these guys really liked you, but they don't. They think about good-looking secretaries but not about you. So I go out with guys who have a different kind of act. They're up front and they're fun. They like mature women and are not hung up, so there's a certain equality. I could never have dated a black guy before coming down here. My father would have killed me, my husband would have had a heart attack, even *I* would have had a heart attack back then. But now I know they really are just like everyone else, and some of them are even better.

"You have to remember that lying and posing are all a part of the game. I would rather go out with a guy who pretends to love me and worship me even if he doesn't than with a man who loves me and can't show it. Some guys are too hung up on analyzing their own feelings and too afraid to commit themselves. Well, loving somebody doesn't have to be forever. It can sometimes be for just one night, and I would rather have him tell me how much he loved me and how turned on he was that one night when he felt it than for him to wait ninety days to see if the feeling wore off.

"Love doesn't need a warranty. It just needs the right chemistry for a little while. And sometimes it takes a few lies to get that chemistry right—to prime the pump, so to speak. Then once they say it, they sometimes start to live it. How will you even know that it is love unless you first say that it is and try it out? If it doesn't work, you didn't lose much. There are lots more men out there, and at least I don't lose everything and have to divorce each time it doesn't work out perfectly."

Myra seeks out men from the Strip for the same reason that so many married men visit prostitutes on the Strip: "I can get from them what I can't get at home—good sex." In her case one of the major types of good sex is cunnilingus, but that is one of the few sexual taboos on the Strip. It is supposedly the most degrading thing a man can do and shows complete subservience on his part. Yet according to Myra, some of the men on the Strip do it, and do it extremely well.

"I just learned you can't ever mention it in front of them. This first guy that I dated down here was so good at it, and one night we were in the bar and somehow we were talking with these people about what we liked. I said that he was the best I had ever had for going down on a woman. I was trying to brag on him, you see. Well, you would have thought that I said he humped his mother or something. He said I was on drugs and crazy, and he really did get mad about it. That was before I knew you couldn't talk about such things. It suits me just fine not to talk about it anyway, because that makes it a little more special."

Whether men such as the ones Myra dates are called popcorn pimps or gigolos, their brand of prostitution differs in major ways from that of the female prostitutes on the strip. The reason for the differences seems to lie in the differences in the clientele: Lonely or neglected women do not want the same forms of attention as lonely and neglected men. Men like Gary do not walk the streets waiting to be picked up by anonymous women, they do not have pimps, and they are not necessarily paid for each individual meeting with a woman. These women want attention more than anything else; some of them refuse to have sexual relations with these guys for fear of herpes, AIDS, or other sexually transmitted diseases. More than the physical aspects of intimacy, they enjoy the companionship of younger men and the ritual of courtship that accompanies their evenings out together.

The sexual involvement of older women with younger men finds open expression primarily on the margins of our society —in areas like the Strip and among some of the women who go to the male strip clubs located well off the Strip in suburban areas. Though lip service may be paid to the idea that older women can pair off with younger men as freely as older men with younger women, in actuality this is still frowned on. Regardless of social stratum, relationships between older women and younger men are criticized and mocked. The male is assumed to be a gigolo or gold digger, and the woman deluded and ridiculous.

Physiologically, however, such a relationship may be ideal. Sexually, men peak early in adulthood, while women do not usually reach their full sexual potential until their mid-thirties.

The young male maintains a harder erection for a longer time, and can get another erection more quickly than he will be capable of in his thirties or forties, much less later in life. Because the life expectancy for women is higher than for men, and because husbands are usually several years older than their wives, a large gender gap occurs in the later years, with women outnumbering men and often widowed for ten to fifteen years before they die. If it endures, a match between a younger man and an older woman makes the woman less likely to be left a widow.

Among many of our primate relatives, there is a decisive male preference for mature female partners. In studying chimps on the Gombe reserve in Tanzania, for example, Jane Goodall observed that one of the most popular females was Flo, who was somewhere between forty and fifty years old. Flo's body clearly showed the ravages of having borne and nursed a dozen or so offspring. Her face showed scars from numerous accidents in the bush and from skirmishes with attackers. Both of her ears were ragged from having been chewed on so many times in fights. Despite this, Flo was the most desirable female in the troop, and when she came into heat, every male was interested in her and willing to ignore the much younger females. Even when she was not in heat, the males treated her with special attention and jockeyed for positions close to her. They groomed her, reached out to touch her, and spent what time they could closer to her than to the frisker younger females.

The preference for older females can be at least partly explained by evolution. The male who spends his energies courting a young female may find that she is incapable of carrying a pregnancy to term, or too weak and inexperienced to care for and protect the infant she does bear. The older female, who has already reared a child or two generates no such doubt. She has proved perfectly capable of both having the child and rearing it; therefore the procreative efforts of the male are more successful when he directs his attentions to the experienced female. Lower-status males continue to copulate with the younger females until these females prove themselves mature enough to be of interest to the older males.

When anthropologist Anne Sutherland started work on one of the Caribbean Islands off the coast of Belize, she found a set of cultural values quite different from those of Western society regarding age and sex. Many middle-aged and older women had long-term ties with men in their teens and twenties. Despite years of hard work in the sun, stretch marks from repeated pregnancies, and sagging breasts from years of nursing, the women were sought after and wooed by the young studs on the island.

While husbands went off in the daytime to fish and tend their lobster traps, the teenage boys slipped into the homes of their special lovers for an afternoon romp. If the husband was on an overnight trip, the young man often stayed the night. After putting the children to bed, the middle-aged mother and the teenage boy might take a stroll on the beach and use an upturned boat as a love grotto. If the relationship endured for more than a few weeks, it became known to everyone on the island and was usually accepted perfuntorily. In one love affair, the mother of seven children ran away from the island with her seventeen-year-old lover. The two of them remained together thereafter in another community as husband and wife. By island standards, the affair was scandalous not because of the age discrepancy but because the mother had left all seven children for her husband to raise.

On this island, women in their sixties often had lovers in their forties, and in some cases these men were the same lovers the women started cultivating when the men were teenagers. As circumstances permitted, the older women sometimes married their younger lovers when their husbands died or left them, but more often they remained as independent widows. That way, if the inclination struck her, each woman stayed free to have affairs with more than one younger man at a time. In turn, those younger men with enough stamina tried to have more than one older mistress, as a macho display of prowess. The more women a man could attract and keep, the higher his prestige.

Many societies institutionalize such relationships both inside and outside of marriage. Young male aborigines of western Arnhem Land in Australia usually seek sexual partners among the older women of the tribe. The boys prefer the fully developed bodies of older women to the skinny, narrow-hipped bodies of young women. These relationships are considered fun, a diverting break from the routine of daily chores for the woman and a chance for the boy to learn a little about how to make love.

This need for young men to learn how to make love is the rationale that societies often offer to encourage older women to take young boys as lovers. On the island of Magaia in the Cook Islands of the South Pacific, boys have a slit made in their foreskins as an initiation into manhood. The man who makes the incision also teaches the boys about sex, explaining the arts of kissing, intercourse, cunnilingus, and the various coital positions best able to bring the woman to a powerful orgasm. The boy then experiments with what he has learned on an older, mature woman. He learns how to make sure that his partner has two orgasms for each one he has, and he learns how to have an orgasm with genital-to-genital touching only.

Sometimes a female who is already married to a boy's older brother or to one of his uncles will be the one to train him in sex. Just as his older male kinsmen teach him to make a spear, to set a trap, or to play the sacred flutes, the wives of these men teach him how to be a good lover. On the island of Truk, for example, a young man may have sex with any of his older brothers' wives who are interested in him. According to the Trukese kinship system, however, the category of brother includes a large number of cousins as well as what Westerners define as brothers. A large group of young sex partners is thus available to any older woman, and as her husband's prowess fades, she will have ample sexual opportunities with other younger men in his family.

Among the Canela Indians of central Brazil, a boy first experiences sex with the wife of his "naming uncle," a ritual relative something like a godparent. Once the boy undergoes this sexual initiation, he is forbidden to have sex with anyone except women past middle age—young women are all taboo.

Older women not only teach the boys the right sexual techniques, but, more important, also help make the young men into better moral beings. The older woman is considered a repository of virtue, and through copulation the youth acquires some of this virtue and wisdom. Since the most virtuous women are the most sought after by the young men, some of these women will share their virtue with a whole troop of adolescent boys in sequence, thereby helping them to build better character.

The Ilahita Arapesh of New Guinea have a similar form of sexual initiation, according to the research of Donald Tuzin. At the time of puberty, a young man is initiated into sex by a woman of his grandmother's generation. She is the wife of a special, ritual friend of his grandfather called a *mundu*. There is no counterpart for the initiation of the female, but when she marries, her marriage is consecrated through intercourse in a special goblin hall, not with her husband but with the elderly *mundu*. She returns to the hall repeatedly for intercourse with this colleague of her grandfather until she becomes pregnant. Only after the birth of the first child may she begin sexual relations with her own husband.

Females in another New Guinea group, the Akuna, generally take the initiative in courtship and seduction and usually pursue younger males. They lure the boys into the bush, seduce them, and try to persuade them to marry. Boys as young as twelve may be talked into marriage by teenage girls. Once married, the couple must refrain from sex for up to a year and a half, but during this time the young wife often finds sexual companionship with the older males of her husband's family.

On Tikopia, another South Pacific island, older women do not marry young men, but they enjoy sex play with them. An older woman may call a young man over, pull him under a blanket with her, play with his penis until he is erect, then copulate with him. Despite this traditional form of sex play between the older women and younger men, the older males show no analogous interest in the younger females.

In Australia a Tiwi aborigine girl is ready to assume full marital and sexual relations at about age fourteen. At this time she will go to live with the man who contracted for her at her birth and has been giving meat to her mother all these years. Because the man had to be fully grown at the time he made the contract, he is likely to be around forty by the time she is fourteen and old enough to live with him as his wife. With the much lower life expectancy among the Tiwi than among Westerners, this young woman will probably be widowed before she is past her fertile years. On the grave of her husband, she will marry another man. The older she is at the time of her husband's death, the younger her new husband is likely to be. If she has passed her childbearing years and is too old to be a very efficient food gatherer, she will have only limited appeal to vigorous men who want to father children and can hunt to feed a large family. Instead, she will probably be taken in marriage by a very young man who has not yet reached his full potential as a hunter.

The fact that the marriages of the Tiwi cross age lines does not mean that young people are limited to sexual relationships with older people only. Younger people can still have adventurous affairs, which are not approved of but are tolerated anyway. Thus if an older and very successful man has several younger wives while some of the young men have none, there is a great chance that the young men will pursue the younger wives and have affairs with them. Despite the turmoil and fights that often result from such affairs, they are still tolerated.

As odd as this system may be by European and American standards, it solves a large number of social problems very simply. It provides for elderly women in ways our Western societies do not. It assures that young men receive skillful sexual training while they are waiting for a wife young enough to bear them children. Older women train the boys; the boys train the girls; and when these girls grow into women, they train the next generation of boys. This allows for the accumulation and transmission of sexual culture, rather than forcing each generation to grapple with it anew.

Western nations have not always been as opposed as they are today to younger men having relationships with older women. In the past these relationships were often fashionable, and older women were ardently sought after by younger men. A wave of such relationships began in the latter part of the eighteenth century, emanating from the royal courts—that of Catherine the Great of Russia, for example, and later Napoleon's court in Paris.

Between the time of the Enlightenment in Europe and the full flowering of Victorianism, the literary and artistic circles of Europe, as well as the aristocracy, developed something of a cult of the younger man in love with the older woman. This centered around people such as George Sand, Chopin, Madame de Staël, the Schlegel brothers, Dorothea Mendelssohn, and Jules Sandeau. Much like modern film stars, they had very public affairs, inspiring one another's books, plays, and musical scores, and then exposing, satirizing, and scorning one another in the next set of works.

The acceptance of these relationships in continental Europe eventually gave way to prim Victorianism, which emanated from Britain and assigned women once again to their asexual roles as mother and housekeeper. With this came the notion of the husband as an older man guiding his younger wife, and in many cases she was much younger than he. Overall, the practice of older women taking younger lovers is incompatible with the general ethos of a patriarchal society. When society is controlled by men, the men choose the mates (either for themselves or for their sons). This is true not only in the West but in China, Japan, and most parts of India. Wherever there is a strong power structure, it is likely to be dominated by males; and so long as males have they power, they will seek to use it in their own favor. Thus, it is primarily among the more primitive peoples, those that lack strong centralized social systems, that greater freedom is allowed for older women to have liaisons with younger men.

Though Western society denigrates any kind of sexual or amorous tie between older women and younger men, people interested in such relationships can still find them. For the wealthier women, gigolos float around places such as Palm Springs, Beverly Hills, and other gathering spots for the rich. For women who are not rich but have a steady income, there are urban enclaves such as the Strip where men hang out waiting to meet them.

By and large, however, contemporary society has very few institutionalized ways of meeting the sexual needs of women outside of courtship and marriage. Although there are some young men such as Gary working as prostitutes, no extensive form of prostitution exists for women. The whole of the Strip is designed to meet sexual needs, but exclusively male needs. Theaters, bookstores, bars, strip clubs, massage parlors, and street prostitutes all offer sexual opportunities of many types to men, but not to women, and especially not to middle-aged or older women.

Fifteen

ROUGH TRADE

Stacy's yell pierced the monotonous traffic noise early one Wednesday evening in May. The street still swarmed with rush-hour activity as Stacy, wearing shorts and a simple striped blouse, ran to the curb and shrieked at a passing car, spewing a barrage of obscenities at the driver.

The car lurched into an illegal parking spot in front of a fire hydrant, and as Stacy paused for breath, a petite redhead in a short skirt and very large earrings jumped out of and confronted Stacy defiantly but not aggressively. Each threw vulgar names and accusations at the other. Stacy lived with Carl the bartender and his name flared repeatedly, so I assumed the argument was over him. Before I could be sure, however, Stacy lunged at the redhead, slapping her across the face with her open hand. The redhead kicked Stacy but only grazed her left leg. Stacy then grabbed the other woman's hair and slung her facedown on the sidewalk.

By this time a small crowd had collected, but kept a discreet distance from the action. Two men who often frequented Carl's bar grabbed the two women and pulled them apart, guarding against further physical contact but intensifying the screaming.

Darlene, the transvestite, led the redhead into the Pink Pussy and asked if they could use the sink in the back. Only rarely did I unlock the bathroom for anyone who did not work for the Company, but the young woman was bleeding profusely from her lip or mouth. Stacy remained on the street with her two guards, who continued to calm her, and the crowd lingered on a little while longer just in case anything else exciting happened. Stacy fluffed her dyed black hair, repaired her lipstick, and seemed calm as she left the two guys and strode along the street. When she passed the redhead's car, however, she erupted again. She kicked the side of the car several times, then grabbed a rock lying on the sidewalk and carved a deep scratch in the front fender. The redhead, hearing or sensing the commotion outside, dashed out of the bathroom, through the store, and out to the street. She ran straight for Stacy, clutching a small stiletto that I knew belonged to Darlene.

Before Stacy knew what happened, the redhead raised her arm and let it fall directly into Stacy's face, tearing through the flesh with the knife blade and releasing a rivulet of blood that first trickled down her cheek, off her chin, and onto her blouse, and then gushed in a torrent. Stacy fell backward but was caught by one of the audience before she hit the ground. He lowered her onto the cement and held her down. The two guards rushed back in time to stop the redhead from delivering a second blow and dragged her away. One of them jumped into her car while the other pushed her into the back seat. They sped away before the police or the ambulance arrived to carry the nearly unconscious Stacy to the hospital.

The spectators watched closely until the ambulance pulled away, and many of the men in the group then strolled into the Pink Pussy. Some of them went straight to the booths to watch a film and masturbate; others raced about searching for a sex partner. There was a frenzied tone to all this activity. The air was almost literally charged with excess electricity, much like that peculiar quality it has just before a big storm or tornado. For an hour after the incident, people continued to reenact the scene, to analyze it, add information about the two women, speculate on what would happen next, and compare it with other episodes. Only after the event had been thoroughly rehashed did the Strip lose interest, the business for the hookers slack off again, and the customers jamming the peeps disperse.

Such scenes did not play out every day in front of the Pink Pussy, but they occurred with reasonable regularity. Every day a few people were taken away in ambulances from some part of the Strip, and two or three times each week the ambulance carted off someone from our block. The victims were cut, pummeled, shot, stomped, bitten, but seldom raped. If the victim had merely overdosed on drugs or alcohol, had a heart attack, or just dropped dead on the street, the event generated curiosity and black humor but no real excitement. Only when there was a visible confrontation did the crowd seem provoked to the sexual frenzy that followed Stacy's fight with the redhead. Even one of the comparatively mild scuffles with customers that I had several times a week provoked a momentary surge of sexual excitement in the peeps, triggered by the yells and the crack of the stick against the doorjamb. The violence made everyone's heart pump harder, and once the danger subsided, the spectators were left with their bloodstreams full of adrenaline. This arousal could quickly turn sexual.

Western tradition depicts sex as a "naturally" warm and gentle act. Those who mix violence with sex or are sexually stimulated by violence are "perverted." Violence and sex combine only in the psyches of individuals who have been brutalized or warped in childhood or are a part of a social group that is grossly abused by the greater society. Violence and sexuality are antithetical aspects of human nature, the one involving love and good things, the other pain and bad things. Yet on the Strip the two are interwoven in ways that indicate this is not only simplistic but invalid.

In his study of sex in public bathrooms, Laud Humphreys made a similar observation one night when one of the bathrooms was under siege from eleven teenage toughs. The youths had barred the door to trap the men inside, and they then proceeded to bombard it with stones and bottles, breaking the glass and threatening the men within with worse damage. This very real danger provoked a small orgy of sexual activity among the besieged men.

Although the evidence that fear, danger, and the excitement generated through violence are closely connected to sex is better documented for males, this does not mean that women are immune to it. Women comprise a major segment of the audience for some of the most violent sports, such as boxing and hockey, and were also avid fans of the gory spectacles performed in the coliseum of ancient Rome. With sufficient license, they seem to be no less sadistic than males.

Throughout the animal kingdom, and in the primate order in particular, the connection between violence and sexuality is a great enigma. Aside from the apparently violent aspects of some courting and mating behaviors among animals, sexuality and violence often seem closely connected to dominance and submission, particularly among males. This odd mixture is seen when the male spider monkey "approaches a female or another male head on, places one or both hands on his back and thrusts the erect penis towards the face. . . ." Such behavior lacks any erotic component; yet the primary feature of the act is the erect penis. Similarly, male squirrel monkeys greet each other by grimacing to expose the teeth, shrieking, and displaying the erect penis.

In most primates, subordination appears when the weaker one, whether male or female, bows in front of the stronger and assumes the position of copulation. The stronger one, even if a female, then thrusts a few times as though inserting a penis to copulate with the subordinate, but coitus does not occur. In this way the status hierarchy of primates is tested and reformed constantly. Over his whole adult career, a dominant male may use his penis much more as a mechanism for dominating others than as a sexual tool. If urination is the primary function of the primate penis, dominance is probably the second, and sex ranks only third.

Hierarchy and domination among humans are not expressed through such apparently sexual rituals; yet the connection between violence and sexual arousal persists in humans, too. For centuries European prostitutes kept flogging switches in their brothels. Even though very few clients showed interest in masochism or sadism *per se,* it was well known that switching the thighs and buttocks of elderly men could bring them to erection. The practice had little to do with the dark, hidden currents running through the man's psyche; rather, it resulted from the simple physiological response of the human, which floods the flogged area of the body with blood and increases overall blood pressure.

Similarly, male infants produce erections whenever they are angry or scared. Studies of small infants reveal that if a male baby is momentarily denied the mother's nipple before he finishes nursing, his body tenses, his hands automatically form into fists, he cries, and his penis invariably erects. The same erectile response occurs when a young boy is spanked or mildly frightened. The erection has nothing to do with culture or individual psychology; it is a physiological response.

As the boy grows older, the variety of stimuli that provoke erections decreases, but violent stimuli continue to cause them. This was noted by Sigmund Freud when many of the males he interviewed "reported that they experienced their first signs of excitement in their genitals during fighting or wrestling with playmates." This is an ancient observation. In the prehistoric cave paintings that abound in southern France and northern Spain, men frequently show erections during the excitement of the hunt. Other pictures show shamans with erections while under the extreme tension of a trance. One of the most interesting pictures of all, however, is in Adaura Cave in Sicily, near the city of Palermo. It shows two nude men wrestling, each of them wearing around his neck a cord strung in such a way that if pulled, could cause strangulation, and each of them displaying very prominent erections.

If the wrestling itself and the tension ensuing from the violence did not produce the erection, the tight cord certainly would. As hangmen have long known, a tight noose around the neck invariably causes an erection in males well before they die. All men who are executed by hanging produce strong erections during the death agony. This physiological response to strangulation is sexually exploited by the many men who persuade their partners to choke them briefly during copulation. This induces a much more powerful erection than usual and, according to the men who practice it, produces a much more powerful orgasm. Men lacking partners to choke them often use ropes strung from showers, closet rods, high bedposts, or the back of a door. The man achieves the erection from the temporary hanging and then masturbates. He risks passing out from lack of oxygen to the brain, of course; and if he does, his body will continue to pull against the rope and he will gradually strangle. In the United States such accidental hangings probably number in the hundreds, if not thousands, each year. The exact figure is difficult to ascertain because of the various ways in which suicides and accidental deaths are classified in different locales.

The hanging fetish is too odd to be relevant to the sex lives of most people, but the same connection between male sexual arousal and violent acts arises in virtually every community in America every night of the week. Frequently men and women who fight end their struggle making love. This pattern, expressed frequently by the cliché "kiss and make up," seems to occur spontaneously among many couples. After a certain amount of pushing, pulling, and sometimes pounding, the fight slips into passionate reconciliation and lovemaking. Over time more violence may be required to arouse the husband, and the escalation of violence may eventually result in the serious injury or death of one partner. It is no coincidence that Saturday night in the Western world is the night for violent domestic rows as well as for amorous adventures and love.

Because the connection between sex and violence is deeply rooted (though poorly understood), domestic violence occurs as frequently in middle- and upper-class homes as in lower-class ones. This contradicts the myth that such violence flares more commonly among the working class and the poor, where the male feels suppressed by society and takes his frustrations out on his partner. These same patterns of violence probably also precipitate much of the child sexual abuse perpetrated by the same men who abuse their wives. Men can become just as sexually excited beating or fighting with a daughter or son as struggling with their spouses. This link between violence and sexuality may be part of the reason why men interested in sexual relations with children do not discriminate on the basis of sex. Fathers who batter and have sex with their daughters quickly jump their sons as well.

Everywhere in the world, most of the acts of sexual violence are committed by men. Such a consistent pattern indicates a physiological process that transcends individual cultures and psychology. Rape has been a part of human warfare as far back as we have records. Sometimes it is condemned, as when a soldier is tried for the crime, and other times it is glorified, as in the rape of the Sabine women by the Romans.

The opening line of Homer's *Iliad* is usually translated into English as "Sing, ye goddess, of the wrath of Achilles." In the original Greek word order, however, the first word is *wrath*, making this the first word of written European literature. The particular wrath to which the poem refers is the wrath that Achilles feels when Agamemnon takes for himself the woman Achilles has seized in a raid. This poem set the tone in Western literature for many subsequent works that mixed large measures of sex and violence.

The mix of sex and violence also appears in many primitive groups, such as the Yanomamo of Venezuela, for whom warfare and the capture of women are one and the same process. Called by anthropologist Napoleon Chagnon "the fierce people," they live in a state of perpetual warfare, always subject to raids and the abduction of their women by surrounding groups, and always raiding these groups for their women. Practices like this in the ancient history of many societies may explain why the marriage ceremony in so many parts of the world simulates some form of capture. Even in modern America, the bride and groom are often chased from the church by friends throwing harmless objects and ritually harassing them. Then, when they enter their home for the first time, the groom lifts the bride and carries her in. Such practices are a long way from rape, but a connection may survive in even these very innocuous rituals.

The potential violence of male sexuality, in contrast to female sexuality, is evident in the prison behavior of the two sexes. Even though homosexual activity among female prisoners is generally considered more common than among male prisoners, violent homosexual attacks by male prisoners occur much more frequently than among female prisoners. Women form reasonably tender domestic bonds even in prison, though the tie may provoke sporadic arguments and sometimes fights. Men, on the other hand, rape one another in prison. Men in prisons build elaborate dominance hierarchies based on anal rape in precisely the same ways other primates do, except that while the other primates do not actually penetrate the subordinate, male prisoners do.

Reliable national statistics on male prison rape do not exist. Based on one thorough study by the former chief assistant district attorney of Philadelphia, Alan F. Davis, the rate may be much higher than is generally assumed. According to his data, 2,000 violent rapes occurred in the Philadelphia prisons in a twenty-six-month period. This figure included only those rapes in which actual violence was used, not the ones in which violence was merely threatened, nor those involving forced prostitution by a prison pimp. Thus, excluding these other forms of force, fifteen violent rapes occurred per day in the prisons of that one city.

Even if men have this biologically rooted propensity for violent sex, however, it is the culture in which they are reared that determines whether it will be sublimated or will be accentuated. Western cultures do not train men to be nearly as violent in sex as the men of some other societies. This is evident when we compare men in our culture with the East African Gusii, who live in a society that trains them to be particularly violent in sexual acts, as well as in other interactions between the sexes.

The Gusii comprise seven Bantu tribes living just east of Lake Victoria. They sustain themselves by a mixture of agriculture and animal husbandry. According to a study by Robert LeVine, the Gusii had a reported rape rate over three times that of the United States, and possibly much higher even than that. Violence was not only manifested in rape, however; it was a

196

part of all acts of intercourse. In Gusii culture, a man was not a real man unless he could make a woman cry from pain during the sex act.

A new bride among the Gusii was taken from her family and ritually harassed and insulted by the groom's family, who sometimes rubbed cow dung on her lips as a sign of their dislike. Once inside the marital chamber of her new in-laws, she was expected to resist intercourse, as her husband was expected to struggle for it. To do this, the husband often enlisted friends who helped to strip off the wife's clothing and then hold her legs apart while he penetrated her. The man was expected to follow this violent penetration with a minimum of six acts of copulation during the first night. If he could not leave the woman physically devastated, her family and friends would insult him for having a small penis and not being a real man. Sex was always viewed as a struggle between the woman, who does not want to copulate, and the man, who tries to force her. Gusii women traditionally cried during coitus and articulated their pain in standardized phrases such as "You're hurting me, you bad man!"—all of which increased the sexual excitement of the male.

Gusii females were given only one opportunity to express aggression against males. When boys underwent circumcision at age sixteen, young girls came to the hut where the boys were recuperating and danced naked, taunting them in an effort to stimulate erections that would rip open the cuts and start them bleeding again. This act at an important rite in male development exemplified the aggressiveness felt by both sexes.

Similar patterns linking extreme cruelty and violence with sexuality are reported from certain groups in the highlands of New Guinea, and in comparison to some of these peoples, the rape rates in our society seem low. There is an additional element that may need to be considered in evaluating the sexual violence found among some of these primitive peoples, however: the existence of extreme environmental or aggressive pressure. These societies often suffer from lack of adequate food and are subject to continuous raids by other peoples.

But however violent they may be in their sexual behaviors,

these groups do not show the Western interest in violence and sex as entertainment. In recent years the combination of sex and violence has become one of the primary themes of the film industry. Current "screw and slash" films have replaced the detective story that focused on the mystery, the cowboy story with a minimum of love interest and relatively bloodless killings, and the war films that glorified bravery and defending one's country but not gratuitous violence and gore. Contemporary society seems to have an insatiable appetite for sex and violence in films, television, books, cartoons, song lyrics, and musical videos.

The Pink Pussy carried a full line of violent pornography, but ours differed from that offered in feature films and magazines. Our books and magazines focused directly and solely on violent sexuality, omitting all other themes. On our shelves such magazines were divided into two main categories: "bondage and discipline," which focused on tying up the partner; and "Sadomasochism," which covered all the other types of violence. Within these two groups, however, were subcategories. Our customers seemed to make a clear distinction between those magazines in which the male was the victim and those in which he was the perpetrator of the violence. Some men preferred B&D magazines that showed men tying up women, with close-up photographs of the women's breasts straining against the tightly bound ropes, cords, or wires. Other men bought only magazines that showed women tying up men, with special emphasis on different ways of tying down the penis with every variety of material. Similarly, men who bought S&M magazines depicting women torturing men in dungeons and basements were not the same men who bought magazines that showed the torture of women.

There was no homosexual equivalent of the B&D magazines, but there was a section of the gay rack that featured homosexual S&M magazines and S&M magazines with transvestites. Our best-selling violent homosexual pornography, however, was not these picture magazines. The greatest demand was for paperback novels such as *Motorcycle Love Slave, Army Black Boot, Cowboy Captive,* and *Prison Orgy.*

Though books like these were available with both homosexual and heterosexual themes, the homosexual ones far outsold the heterosexual ones. The men who bought heterosexual violent pornography preferred it in the form of pictures, while those who bought homosexual violence preferred it in words.

These differences were probably related to age. Violent homosexual books were bought by males of various ages, including some who were very young. Violent heterosexual pornography, however, was purchased primarily by men in their thirties or older. Heterosexual men in their twenties showed no interest in either S&M or B&D material other than to mock it and the "dirty old men" who were attracted to it.

There were other differences as well. Men who bought violent heterosexual pornography rarely bought any other kind of pornography. This kind of focused interest was not true of the homosexual purchaser; he might buy an S&M book along with other homosexual or heterosexual material, or an S&M book one week and another type of book the following week. It seemed to me that there was a more pervasive but much less intense interest in violence among the homosexual customers. There was a much sharper division between the heterosexual men who liked violent pornography and those who did not; and those who did like it purchased it to the exclusion of all else.

The Strip outside the Pink Pussy offered a range of opportunities for violent sexual acts in the flesh rather than only in words and pictures. The prostitutes called this the "rough trade." The majority of them offered various forms of sadomasochism as standard services, and some even specialized in it. All the people involved with sadomasochism stressed the element of fantasy in their activities; they claimed they hurt one another only to a certain point, with imagination taking over thereafter. These limited amounts of acceptable pain were supposed to enhance the orgasm of both the person giving the pain and the one experiencing it. Practitioners of S&M made a great effort to distance their image of their activities from the newspaper and television accounts of men who kidnapped unwilling victims and then tortured them. Even though the themes of their sexual play might involve similar scenarios, the customers on the Strip claimed to be only play-acting with willing partners.

While rough trade was important to the economy of the Strip and many prostitutes engaged in it, it was viewed negatively by most people. The women called the men who were interested in it "pain freaks" or just plain "freaks." Despite the client's and the prostitute's insistence that the trade was chiefly acting and fantasy, such men were the most feared on the Strip, because the women who serviced them never knew when one of them might turn the fantasy into a real-life episode. There were many stories about supposedly high government officials in Congress or the White House who had actually tortured some prostitute to death and had the story suppressed. Similar rumors circulated constantly about the gory fate of one prostitute or another who was tortured to death by a maniac or used in the making of a "snuff film" that showed the actual sex murder of a woman. Even though the newspapers did sometimes report on prostitutes and homosexuals tortured to death by unknown assailants, I never saw any of the snuff films.

Although the term *rough trade* was usually applied to only this sadomasochistic fringe of the strip, in a certain sense it was applicable to everything and everyone there. As frequent episodes of violent confrontation, such as the one between Stacy and the redhead, indicated, all the men on the Strip responded on a visceral level to violence. And this response was easily translated into sexual activity. The sadomasochists showed a more specifically focused taste for this kind of arousal, but they differed in degree, and not in kind, from the average man on the Strip.

Sixteen

THE SEXUAL OBSESSION

After five months of working in the Pink Pussy, I found life there fairly routine.

George did not come to work one day because he had spent the entire night before in an orgy with two lesbians and a vibrator.

Space Man, one of the street nuts, attacked several commuters' cars with bricks; police took him away to Saint Elizabeth's, the District's mental hospital.

A brother-sister dance act cut so deeply into Violet's tips that she threatened to quit her job and go to work teaching aerobics to secretaries.

A very short albino of indeterminate sex and race tried to solicit in the peep booths.

Dodge decided to tattoo his entire body, beginning with a large firebird on his chest.

An elderly woman wandered away from the bus station and was found raped and robbed but still alive behind the Pink Pussy.

A young deaf boy tried to hustle and failed, but did get a job dancing even though he could not hear the music.

Tex took up eating tar, claiming that it helped him to sustain erections longer.

Working fifty-four hours a week in the Pink Pussy and spending almost all my spare time with people on the Strip, I began to see life on the Strip as normal and its everyday events as too unremarkable to warrant much investigation, and certainly not worth much analysis. The Strip became less of a place and more of a way of life to me, differing in nuance but not in kind from the rest of the city.

I realized I needed to restore my perspective, so I made a conscious effort to stay away from the Strip outside working hours. I wanted to read books that were not pornographic, to go to films that had real plots, to talk to people not involved in the buying and selling of sex. I decided to spend more time with my former colleagues working in the Congress, to talk more often with my fellow anthropologists in town, and to catch up on new exhibits at the museums. Above all, I wanted to eat something that was not fried in one of the fast-food franchises on the Strip.

I resolved to eat lunch at the Southern Cafeteria before going down to the Strip each day to begin work. I usually came in just before 2:30, when the lunch line closed for the day, and ate my meal while the women who worked there came out for their own lunches. Frequently I sat next to a large booth where a group of the older women gathered. They took off their starched uniform hats, put their feet up on chairs, and began talking about gardens, grandchildren, traffic, and television as they ate. The shift supervisor always sat at the head of the table reading the *Washington Post*, the *National Enquirer*, or any other newspaper abandoned by a customer. Sporadically she would interrupt their chatter in an officious tone and, with a snap of the newspaper as she folded it back, would announce, "Now listen to this one."

The article she chose invariably dealt with murder; rape; a steamy divorce involving strange sex practices; child sexual abuse in Texas; prostitution in Calcutta; or some other bizarre sex story. She would read the story in a very dramatic fashion, stopping from time to time for editorial observations. As soon as they had heard the first few paragraphs, the women started adding their own comments, other information they had heard about the story on the television, their knowledge of the area where the event took place, and any other details known or conjectured.

"Well, if you ask me, I jest don't know how they could've gotten a whiskey bottle up her without her being passed out or on drugs or something."

"Jest remember that gal they found out in the park here half-buried, about a year ago. She had been plunged with a whole baseball bat and hadn't been drinking or on drugs or nothing."

"Anyhow, look how big a baby's head is, and you gave birth to four of them. They's a whole lot bigger than a whiskey bottle."

"Yeah, but birth is natural. God made the woman to bear children, not baseball bats and whiskey bottles and what not. Anyways, the baby's coming out, not going in. There's a whole lotta difference."

"What comes out must go in. You remember that woman what was arrested for doing the hootchy-kootchy dance with Ping-Pong balls. She shot out nearly a dozen of them Ping-Pong balls—bang, bang—and if she shot 'em out, she shore as the Lord had to take 'em in. She didn't swaller 'em, you know."

"We don't know what went in this dead woman, anyway. Nobody said it was a whiskey bottle that abused her. They said she was abused by a very large cylindrical—or however you say that word—thing that had been used to rape her. Maybe it was just a really big man who had drunk the whiskey."

"Men don't come that big—and anyways, flesh pushing on flesh don't tear, least not as bad as they say she was tore up."

"Don't tell me flesh don't tear flesh. I mean to tell you, I bled from one month straight to the other after I first married Big Frank. I couldn't even go to the water's edge the whole time we was at the beach. I could hardly walk, I hurt so bad."

"And didn't you see what happened to Susanna after her

brother raped her so bad that time when he was all involved with those drugs? They held her in the hospital for six weeks or so."

"That was only because the producer wanted to fire her from the story, so he had to think of a way to get her out of the picture for a while. I read it was because she was having an affair with that actor, anyways."

"Honey, I've asked for a hell of a lot of things in my day, but I have never known a woman ask to be raped. Now she might ask for some attention, or she might even get out of hand with some of her carrying on, but she ain't gonna ask to be raped."

"Hey, girls, you won't believe this one. . . ."

Each day while I ate my plate of soggy, overcooked vegetables, I listened as work, gossip, Sunday sermons, and grandmother talk wove a seamless tapestry with sex and violence from the newspapers, television, and personal experience. There were many times when I could have been listening to Violet and Cissy during a break at the Western Beef House, or to two of the hustlers hanging off the firebox on the corner. The Southern Cafeteria offered no haven.

I also resolved to visit a proper bookstore twice a week for decent reading material to read at work. Yet at each visit I could not help comparing the magazines and books I found there with those on the Strip. I thumbed through a variety of women's magazines. Not only were many of their articles about sex, but the pictures in the advertisements differed only slightly from the pictures in the magazines sold in the Pink Pussy. By acquired response as a censor at work, I flinched each time I saw an advertisement that showed a partially nude young girl, knowing that if it were on our racks, I would have to send the magazine back to the publisher under our "no kids and no pets" rule.

I did not need to pick up any of the men's detective magazines to know that they, too, would be barred from the Pink Pussy. Invariably they showed a murdered, kidnapped, or tortured woman who was bleeding all over her scantily clad body.

Though the magazine always took the point of view of the police, thus making the reader feel like a helper of the wounded woman, the material was far too kinky for our store. The articles seemed never to be about men murdering other men, always about men attacking women and children.

Not all the material in the paperback racks was objectionable by Pink Pussy standards. In fact, the long rows of "historical novel" paperbacks would have been right at home in our shop. I bought a few of them to read at work. The story was always recounted with the same breathy passion and with continuous doses of sex and violence. Only the backgrounds and settings changed, from a lost Viking ship near Greenland to the court of a feudal lord in rebellion against the Manchu dynasty; from the murky moors of England to a rubber plantation along the Amazon; from the wild West to a Bavarian palace.

To keep up the pretense of being historical novels and not mere "bodice rippers," they stuffed pseudo-information in between the passages of gore and passion. The reader learned the process of making indigo dye and its history from discovery to modern times. The silk industry of China and the making of Viking swords were examined in detail, as were the lost-wax method of bronze casting, the Aztec method of stone carving, and the way to cure an ermine pelt. Then the narrative quickly returned to the important issue of how she became a prostitute against her will, but after being sold back to the Saracens, fell in love with Juan, the Viking-Inca mestizo who first raped her and started her on her life of misery.

In a few cases I found books in legitimate bookstores identical to those we carried in the Pink Pussy. These were usually "how-to" sex books, guaranteeing the reader a better sex life in twelve easy steps and offering illustrations and photographs as guides.

I had thought of pornographic books and magazines as a distinct genre before I started working at the Pink Pussy, but the more I looked, the more the boundary between pornographic and nonpornographic materials seemed to dissolve. Printed matter as varied as the Sears catalog, the daily newspaper, psychoanalytic tomes, and literary masterpieces began to appear just as salacious and sexually explicit to me as the works for sale in the Pink Pussy.

Television offered an only slightly modified version of this printed matter. It was certainly no surprise that many of the programs depended on sex as a part of the story and used attractive bodies to hold viewer attention. What did surprise me was my new awareness of sex—especially bizarre, weird sex and violence—in "serious" television.

"The Aspen Hill Rapist stalks another teenage victim—details tonight at eleven on Channel Eleven."

"Don't miss the third in the series 'Fathers Who Rape,' a penetrating look at child sex abuse in the metropolitan area by award-winning reporter Allison Crindon."

"Coming up next: Officials respond to charges of neglect after the pregnancy rate among inmates in the state hospital zoomed last year."

"Should AIDS victims continue to have sex? This will be the special topic of 'News Five' at five tomorrow."

"Should rapists be castrated? That's the focus of our audience call-in this week on 'You Should Know.' "

The accompanying visuals, though edited to conform to broadcast standards, often seemed even more lurid than the full picture might have been. The news camera lingered on blood-soaked cement, a broken toy, clawing handprints in the dirt, or the everyday household item turned into an instrument of torture. The particularly erotic or gruesome story might play for months as "Eyewitness News" and "Action News" followed the principals through repeated court appearances; interviewed survivors, witnesses, and other victims; and provided detailed testimony and drawings from the court appearances.

Cable television and video cassettes have opened up whole new vistas in undisguised home pornography. Now in the privacy of their own homes, viewers watch shows that differ very little from the films shown in the peeps at the back of the Pink Pussy. If anything ever succeeds in putting pornography stores out of business, it may well be television and the proliferation of cable-TV shows and easily available video cassettes.

The longer I worked on the Strip and the more I tried to break away and find a nonsexual haven, the more difficult it became. In the aisles of the Swinging Singles Supermarket in Georgetown, I saw people cruising for sex in much the same way that I had learned to accept on the streets of the Strip and in the back rooms of the peep shows. Cruising appeared to be one of the favorite sports of the city's young professionals, along with running, handball, or tennis, having replaced the practice of flirting over cocktails as the sexual game of the new generation.

I frequently sought refuge in the various museums along the mall, where I could browse through miles of exhibits and sit for hours at little basement tables staring at the tourists or reading. But gradually I realized that in looking at the paintings on the walls, the same questions were always in my mind: Is there any urine, feces, or blood? How about kids and pets? I began to see more and more of these five forbidden subjects in the pictures before me, used in ways either deliberately sexual or easily interpreted as sexual.

I saw in a fresh light the often portrayed story of Zeus coming in the form of a swan to copulate with Leda. I saw with new eyes all the Greek myths about humans copulating with animals. Zeus, in the form of a bull, raped Europa. Io, whom he also wanted to rape, was turned into a cow by his wife, Hera, but he still managed to impregnate her and father more children. Pasiphae, the queen of Crete and wife of Minos, copulated with a bull and from that union bore the Minotaur, which lived in the labyrinth and destroyed the seven virgin girls and seven virgin boys sent yearly from Athens. The gods and goddesses of Mount Olympus also sought out girls and boys, whom they tricked into sex or raped. Zeus, in particular, showed as much fondness for seducing young boys, such as Ganymede, as he did for young girls and cows.

Even the football stadium offered me little respite. The great popularity of spectator sports took on new meaning when I began to see the excitement generated among the viewers as little more than extended foreplay. The fascination in the eyes of football fans in the stadium closely paralleled that shown by the men who watched the frequent fights on the Strip. I wondered if the mixture of long-legged cheerleaders and sex-symbol athletes in this setting of ritualized violence stimulated the spectators to amorous adventures after the game. Did weekend ball games on television rekindle sexual desire in the home the way violence did on the Strip, or were the two settings too different?

No matter where I was—whether in a restaurant or a museum, the movies or a theater, the park or the grocery store—and no matter whether I read, watched television, or listened to other people's conversations, sexual themes abounded. People laughed about sex, joked about it, worried about it, complained about it, bragged about it; it was always there, as a part of every interaction. Of course, this was no great discovery. We are all aware that sexual themes form the continuous background noise of our society. Working in the Pink Pussy, however, made it more audible to me; the experience so amplified the background noise that I had difficulty hearing anything else.

Each society creates its own set of dilemmas, and contemporary Western society has created a peculiar sexual dilemma. On the one hand, it is a society whose people have fewer sexual opportunities than almost any other people in the world. On the other hand, it constantly bombards its members with messages promoting sex as the way to happiness, ego fulfillment, balanced character, fun, love, liberation, and everything else good. But even those who flaunt the topic of sex harbor doubts about it, test it, compare it, vary it, and worry that it is not perfect. Our culture creates people who are expert at talking about sex, clever with sexual puns, full of boisterous jokes, yet are unfulfilled by it or cannot find it at all. Just as in a rich society, surrounded by ample food, people suffer malnutrition, obesity, anorexia nervosa, bulimia, ulcers, and a thousand other dietary disorders, so too in a land full of the promise of sex, people suffer from myriad sexual disorders and deprivations.

Each person faces this dilemma and must find his or her way out of it. Some people denounce the culture's myths and attitudes toward sex; they spend a lifetime fighting and reforming them in the name of religious morality, political righteousness, hygiene, or the social good. They want to end adultery, ban public sexuality, purify television, put moral lessons into films, purge sexy advertisements, and cure, imprison, castrate, or exile sexual deviates.

Other people believe completely the myths about sex as bliss and seek their own ways of reaching sexual nirvana. They frolic in the discos and singles bars on the weekends, and on Mondays they write personal ads describing the perfect partner and their idealized image of themselves. Some of them adopt monastically rigorous regimes of exercise, diet, and self-improvement in the belief that if they make themselves into the right kind of person, they will achieve sexual salvation. Others seek succor in the arms of physicians or psychoanalysts, awaiting the diagnosis and cure of the peculiar disease that mars their sex lives, and prevents personal growth. Still others seek out the Strip, where they buy sex or at least buy pornographic fantasies. Others find sexual satisfaction through children, anonymous encounters, masturbation, rape, pets, obscene phone calls, and countless other deviations.

Some people elect none of these options and instead withdraw from the dilemma entirely. They choose a sober chastity, but keep this secret and as a rule continue the public pose of being just as sexually obsessed as the rest of society. They often bury themselves in other addictions—work, hobbies, compulsive watching of soap operas, listening endlessly to news broadcasts. Some plunge into the blurred haze of alcohol or coast from the almost sexual highs of cocaine to the mellow lows of tranquilizers. It is no coincidence that our sex-obsessed modern society is also one of the most alcohol- and drug-addicted societies known to history.

I knew that somewhere outside of my world there were still people for whom sex was a natural and enjoyable part of life, and not an obsession of any sort. Yet I had lost sight of them entirely. The lens through which I now saw the world converted everything into the culture of the Strip.

At the start of my research on the red-light district, I had undertaken to investigate a clearly demarcated zone. I knew precisely on which block it began and on which it ended. The people there were of a special type: prostitutes and pimps, pornographers, hustlers, dope dealers, and the customers they served. But as the months passed and I became ever more accustomed to the Pink Pussy and to the world it inhabited, the outside world not only became indistinguishable from the Strip, but in some ways struck me as even more grotesque, because it had chosen to obscure what the Strip made clear and distinct. The differences, I decided, were illusory.

Seventeen

HARD TIMES IN THE SMUT STORE

"Hey, are you Jack?"

"Yeah, sure."

"We need to talk—alone."

"Sure, no one is here."

"Then lock the door; we don't want any interruptions."

When the two men first walked in, I assumed they came because of something to do with the racing part of the business or the early-morning limousine service for bettors. They looked the part. The one ordering me to lock the door spoke through thin, mean lips. He wore a dark blue sport jacket and a gaudy tie. His partner was a little shorter and had already lost most of his hair, though he seemed no older than I was. His paunch was exaggerated by his plaid jacket and very white shirt. Just as I was thinking that he did not look too dangerous, he pulled open the jacket. Inside I could see the end of a pistol protruding from a shoulder holster. I had better do as I was ordered.

Still, as I crossed the room toward the door, I wondered if I should dash outside and run. But running seemed silly. What would I do, race up the street yelling that two armed strangers were in the store? Should I run to headquarters and tell them that I had left the store and the money in the custody of those

211

two strangers because I was afraid of them? What if they pursued me? Shot at me? I stayed and I locked the door.

Only then did I notice the unusual silence. The Strip seemed lifeless. No kids loitered around the front of the store; all night none had come into the store pestering me for change, cigarettes, or a chance to look at the peeps. Even the walls were silent, lacking the incessant banging, whizzing, wheeping, zipping, and zapping of the video arcade next door. Nothing but an eerie quiet. For some reason the video arcade had been closed down, and I assumed that the two men must have something to do with it. Even the Pink Pussy was deserted when the two men arrived.

Fine anthropologist I am. My whole tribe moved away and left me, and I had not even noticed. What would have become of Margaret Mead if she woke up one morning on Samoa to find that all the people had moved to Tahiti during the night? An anthropologist losing his people is like a captain losing his ship or a policeman losing his motorcycle. I deserved to be shot.

"I'm never supposed to lock up with anyone inside. It's against Company policy and whoever does it can get fired."

The men did not seem impressed with Company rules and regulations, and I began to wonder if the Company had sent them to check up on me. Maybe they had come just to see whether I would violate Company policy by locking the door when confronted by a man with a gun. I dismissed the idea as quickly as it had come, but thinking of the Company reminded me that I had not pushed the emergency buzzer before coming out from behind the counter. I should have punched it—help would have immediately arrived from headquarters. I started back across the room to my seat behind the counter in hope of pressing that buzzer as soon as possible. Why had I waited so long? That was the first thing we were supposed to do.

"Let's step into the Red Room," said one of the men brusquely.

I reacted as though he had snatched me away from the buzzer and pointed me toward the far side of the store. Curt suggestions feel like commands when they come from a man with a gun. Silently the three of us crossed that room full of enticing eyes, gaping vaginas, protruding buttocks, ejaculating penises, and red tongues sticking out from between even redder lips. As we walked I imagined the echo of hard boots on cold, wet cobblestones, but the only thing I heard was the familiar squeak of my tennis shoes on the threadbare harvest-gold carpet.

Once inside the Red Room, I fumbled, unable to find the light switch. In the pause, one of the men tripped on the vacuum cleaner, swore at its mother, and kicked it. While I continued fumbling, Plaid Jacket flicked on the lights. Obviously he had been in the room before. I could not help but wonder if perhaps he had been in the basement as well. I was about ready to ask him if he knew Mickey who used to have my job, but Blue Jacket spoke first.

"We're here representing some interests who want to know about the video arcade next door. It's all locked up tonight, like maybe the people moved away or something."

I felt a slight sense of relief. "You're real-estate agents?" I knew that plaid jacket looked familiar.

Both of them looked at me as though debating whether I was crazy or just plain stupid. I tried to chuckle, as if I'd been only joking; of course they were not real-estate agents. Silently I wondered if universities could recall incompetent Ph.D.'s.

"We have a lot of interests to represent, and real estate is one big one. Yeah, we're sort of real-estate agents." Plaid Jacket sneered at me as he spoke. "What do you know about the place?"

"I don't really know any of the people over there at all. They're mostly fat and drive motorcycles. The big guy with the beard seems to be the head honcho, but he never comes in here. His girlfriend comes in sometimes—she wears that big kind of white apron with pockets all across the front for giving out change, but she's always running out of change and coming in here to get more quarters."

I knew I was babbling and that this was not exactly the information they wanted, but I felt the need to keep talking. As long as I was talking, nothing else was going to happen, and it made me appear cooperative. I decided to go through my whole ethnographic analysis of the video arcade, with some editorial thoughts on what it means for contemporary civilization as we have known it. I would treat them like students who won't leave my office; I would bore them to death with endless ethnographic facts from around the world until they retreated voluntarily and left me in peace.

"Sometimes the woman from next door comes over here to use the telephone and bathroom," I continued, "but, of course, it's against Company policy to let somenone else use our phone and bathroom. I only let her do it if it is an emergency and she can't make it to McDonald's where—"

"How many machines in there?" Plaid Jacket interrupted.

"Seventeen," I answered quickly and precisely. Why did I say seventeen? I had no idea how many machines were over there. The instinct on the Strip is always to avoid answering until you have to, and then to lie with great precision, authority, and sincerity. "Or maybe eighteen—I think they added a new form of Pac Man last week."

"Is that all?" asked Blue Jacket.

"Well, they threw out all the beds that used to be in there, and I'm not sure how much room that left for machines exactly. I thought they told me seventeen, but . . ." I did not know what I was saying. This was uncomfortably like my dissertation orals. This guy reminded me a lot of that smiling sociologist who always wanted more exact information about everything.

"Hey, man, cut this stuff, just tell me are they in there now?" said Blue Jacket.

"Of course." Why did I *say* that?

"You're sure that right now, as we are talking, those machines are on the other side of this wall."

What was this, one of those trick philosophy-of-science questions, where they ask you how you know the refrigerator light is off when the door is shut? I could never answer that one in graduate school, and I was still not sure.

"I'm only the clerk, you know. The manager will be here in the morning and he'll probably know." Always appeal to a higher authority. "He said there were seventeen in there yesterday; that's all I know." I felt a renewed sense of confidence. If

I could only keep thinking of this in terms of school, I was sure I could get through it just fine. All the blood would be metaphorical and the struggle could stay at the verbal level.

"Have you been in the basement?" Blue Jacket seemed to be threatening me. Or was he only asking a question?

I could tell they were not playing school. I tried to think of another silent joke to keep myself calm while I formulated the right answer to this one, but naturally nothing came into my head. "No!"

"Do you know how to get into it?" asked Plaid Jacket with a tone of forced patience in his voice.

"Well, through that door, but I don't have the key. It's against Company policy for me to go down there. Seems there was some trouble once or something." I had decided firmly that if I was going to die, I would do it in the Red Room. I did not want to die underground. The Red Room was something like the parlor of a nice Victorian whorehouse, and that wasn't a bad place to die. It was not quite the same as being attacked by lions at the foot of Mount Kilimanjaro, having my head shrunk by the Jivaro, or being eaten in New Guinea. Still, I would rather die in the Red Room than in the basement. Anyway, Mickey had already died in the basement.

"Can't you get into the other building through your basement?" Plaid Jacket's voice seemed a little softer, as though he were really wondering about the answer and did not already know it.

I tried to screw up my forehead into a totally puzzled expression, as though asking "What, are you crazy? Of course not." But since I claimed never to have been in the basement, I answered with a meager "Not that anybody told me." That, too, was a lie. I knew that the two buildings had once shared a common coal bin and furnace—Violet had shown me how to crawl through the coal door into the bin and then through another small coal door into the next building. But I figured that these guys wanted a real door, so I didn't mention the little one.

Plaid Jacket reached up inside his coat. For once I prayed that someone was about to light a cigarette in my face. He was obviously reaching for something. Slowly I saw his wallet emerge.

"I would pay ten dollars a minute just to be inside that building." His tone was positively unctuous.

"God, I wish I could get you in. I could sure use the money. But headquarters keeps the key."

For a silent moment the two of them stared at me. Plaid Jacket furrowed his brow and leaned forward. "Look here now. I've dealt with you boys before. Sometimes you have ways of getting keys when you need them. And even if you couldn't let me into the room, you might be able to find out the serial numbers on the machines. Do you know how much those machines cost?"

"No, how much *do* they cost?"

"Some of them are over twenty thousand apiece. That's why it's important to know exactly which ones are in there and how many. I could pay ten dollars a machine to let my company know just which machines are in there and what the numbers are."

I wondered just which company he worked for, anyway. I worked for the Company. His must be the Other Company. I suddenly realized that I was caught in the middle of a corporate war. My father-in-law had always wanted me to be a part of the private sector—out in the arena of life. I wondered if he had really thought through all the ramifications of this free-enterprise stuff. I really did not think that monopolies were so bad. I had liked it much better when we had only one phone company, and I think I liked it better when the Company did not have competition.

Plaid Jacket handed me a card. The card had a telephone number written on it, but no name. "Just call this and let us know," he explained.

I felt a great sense of relief throughout my entire body. That was the first real indication I had that I would live through the interaction. If he expected me to call him, he was obviously not going to kill me.

"Who should I ask for?"

"Just say you want to talk about the video machines. We'll

know who you are." As he spoke, Blue Jacket started to open the door out of the Red Room. But I did not want them to leave. Now that I knew I would live, I wanted to know exactly who they were and what was going on. My anthropological training was returning.

"How about turning out all the lights before we leave?" Blue Jacket suggested.

"Oh, I'll get those when I clean up." I didn't want to think about such pesky details now that I was after knowledge again.

"We want the lights off so no one sees us going out." Again Plaid Shirt spoke with a condescending tone.

"No one's going to bother you around here. I know everybody on the block," I tried to reassure them.

"Thanks, but you're the one we're worried about. We would hate for your company to know that you had been talking to us. You know how they are sometimes about employees talking to the competition."

Blue Jacket had explained it adequately. I switched off all the lights, including the marquee and the lights in the rubber-goods case. The only thing I could see was the tie that Blue Jacket was wearing.

"Remember," said Plaid Jacket, "we're talking about over a quarter of a million dollars in machines. This is serious, not petty street stuff. You help us on this one and we could help you get a new job. You seem like a bright enough kid." I strained for a note of mockery in his voice.

As soon as they were safely out the door again and I had locked it, I raced for the bathroom. After washing my face and hands in cold water, I returned to the front, switched the lights back on, and immediately fished the basement key from behind the cash register. As I walked down the broken stairs, I half expected to find a small piece of a plaid jacket lying on the floor where Mickey had been killed. I looked carefully all around the spot but saw nothing new. I then took the flashlight and, using both hands, pried open the iron gate into the coal bin. I stuck in my head and the hand holding the flashlight. On the other side, I could see the slightly ajar door leading into the other building. I did not go farther. I decided to wait and think about it. Anyway, I didn't have a pencil and paper to write down the numbers. Instead I went back upstairs and closed out my nightly reports.

On the walk up to headquarters that night, I decided that I would report the whole incident to someone. After all, I had been with the Company over half a year and was in good standing. If I reported this immediately, maybe I would get a raise. Or at least I could get these other guys off my back. I did not know them. Maybe they were lying and would not even pay me. Maybe they were checkers from the Company testing my loyalty. I definitely had to tell someone at headquarters.

Once in headquarters, I handed my reports and the money to JP as usual and exchanged the usual inane comments and vulgarities about the weather and the weirdos. I knew I could not explain my situation adequately to JR; he was too stupid. I asked casually if Ted or Danny or Shorty was around, and he casually told me that they were not. Before I knew it, I was outside again, walking toward the bus stop as always, not having found a way to mention the episode.

By the light of the following morning, I laughed about the whole incident. I assured myself that the two men had been bluffing me. They were too much like detectives in the old movies—bad stereotypes. I certainly did not take seriously the whole matter of serial numbers on video games. After all, this was not cocaine, stolen jewels, or State Department secrets. Who ever died over Pac Man, anyway? Besides, Pac Man was too old-fashioned now, and the machines were probably not worth one-tenth of what those men claimed.

It was Memorial Day, and the street in front of my apartment was empty when I left for work at my usual time. I looked up the street carefully since I was accustomed to Massachusetts Avenue crawling with traffic at four in the afternoon. I stepped out onto the empty street and suddenly, before I was halfway across, a rusty Buick lunged out of a parking place, headed directly at me. I jumped as the Buick shot past me, gently brushing against my backside and pushing me forward between two parked cars. As I steadied myself on the hood of one of the cars, the Buick squealed to a halt, reversed, and came racing backward toward me again. It stopped just beside me, sealing me into the small space between the two parked cars. My legs seemed much too wobbly to run anyway.

"Hey, you know where the Suitland Parkway is from here?" the man on the passenger side of the front seat asked in a heavy accent I could not recognize. He had dark curly hair and a thick moustache. Both he and the driver looked very much alike, almost like brothers.

"I've never heard of it" was all I could say. I was rattled. The night before I had felt fairly alert when the two men came into the store. Now I was caught totally off guard, on my home territory where I had always felt safe.

The man asked me another question, but I could not answer. I was trying to formulate my own questions: Why had they just tried to run me down, and why would they then do something so stupid as to come back and ask me for traffic directions? But I couldn't put the questions together in my own mind, much less articulate them.

In my peripheral vision, I saw a third moustached man rise up unexpectedly from the back seat. He was pointing something metallic at me. Then I heard a click, followed by another click and another. It seemed to take me forever to realize that the man was pointing a camera at me and snapping pictures. I put my hands in front of my face. "What do you think—" But even as I spoke, I did not know what I was asking. Nor did the occupants of the Buick seem very interested, for the car raced away as quickly as it had come. I watched it round the corner, the man in the back seat continuing to snap pictures of me out the rear window until the car was out of sight.

I looked around, hoping that someone else had witnessed this inexplicable scene, but no help was forthcoming. I turned slowly and walked in the direction of the subway. I refused to look back in case the men were following me. I did not even allow myself to look to the left or the right. If someone wanted to run me down or shoot me or whatever, I did not want to see it coming. My mind ached in confusion, and my legs were still rubbery from the near-miss of the car. I could not understand any of this. Were these the guys from the Company or the Other

Company? Why would no one tell me anything? Is this what Mickey went through before they took him down to the basement and shot him? Did he understand what was going on? I felt as though I were playing a game in which both sides assumed I knew the rules, but I did not. Everyone knew them but me. I was stranded without knowing what it was I was in the middle of.

At work I told George the story about the two guys the night before and about the three that afternoon. He half listened as he finished the paper work; the story seemed no more interesting to him than yet another set of street rumors. He tossed me a few platitudes about all the strange people in the world today, all the crime on the streets, and how I should be more careful. Then he told me that I worried too much and made a big deal out of very simple things. "Flow with the situation a little more," he told me. "Don't get so riled up." He even accused me of being too damned academic and thinking about everything too much.

I felt a bit naïve and embarrassed, until he said I should probably spend a couple of nights at headquarters just to be on the safe side. I realized then that he was taking the incident seriously, but that he, like everyone else, did not want me to know what was going on. When he left, he said he would send Shorty from headquarters to keep an eye on the store with me.

The evening passed normally except for the spooky silence emanating from the closed video arcade. I heard from no one at headquarters until Mike barged in around ten o'clock, telling me to close the whole store immediately. I grabbed my stick and hit it on all the closed peep-booth doors, shouting, "Everybody out! Everybody out! We're closing now—we have a fire in the electrical system. Everybody out! We have to evacuate immediately!"

There were only five men in the store, and despite some grumbling about lost quarters, they left peacefully, knowing they could probably find the same film in the next store down the Strip. After I had locked the door behind the last customer and switched off the marquee, Mike left too, saying that I was to wait for a truck that would soon arrive.

I waited for two hours alone in the dark store, but nothing happened. It was well after midnight before a rental truck parked in front and three unknown guys jumped out of the cab. At the same time, Mike and George walked up together from the Slipper. Everyone but me seemed to be on a synchronized schedule.

"How about you staying out front with the truck and keeping an eye for us?" Mike said to me.

"Keep an eye out for what?" I asked.

"That reminds me of this old whore I used to know with a glass eye. She was always keeping an eye out for the sailors. If you buy me a drink sometime, I'll tell you the story. But tonight you just keep an eye out for any of your friends, for cops, for spectators, or for boys on bikes. If you see any of them, you holler for me." As he talked, Mike was already removing some of the locks and chains from the door of the video arcade.

I scampered up on top of the truck, as Mike had motioned me, and watched. Once the group entered the arcade, I listened as they banged and thumped around inside. Twenty minutes later they all appeared together, maneuvering a dismantled video apparatus through the narrow entry. Over the next four hours, they brought out at least twenty machines. Even *they* did not seem sure how many machines they had, since they broke them down into so many parts. They also loaded the truck with a cash register, a refrigerator, a desk, a complete stereo system, seven cases of beer, some miscellaneous electrical equipment, and nearly three dozen carefully sealed, identical boxes. I never did find out what was in those boxes, but they oozed a sense of mysterious importance, as though they were the real cause of this whole operation and not the video games. I offered to help carry the boxes, but Mike refused firmly and told me not to get off the truck.

In retrospect, I doubt that the men moving the boxes had any more idea what they were doing than I did. All they knew was that the Company had told them to empty the video arcade and to get the contents out of the District of Columbia before daylight. So that was exactly what they were doing, not knowing themselves whether it was the video machines, the boxes, or maybe even the cash register that was the real object of the mission. They simply removed everything as ordered.

Even though the operation did not end until nearly dawn, it attracted virtually no notice from anyone. Few people were on the street that night because of the holiday, and even the police on their usual patrol seemed uninterested in the affair, never stopping to ask if we were moving.

With the truck finally loaded, Mike sealed the building once again, and one of the men drove the truck up the street to park in the alley behind headquarters. Then all of us went out for breakfast, and I overheard one of the men say that they were taking the cargo to a warehouse in Maryland. At breakfast Mike cautioned me not to say anything to anyone about the evening's activities. "Remember, you saw nothing. No truck, no games, no boxes, no people—nothing. As far as you know, everything is still in that building and nobody has a key to get in. You understand?"

I understood at least that much. But I was not really as interested in the truck and what had just happened as I was in the men who had tried to run me down and then taken pictures of me; and in Blue Jacket and Plaid Jacket, who might return for another visit. I just wanted to know where I fitted into all this and whether I was truly in danger. Was I making too much out of trivial events? Did any of this have anything to do with Mickey's death?

In a way, I wanted out. I was ready to pitch it all and end the study. But I felt that the work had just begun. Now that I knew the area and the cast of characters, I could finally begin to study it seriously. I wanted to know if Violet would find a new job and what kind of a transition she would make into the legitimate world. I wanted to follow Jerry and see whether or not he'd be able to get out of prison and become a successful new pimp. I wanted to evaluate the impact of the higher drinking age on the Strip. I wanted to see what would happen with the growing antipornography movement. I still did not know whether life on the Strip in the summer would be different from life in the spring, or whether summer customers were different from those of the spring and winter. There were far too many questions left unanswered, and a lot of questions that had not even been framed properly.

The next day I resolved to begin my research afresh. I was there to study life on the Strip, not to waste time on the melodramas of petty criminals. I was studying sex and pornography, not organized crime. I wanted to forget the episode of the past few days and get on with my work. I made new lists of questions to be pursued, new people I had seen around the area to get to know, and some old acquaintances with whom I needed to catch up and find out what was happening. Although I was very tired from the long night of sitting on top of the truck, I worked with the frenzy of new determination.

Around 7:30 that evening, George came into the shop, reeking of alcohol and smoke. He was on one of his drinking binges and he wanted to borrow $20 from the till. Sometimes he made as many as three trips for cash over the course of a single night. I made a mental note that I should investigate this more. Did George really pay back the money the next day, or did he just juggle receipts and cash to cover the drinking money?

While I was thinking about this new little problem for my research, I saw Plaid Jacket and Blue Jacket coming toward the store. Before I could say anything to George, they were inside, but George did not seem at all surprised. As though following some ritual of which only I was ignorant, the three of them walked directly into the Red Room. I stared at George as they walked away from me, searching for a sign to indicate what he wanted me to do. Should I go with them? Should I buzz headquarters for help? Without even looking at me, George closed the door behind him. I could hear nothing in the well-padded room, not even muffled conversation. Now thoroughly distracted from my whole new set of notes, I pulled out my knife and wiped it down, ready for action. I made sure the stick was close at hand and debated moving it over to the door just outside the Red Room in case George wanted it. I straightened my books and papers and made sure there was a clear path if I needed to hit the buzzer.

But still, nothing happened. After ten minutes the three of them emerged, as expressionless as when they had entered.

Without acknowledging that I was even there, the Jackets left. George seemed interested only in returning to his drinking companions at the Slipper.

"They're nothing but some two-bit hoods. Just ignore them." George seemed to be explaining the situation to me as best he could. "They think they have a little class and are better than us just because they wear ties and we don't. But still, don't go talking to them. Remember to keep your damn mouth shut. You still don't know nothing. All right?"

George left before I could even answer. "I know, I know, I know," I said to the empty store. I was tired of being treated like a dumb student. Maybe the reason I did not understand this game was that I was not really a player at all. I was merely a peripheral. George, Mike, Blue Jacket, and even the guys on the motorcycles could talk to one another in this game. They were the ones on the two teams. The rest of us—the porno clerks, the whores, the drug pushers, and the street people—were no more than faceless supporting actors in their dramas. We were good for working the streets but had no role in running things. At most, we could be used to convey messages between competing sides. I no longer needed to know the exact cause of Mickey's death; I knew that he was just a message from one faction to another, written in a code I did not understand. The two teams would not harm each other, for that would be war, but they could beat up a whore, scare me with a gun or a car, or shoot an insignificant clerk like Mickey without compunction.

It was very easy for George to be complacent. He had nothing to fear. In the skirmishes with the police when the girls had worked inside the Pink Pussy, it was always the girls who went to jail, not George. This time a few of the minor clerks might get hurt from time to time, but the bigger players were clothed in a smug immunity that made them a different caste on the Strip.

The night was very quiet. I was extremely tired from having kept watch on top of the truck the whole night before and I was disgusted with this place. I decided that I would just close the store and go home early. I finished my paper work, carried it up to headquarters, and handed it to JR as usual. I knew he didn't care that it was only 11:30. As long as I didn't interrupt his television programs, he didn't care what I did.

The next morning, the phone woke me up around ten o'-clock. Shorty was calling me from headquarters. "Get down to the store right away. George will meet you there." I assumed that I was about to be interrogated for having closed the store early, but I was ready to answer all questions. After the long night vigil on the truck, I felt they owed me something, at least a few extra hours of sleep. I rehearsed my rationalizations and excuses on the subway and as I walked the three remaining blocks to the shop.

George was sitting on the curb in front of the store smoking a cigarette and drinking a cup of coffee. The wrapper from an Egg McMuffin lay beside him. "What time did you leave last night?" he asked accusingly.

"The usual time. Why?" I had learned to never admit anything until they could offer proof that you did it.

"Did you lock up good and put on the alarm and everything?"

"Yes." I resented the questions, especially since I remembered clearly doing all those things. Most nights I would do them by rote and then not even remember if I had actually done them, but having left early the night before, I remembered being extra careful to lock everything up properly.

George rose from the curb and silently led the way into the store. The Pink Pussy was wrecked, totally and completely trashed. Smashed smiles and large hunks of moist-looking, naked anatomy littered the floor like oversize confetti. The shattered glass of the display counter mixed with spilled potions, lotions, and pills. The blowup doll had been sliced across the face with a razor, the wires had been ripped from the vibrators, and the dildos had been cut into large chunks. In the back room, the smashed projectors littered the linoleum floor while the films draped the doors and light fixtures like vines in a jungle. The screens had been slashed and the coin boxes pried open, spilling thousands of quarters into the mess of broken glass on the floor.

Amid the wreckage, the cash register stood apparently unscathed. As I picked my way over to it, I kicked some of my own shredded books out of the way and realized in embarrassment that some of my notes now lay scattered around on the floor as well. I hit the cash key on the register and the drawer popped open revealing the same $20 in change that I had left there the night before as usual. "Whoever came in didn't want money," I volunteered.

"No, they didn't," George agreed.

"How did they get in?" I asked, realizing that there was no broken door or sign of forced entry.

"Through the basement," George answered.

As I searched for my notes underneath some shredded video cassettes, George said sharply, "Look at the radio."

I picked it up and inspected the broken top, which seemed to have been dealt a single heavy blow with a pipe or hammer. It was obviously ruined and would probably never play again or tell time. I was about to toss it onto the floor when George said, "Wait, look at the clock." The hands on the clock pointed to 11:37. The clock was stopped at a time when I still would have been in the store—twenty-three minutes before I was supposed to have locked the doors. I wasn't sure whether George was blaming me for not being there to punch the buzzer when the guys arrived or whether he was glad I had escaped before they entered.

As we cleaned up and tried to dig out the quarters from the garbage, we talked about how the place should be remodeled and what kind of new name it should have. George wanted to move the counter farther back from the door, and change the peeps into an exclusively video format. I suggested ripping out the wall separating the Red Room and making that into a special section to sell video tapes and some of the more expensive items.

The Pink Pussy was no more. Within a week the new marquee was up, advertising new delights under a new name. The interior was little changed; the Company restored it much the way it had been, and stocked it with new goods. George continued to work there, but he had to find another night clerk because I quit.

Exactly two weeks from the night the Pink Pussy was destroyed, some men came in and attacked the clerk who replaced me. They cracked his skull with a pipe, knocked out one eye, shattered his jaw, broke some ribs and most of his teeth, and left him for dead, another message on the new harvest-gold carpet. Not long after that, a fire of unknown origin destroyed headquarters and several adjoining businesses, killing one man in the blaze.

Notes

Chapter 1: Junk-Food Sex

P. 3   I WANTED TO INVESTIGATE . . .: The names of many of the businesses have been changed, and the geography has been slightly distorted to protect the privacy of individuals. Similarly, the names of the people in the book have been changed and facts about them altered to protect their anonymity.

Chapter 3: Sex without Partners

P. 38   TROBRIAND ISLANDS: Bronislaw Malinowski, 1929.

P. 38   MURIA: Verrier Elwin, 1979.

Chapter 4: The Newest Vice

P. 46   GREEKS: Reay Tannahill, 1980, pp. 84–105; K.J. Dover, 1978.

P. 48   "ONAN KNEW . . .": Gen. 38. 9, 10.

P. 48   ONANISM: Oxford English Dictionary.

P. 48   TISSOT: Lawrence Stone, 1979, p. 320.

P. 49   FROM APPROXIMATELY THE MIDDLE . . . : Edward Wallerstein, 1980, p. 36.

P. 51   SYLVESTER GRAHAM: Vern L. Bullough, 1976, pp. 544–548.

P. 52   THE INVENTION OF NEW ANTISEPTICS . . . : Rene Spitz, 1952, 490–527.

P. 53   IN 1870 APPROXIMATELY 8 PERCENT . . .: Edward Wallerstein, 1980, p. 29.

Notes

Chapter 8: The Gift of Sex

P. 97   A MALE ROADRUNNER . . .: Clellan Ford and Frank Beach, 1971, p. 99.

P. 97   "IN THE COURSE . . .": Bronislaw Malinowski, 1929, p. 319.

P. 98   "WHENEVER MEN PROVE . . .": Janet Siskin, 1973, p. 324.

P. 98   IN A SAMPLING . . .: Donald Symons, 1979, p. 257.

P. 99   IN THE BOOK . . .: F. G. Bailey, 1971.

P. 99   THE GIFT: Marcel Mauss, 1975.

P. 100   A STARVING IK WOMAN . . .: Colin Turnbull, 1972.

P. 101   GUADALCANAL: Ian Hogbin, 1964.

P. 101   IN THE SOUTHERN NEW HEBRIDES . . .: Arthur Deacon, 1970.

P. 102   EPIC OF GILGAMESH: Penguin Books, 1960.

P. 102   "AND A'BRAM WENT UP . . .": Gen. 13. 1, 2. "SHEEP AND OXEN . . .": Gen. 20. 14–16.

P. 103   "YOU WILL POLLUTE . . .": Augustine *De Ordine* 2. 4(12).

P. 104   "TAKE AWAY THE PROSTITUTES . . .": St. Thomas Aquinas *Summa Theologica* II–II 10, 11.

P. 105   ON JUNE 3, 1358 . . .: Paolo Mantegazza, 1935, pp. 275–280.

Chapter 9: Trade

P. 120   WHEN CAPTAIN BLIGH . . .: Robert Levy, 1973.

P. 122   "IT'S JUST LIKE DOING IT. . . .": Robert Levy, 1973, p. 135.

Chapter 10: The New Servant Class

P. 125   THE AZANDE PEOPLE . . .: E. E. Evans-Pritchard, 1970, 1973.

P. 129   WEALTHIER MEMBERS . . .: Thorstein Veblen, 1924.

P. 132   THE JOBS IN WHICH PRESSURES WERE EVIDENT . . .: Laud Humphreys, 1970, p. 112.

Chapter 11: The Sensuous Ape

P. 137   IN SOCIETIES SUCH AS THE YANOMAMO . . .: Napoleon Chagnon, 1977.

Notes

P. 137 EVEN THE CLASSICAL GREEKS ATHLETES . . .: Reay Tannahill, 1980, p. 88.

P. 138 WHEN ESTRUS VANISHED . . .: Helen Fisher, 1982.

P. 140 ALL THESE EVOLUTIONARY CHANGES . . .: Donald Symonds, 1979.

Chapter 12: How Much Sex Is "Normal?"

P. 145 COUPLES COPULATE . . .: John Gagnon, 1973.

P. 145 "IN MOST SOCIETIES . . .": Clellan Ford and Frank Beach, 1971.

P. 145 THIS IS A RATE . . .: Robert Dickinson et al., 1931.

P. 145 CONTEMPORARY WESTERN SOCIETIES . . .: Weatherford, 1974, 1978.

P. 145 BENA: Marc Swartz, personal communication.

P. 146 A KGATLA MAN . . .: Isaac Schapera, 1966, pp. 185–86.

P. 146 BALA: Alan Merriam, 1971, p. 90.

P. 146 LEPCHA: Geoffrey Gorer, 1938, pp. 329–30.

P. 147 ARANDA: Clellan Ford and Frank Beach, 1951, pp. 78–79.

P. 147 TURU: Harold K. Schneider, 1971.

P. 148 KAINGANG: Jules Henry, 1964.

P. 149 MEHINAKU: Thomas Gregor, 1977.

P. 150 TALLENSI: Meyer Fortes, 1949.

P. 150 ACCORDING TO . . .: Fustel De Coulange, 1873.

P. 150 SIRIONO: Allan Holmberg, 1969.

P. 151 ABORIGINES: Ronald and Catherine Berndt, 1951.

P. 151 YANOMAMO: Napoleon Chagnon, 1977.

P. 151 GADAGAS: Paul Hockings, 1980, p. 53.

P. 152 ULITHI: William Lessa, 1966, pp. 84–85.

P. 152 ABORIGINES: Ronald and Catherine Berndt, 1951.

P. 152 CANELA: William Crocker, 1974.

Notes

P. 152 MARQUESAN WEDDING: Bengt Danielson, 1956, p. 114.

P. 154 THE SEX REPUTATIONS . . .: Irving Wallace et al., 1978.

P. 154 CHEYENNE: E. Adamson Hoebel, 1978.

P. 155 DANI: Karl Heider, 1976.

P. 155 PILAGO: Jules and Zunia Henry, 1944.

P. 155 YAP: Edgar Gregersen, 1983, p. 254.

P. 156 GANDHI DID MUCH . . .: Irving Wallace et al., 1981.

P. 157 ANTHROPOLOGIST: Weston LaBarre, 1985.

P. 157 THE ANCIENT GERMANS: Tacitus, 1948.

P. 157 DUGUM DANI: Karl Heider, 1979.

P. 158 THE JIVARO . . .: Michael Harner, 1973.

Chapter 13: Kiddy Sex.

P. 169 THE KAINGANG . . .: Jules Henry, 1964.

P. 170 THESE INDIANS, CALLED PILAGO . . .: Jules and Zua Henry, 1944.

P. 171 AMONG THE CAYAPA . . .: Milton Altschuler, 1971, pp. 38–58.

P. 171 SIRIONO: Allan Holmberg, 1969.

P. 172 WHEN THE FUTURE KING . . .: Phillipe Aries, 1962, pp. 100–103.

P. 173 IN STUDYING THE SAMBIA . . .: Gilbert Herdt, 1981.

Chapter 13: Older Women Make Better Lovers

P. 182 AMONG MANY OF OUR PRIMATE RELATIVES . . .: Jane Goodall, 1971.

P. 183 WHEN ANTHROPOLOGIST . . .: Anne Sutherland, personal communication.

P. 184 YOUNG MALE ABORIGINES . . .: Ronald and Catherine Berndt, 1951.

P. 184 ON THE ISLAND OF MAGAIA . . .: Donald S. Marshall, 1971.

P. 184 ON THE ISLAND OF TRUK . . .: Marc Swartz, 1958; Ward Goodenough, 1949.

P. 184 AMONG THE CANELA . . .: William Crocker, 1974.

P. 185 THE ILAHITA ARAPESH . . .: Donald Tuzin, 1976.

P. 185 FEMALES IN ANOTHER NEW GUINEA GROUP: Brian Du Toit, 1975.

P. 185 ON TIKOPIA . . .: Raymond Firth, 1936.

P. 185 IN AUSTRALIA A TIWI . . .: C. W. M. Hart and Arnold Pilling, 1960; J. Goodall, 1971.

Chapter 15: Rough Trade

P. 191 IN HIS STUDY OF SEX . . .: Laud Humpreys, 1970, p. 151.

P. 192 "APPROACHES A FEMALE . . .": Mark Strage, 1980, p. 45.

P. 192 SIMILARLY, MALE SQUIRREL MONKEYS . . .: Carl Sagan, 1977, p. 54.

P. 193 "REPORTED THAT THEY EXPERIENCED . . .": Mark Strage, 1980, p. 45.

P. 193 IN THE PREHISTORIC CAVE PAINTINGS . . .: Philip Van Doren Stern, 1969, pp. 155–66.

P. 195 CALLED BY ANTHROPOLOGIST . . .: Napoleon Chagnon, 1977.

P. 195 EVEN THOUGH HOMOSEXUAL ACTIVITY . . .: David Ward and Gene Kassebaum, 1973.

P. 196 BASED ON ONE THOROUGH STUDY . . .: Alan F. Davis, 1973.

P. 196 THE GUSII COMPRISE . . .: Robert LeVine, 1965.

Bibliography

Allgeier, Elizabeth Rice, and Naomi B. McCormick, eds. *Changing Boundaries.* Palo Alto, Calif.: Mayfield, 1983.

Altschuler, Milton. "Cayapa Personality and Sexual Motivation." *Human Sexual Behavior.* Edited by Donald S. Marshall and Robert C. Suggs. New York: Basic Books.

Anonymous. "French Surgeon." *Untrodden Fields of Anthropology.* New York: privately printed for Rarity Press, 1931.

Aries, Phillipe. *Centuries of Childhood.* Translated by Robert Baldick. New York: Random House, 1962.

Arnold, Katherine. "The introduction of poses to a Peruvian brothel and changing images of male and female." *The Anthropology of the Body.* Edited by John Blacking. London: Academic Press, 1977.

Bailey, F.G. *Gifts and Poison.* Oxford: Basil Blackwell, 1971.

Bailey, F. G. *Morality and Expediency.* Oxford: Basil Blackwell, 1977.

Barnett, Cyndi, Claudia Brewington, Wendy Farrar, Jane Hynes, Carole M. Olson, and Minna Shapiro. *Pride.* Minneapolis: Family and Children's Services, United Way, 1984.

Beach, Frank A., and Clelland S. Ford. *Patterns of Sexual Behavior.* Baltimore: Johns Hopkins University Press, 1977.

Beaglehole, Ernest, and Pearl Beaglehole. *Pangai, Village in Tonga.* Wellington, N.Z.: Memoirs of the Polynesian Society, vol. 18, 1941.

Benderly, Beryl Lieff. "Rape Free or Rape Prone," *Science 82* 3 (1982).

Benedict, Ruth. *Patterns of Culture.* Cambridge, Mass.: Houghton Mifflin, 1934.

———. "Sex In Primitive Society," *American Journal of Ortho-psychiatry* 9 (1939).

Berndt, Ronald M. *Excess and Restraint: Social Control Among a New Guinea Mountain People.* Chicago: University of Chicago Press, 1962.

Berndt, Ronald, and Catherine M. Berndt, *Sexual Behavior in Western Arnhem Land.* New York: Viking Fund Publications in Anthropology no. 16, 1951.

Blackwood, Evelyn. "Lesbian Behavior in the Cultures of the Pacific." Anthropological Research Group on Homosexuality Newsletter 4-1 (1983).

Brake, Mike, ed. *Human Sexual Relations.* New York: Pantheon, 1982.

Broude. Gwen J., and Sarah J. Greene. "Cross-cultural codes on Twenty Sexual Attitudes and Practices." *Ethnology* 15-4 (1976).

Bryant, Clifton, and C. Eddie Palmer. "Massage Parlors and 'Hand Whores.' " *Journal of Sex Research* 11-3 (1975).

Buck, Peter Henry. *Ethnology of Tongavera.* Honolulu: Bernice P. Bishop Museum, Bulletin 92 (1932).

———. *Mangaian Society.* Honolulu: Bernice P. Bishop Museum, Bulletin 122 (1932).

Bullough, Vern L. *Sexual Variance in Society and History.* Chicago: University of Chicago Press, 1976.

Burton Ronald. *Venus Oceanica: Anthropological Studies in the Life of the South Sea Natives.* New York: Oceanic, 1935.

Chagnon, Napoleon. *Yanomamo: The Fierce People,* 2d ed. New York: Holt, Rinehart & Winston, 1977.

Champion, Timothy, Clive Gamble, Stephen Shennan, and Alasdair Whittle. *Prehistoric Europe.* London: Academic Press, 1984. Commission on Obscenity and Pornography. *Report of the Commission on Obscenity and Pornography.* New York: Bantam Books, 1970.

Bibliography

Corbin, Marie, ed. *The Couple.* Middlesex, U.K.: Penguin, 1978.

Crocker, William H. "Extramarital Sexual Practices of the Ramkokamekra-Canela Indians." *Native South Americans.* Edited by Patricia J. Lyon. Boston: Little, Brown, 1974.

D'Andrade, Roy C. "Sex Differences and Cultural Institutions." *The Development of Sex Differences.* Edited by Eleanor E. Maccoby. Palo Alto, Calif.: Stanford University Press, 1966.

Danielson, Bengt. *Love in the South Seas.* Translated by F. H. Lyon. London: George Allen & Unwin Ltd., 1956.

Davenport, William H. "Sex in Cross-Cultural Perspective." *Human Sexuality in Four Perspectives.* Edited by Frank A. Beach. Baltimore: Johns Hopkins University Press, 1977.

Davis, Alan F. "Sexual Assaults in the Philadelphia Prison System." *The Sexual Scene,* 2d ed. Edited by John H. Gagnon and William Simon. New Brunswick, N.J.: Transaction Books, 1973.

Davis, Murray S. *Smut: Erotic Reality and Obscene Ideology.* Chicago: University of Chicago Press, 1983.

Deacon, Arthur Bernard. *Malekula: A Vanishing People in the New Hebrides.* Oosterhout, Netherlands: Anthropological Publications, 1970.

De Coulanges, Fustel. *The Ancient City.* Translated by Willard Small in 1873. New York: Doubleday Anchor Books, undated.

DeMartins, Manfred F., ed. *Human Autoerotic Practices.* New York: Human Sciences Press, 1979.

Denis, Armand. *Taboo.* New York: Putnam's, 1967.

Dentan, Robert Knox. *The Semai: A Nonviolent People of Malaya.* New York: Holt, Rinehart & Winston, 1968.

Devereaux, George. "Institutionalized Homosexuality of the Mohave Indians." *Human Biology* 9 (1937).

———. "Heterosexual Behavior of the Mohave Indians." *Psychoanalysis and the Social Sciences.* Vol 2. Edited by Geza Roheim. New York International University Press, 1950.

Diamond, Norma. *K'un Shen: A Taiwan Village.* New York: Holt, Rinehart & Winston, 1969.

Bibliography

Dickinon, Robert Latou, and Lura Beam. *A Thousand Marriages: A Study of Marriage Adjustment.* Westport, Conn.: Greenwood Press, 1931.

Dover, K. J. *Greek Homosexuality.* New York: Random House, 1978.

Durgnat, Raymond. *Eros in the Cinema.* London: Calder & Boyars, 1966.

Du Toit, Brian M. *Akuna: A New Guinea Village Community.* Rotterdam, Netherlands: A. A. Balkema, 1975.

Dwyer, Daisy Hilse. *Images and Self-images: Male and Female in Morocco.* New York: Columbia University Press, 1978.

Edwardes, Allen. *The Jewel in the Lotus.* New York: Julian Press, 1959.

Ellis, Albert. *The Folklore of Sex.* Rev. ed. New York: Grove Press, 1961. Also published as *Sex-Beliefs and Customs.* London: Nevill, 1951.

Ellis, Havelock. *The Psychology of Sex.* 2d ed. New York: Harcourt Brace Jovanovich, 1933.

Elwin, Verrier. *The Muria and their Ghotul.* Bombay: Geoffrey Cumberlege, Oxford University Press, 1947.

Erikson, Kai. *Wayward Puritans.* New York: John Wiley, 1966.

Evans-Pritchard, E. E. *The Nuer.* Oxford: Clarendon Press, 1940.

———. *Kinship and Marriage among the Nuer.* Oxford: Clarendon Press, 1951.

———. "Sexual Inversion among the Azande," *American Anthropologist* 72, no. 6 (1970).

———. "Some notes on Zande Sex Habits," *American Anthropologist* 75, (1973).

———. *Man and Woman among the Azande.* New York: Free Press, 1974.

Farb, Peter, and George Armelagos. *Consuming Passions: The Anthropology of Eating.* New York: Washington Square, 1980.

Firth, Raymond. *We the Tikopia.* New York: American, 1936.

Bibliography

Fischer, J. L., and Marc J. Swartz. "Socio-psychologcal aspects of some Trukese and Ponapean love songs." *Jounral of American Folklore* 736-89 (1960).

Fisher, Helen E. *The Sex Contract: The Evolution of Human Behavior.* New York: William Morrow, 1982.

Fisher, Lawrence E. "Relationships and Sexuality in Contexts and Cultures." *Handbook of Human Sexuality.* Edited by John Money and Benjamin B. Wolman. Englewood Cliffs, N.J.: Prentice-Hall, 1980.

Ford, Clellan S., and Frank A. Beach. *Patterns of Sexual Behavior.* New York: Harper & Row, 1951.

Fortes, Meyer. *The Web of Kinshp among the Tallensi.* London: Oxford University Press, 1949.

Fortune, Rio F. *Sorcerers of Dobu.* New York: Dutton, 1932.

Foucault, Michel. *The History of Sexuality.* Translated by Robert Hurley. New York: Random House, 1978.

Fromm, Erich. *The Art of Loving.* New York: Bantam, 1956.

Gagnon, John H., and William Simon. *Sexual Conduct.* Chicago: Aldine, 1973.

Gebhard, Paul H. "Human Sexual Behavior." *Human Sexual Behavior.* Edited by Donald S. Marshall and Robert C. Suggs. New York: Basic Books, 1971.

Giraldo, Z. I. *Public Policy and the Family.* Lexington, Mass.: D.C. Heath, 1980.

Gladwin, Thomas, and Seymour B. Sarason. *Truk: Man in Paradise.* New York: Wenner-Gren Foundation for Anthropological Research, 1953.

Goffman, Erwin. "Gender Advertisements." *Studies in the Anthropology of Visual Communication* 3-2 (1976).

Goldberg, B. Z. *The Sacred Fire: A History of Sex in Ritual Religion and Human Behavior.* Secaucus, N.J.: Citadel, 1974.

Goldman, Irving. *The Cubeo: Indians of the Northwest Amazon.* 2d ed. Urbana, Ill.: University of Illinois Press, 1979.

Bibliography

Goodale, J. C. *Tiwi Wives.* Seattle: University of Washington Press, 1971.

Goodall, Jane. *In the Shadow of Man.* New York: Dell, 1971.

Goodenough, Ward H. "Premarital Freedom on Truk." *American Anthropologist* 51-4 (1949).

———. *Property, Kin and Community on Truk.* New Haven, Conn.: Yale University Publications in Anthropology 46, 1951.

Goody, Jack. "A Comparative Approach to Incest and Adultery." *British Journal of Sociology* 7 (1956).

Gorer, Geoffrey. *Himalayan Village.* London: M. Joseph Ltd., 1938.

———. *Death, Grief, and Mourning.* New York: Doubleday, 1965.

Gough, E. Kathleen. "The Nayars and the Definition of Marriage." *Journal of the Royal Anthropological Institute* 89-1 (1959).

———. "Is the Family Universal?" *A Modern Introduction to the Family.* Edited by Norman W. Bell and Ezra F. Vogel. New York: Free Press, 1968.

Gregersen, Edgar. *Sexual Practices.* New York: Franklin Watts, 1983.

Gregor, Thomas. "Privacy and Extra-marital affairs in a Tropical Forest Community." *Peoples and Cultures of Native South America.* Edited by Daniel R. Gross. Garden City, New York: Doubleday/ The Natural History Press, 1973.

———. *Mehinaku, the Drama of Daily Life in a Brazilian Indian Village.* Chicago: University of Chicago Press, 1977.

———. *Anxious Pleasures.* Chicago: University of Chicago Press, 1985.

Griffin, Susan. *Pornography and Silence.* New York: Harper & Row, 1981.

Handy, E. S. Craighill. *The Native Culture in the Marquesas.* Honolulu: Bernice P. Bishop Museum, Bulletin 9, 1923.

Hanson, Allan F. *Rapan Lifeways: Society and History of a Polynesian Island.* Boston: Little, Brown, 1970.

Harner, Michael J. *The Jivaro.* Garden City, New York: Anchor, 1973.

Bibliography

Harrington, Charles. "Sexual Differentiation in Socialization and Some Male Genital Mutilations." *American Anthropologist* 70-5 (1968).

Harris, Marvin. *Anthropological Theory.* New York: Thomas Y. Crowell, 1968.

————. *Cannibals and Kings.* New York: Random House, 1977.

————. *America Now.* New York: Simon & Schuster, 1981.

Harris, Sara. *House of 10,000 Pleasures.* New York: Dutton, 1962.

Hart, C.W.M., and Arnold Pilling. *The Tiwi of Northern Australia.* New York: Holt, Rinehart & Winston, 1960.

Heider, Karl G. "Dani Sexuality: A Low Energy System." *Man* 11-2 (1976).

————. *Grand Valley Dani.* New York: Holt, Rinehart & Winston, 1979.

Henry, Jules. *Jungle People.* New York: Vintage, 1964.

Henry, Jules, and Zunia Henry. *Doll Play of Pilago Indian Children.* New York: American Orthopsychiatric Association, Research Monograph 4 (1944).

Herdt, Gilbert H. *Guardians of the Flutes.* New York: McGraw-Hill, 1981.

Herskovitz, Melville J. *Dahomey: An Ancient West African Kingdom.* Evanston, Ill.: Northwestern University Press, 1967.

Hockings, Paul. *Sex and Disease in a Mountain Community.* New Delhi, India: Vikas Publishing House, 1980.

Hoebel, E. Adamson. *The Cheyennes.* 2d ed. New York: Holt, Rinehart & Winston, 1978.

Hogbin, Ian. *A Guadalcanal Society.* New York: Holt, Rinehart & Winston, 1964.

————. *The Island of Menstruating Men.* Scranton: Chandler, 1970.

Holmberg, Allan R. *Nomads of the Long Bow: The Siriono of Eastern Bolivia.* Garden City, N.J.: The American Museum of Natural History, 1969.

Bibliography

Homer. *The Iliad.* Translated by Richard Lattimore. Chicago: University of Chicago Press, 1976.

Hardy, Sarah Blaffer. *The Woman that Never Evolved.* Cambridge, Mass.: Harvard University Press, 1981.

Humphreys, Laud. *Tearoom Trade: Impersonal Sex in Public Places.* Chicago: Aldine, 1970.

Huxley, Francis. *Affable Savages.* New York: Capricorn, 1966.

Jenni, D.A. "Evolution of Polyandry in Birds." *American Zoologist* 14 (1974).

Karsch-Haack, Ferdinand. *Das Gleichgeschlectliche Leben der Naturvolker.* New York: Arno Press, 1975.

Katchadourian, Herant A. *Fundamentals of Human Sexuality.* 4th ed. New York: Holt, Rinehart & Winston, 1985.

Katz, Jonathan. *Gay American History.* New York: Avon, 1976.

Kaufmann-Doig, Federico. *Sexual Behavior in Ancient Peru.* Lima, Peru: Kompaktos S.C.R.L., 1979.

Kelly, Raymond C. "Witchcraft and Sexual Relations." *Man and Woman in the New Guinea Highlands.* Edited by Paula Brown and Georgeda Buchbinder. Washington, D.C.: American Anthropological Association 8 (1976).

———. *Etoro Social Structure.* Ann Arbor, Mich.: University of Michigan Press, 1977.

Kemnitzer, David S. "Sexuality as a Social Form," *Symbolic Anthropology.* Edited by Janet L. Dolgin, David S. Kemnitzer, and David Schneider. New York: Columbia University Press, 1977.

Kennedy, John G. *Struggle for Change in a Nubian Community.* Palo Alto, Calif.: Mayfield, 1977.

Kenyatta, Jomo. *Facing Mt. Kenya.* New York: Random House, 1965.

Keuls, Eva C. *The Reign of the Phallus.* New York: Harper & Row, 1985.

Kinsey, Alfred C., Wardell B. Pomeroy, Clyde E. Martin, and Paul Gebhard. *Sexual Behavior in the Human Male.* Philadelphia: W.B. Saunders, 1948.

Bibliography

————. *Sexual Behavior in the Human Female.* Philadelphia: W.B. Saunders, 1953.

Klein, Bonnie Sherr. *Not a Love Story.* Film of the Canadian Film Board, Studio D, The Women's Studio, 1982.

Knoche, Walter. "Geschlechtsleben auf der Osterinsel." *Zeitschrift für Ethnologie* 44 (1912).

LaBarre, Weston. *Muelos.* New York: Columbia University Press, 1984.

Landtman, Gunnar, *The Kiwai Papuans of British New Guinea.* London: Macmillan, 1927.

Laria, Roque de Barros. " 'Polyandrous Adjustments' in Surui Society." *Native South Americans.* Edited by Patricia J. Lyon. Boston: Little, Brown, 1974.

Laubscher, Barend Jacob Frederick. *Sex, Custom, and Psychopathology.* London: Routledge & Kegan Paul, 1937.

Lee, Richard B. *The Dobe Kung.* New York: Holt, Rinehart & Winston, 1979.

Lessa, William A. *Ulithi: A Micronesian Design for Living.* New York: Holt, Rinehart & Winston, 1966.

Levine, Robert A. "Gusii Sex Offenses." *American Anthropologist* 6 (1959).

Levi-Strauss, Claude. *Tristes Tropiques.* Translated by John and Doreen Weightman. New York: Atheneum, 1974.

Levy, Robert I. "The Community Function of Tahitian Male Transvestisism." *Anthropological Quarterly* 44 (1971).

————. *Tahitians.* Chicago: University of Chicago Press, 1973.

Lewissohn, Richard. *A History of Sexual Customs.* London: Longmans Green, 1958.

Lindenbaum, Shirley. "A Wife Is the Hand of Man." *Man and Woman in the New Guinea Highlands.* Edited by Paula Brown and Georgeda Buchbinder. Washington, D.C.: American Anthropological Association 8 (1976).

Bibliography

Linton, Ralph. "Marquesan Culture" and "The Tanala of Madagascar." *The Individual and His Society.* Edited by Abram Kardiner. Westport, Conn.: Greenwood Press, 1939.

Little, Kenneth. "The Role of Voluntary Association in West African Urbanization." *American Anthropologist* 59 (1957).

Lowie, Robert H. "Myths and Traditions of the Crow Indians." Anthropological Papers of the American Museum of Natural History 25 (1922).

Malinowski, Bronislaw. *The Sexual Life of Savages.* New York: Eugenics, 1929.

————. *Sex and Repression in Savage Society.* London: Kegan Paul, 1927.

Montegazza, Paolo. *The Sexual Relations of Mankind.* Translated by Samuel Putnam. New York: Eugenics Press, 1935.

Marshall, Donald S. "Sexual Behavior in Magaia." *Human Sexual Behavior.* Edited by Donald S. Marshall and Robert C. Suggs. New York: Basic Books, 1971.

Mauss, Marcel. *The Gift.* Translated by Ian Cunnison. London: Cohen & West, 1975.

Maybury-Lewis, David. *Akwe-Shavante Society.* London: Oxford University Press, 1974.

Mayer, Philip. "Ekeigoroigoro." *Journal of the Royal Anthropological Institute* 3-6 (1953).

McCary, Stephen P., and James Leslie McCary. *Human Sexuality.* 3d. ed. Belmont, Calif.: Wadsworth, 1984.

McCurdy, David W., and James P. Spradley, eds. *Issues in Cultural Anthropology.* Boston: Little, Brown, 1979.

Mead, Margaret. *Coming of Age in Samoa.* New York: William Morrow, 1928.

Meigs, Anna. "Male Pregnancy and the Reduction of Sexual Opposition in a New Guinea Highlands Society." *Ethnology* 15-4 (1976).

————. *Food, Sex, and Pollution.* New Brunswick, N.J.: Rutgers University Press, 1984.

242

Bibliography

Merriam, Alan P. "Aspects of Sexual Behavior among the Bala." *Human Sexual Behavior.* Edited by Donald S. Marshall and Robert C. Suggs. New York: Basic Books, 1971.

Messenger, John C. *Inis Beag.* New York: Holt, Rinehart & Winston, 1969.

———. "Sex and Repression in an Irish Community." *Human Sexual Behavior.* Edited by Donald S. Marshall and Robert C. Suggs. New York: Basic Books, 1971.

Milner, Christina, and Richard Milner. *Black Players: The Secret World of Black Pimps.* London: Michael Joseph, 1973.

Montagu, Ashley. *The Anatomy of Swearing.* New York: Macmillan, 1967.

———. "Physiological Paternity in Australia." *American Anthropologist* 39 (1937).

Morris, Desmond. *Intimate Behavior.* New York: Random House, 1971.

———. *Manwatching.* New York: Harry N. Abrams, 1977.

Murphy, Michael. "Coming of Age in Seville." *Journal of Anthropological Research* 39-4 (1983).

Nass, Gilbert D., Roger W. Libby, and Mary Pat Fisher. *Sexual Choices.* 2d ed. Monterey, Calif.: Wadsworth, 1984.

Newton, Esther. *Mother Camp: Female Impersonators in America.* Englewood Cliffs, N.J.: Prentice-Hall, 1972.

Newton, Niles. "Trebly Sensuous Woman." *Women: Body and Culture.* New York: Harper & Row, 1975.

Paige, Karen Erickson, and Jeffrey M. Paige. *The Politics of Reproductive Ritual.* Berkeley: University of California Press, 1981.

Peckham, Morse. *Art and Pornography.* New York: Basic Books, 1969.

Pierson, Elaine Catherine, and William V. D'Antonio. *Male and Female: Dimensions of Human Sexuality.* Philadelphia: Lippincott, 1974.

Pontius, A. "Dani Sexuality." *Man* 12 (1977).

243

Bibliography

Read, Kenneth E. *Other Voices: The Style of a Male Homosexual Tavern*. Novato, Calif.: Chandler & Sharp, 1980.

Reade, Brian. *Sexual Heretics*. New York: Coward-McCann, 1970.

Redfern, Paul. *The Love Diseases*. Secaucus, N.J.: Citadel, 1981.

Reich, Wilhelm. *The Sexual Revolution*. New York: Farrar, Straus & Giroux, 1969.

———. *The Function of the Orgasm*. New York: Farrar, Straus & Giroux, 1973.

Reiss, Albert J., Jr. "The Social Integration of Peers and Queers." *Social Problems* 9 (1961).

Riesman, Paul. *Freedom in Fulani Social Life*. Translated by Martha Fuller. Chicago: University of Chicago Press, 1977.

Riviere, Peter. *Marriage among the Trio*. Oxford: Clarendon, 1969.

Rosenthal, Leora N. "The Definition of Female Sexuality and the Status of Women among the Gujerati-speaking Indians of Johannesburg." *The Anthropology of the Body*. Edited by John Blacking. London: Academic Press, 1977.

Rush, Florence. *The Best Kept Secret: Sex Abuse of Children*. New York: McGraw-Hill, 1980.

Russo, Vito. *The Celluloid Closet*. New York: Harper & Row, 1981.

Saddock, Benjamin J., Harold I. Kaplan, and Alfred M. Freedman, eds. *The Sexual Experience*. Baltimore, Md.: Williams & Wilkins, 1976.

Sagan, Carl. *The Dragons of Eden*. New York: Ballentine, 1977.

Sandars, N.K., trans. *The Epic of Gilgamesh*. Middlesex, U.K.: Penguin, 1960.

Sanday, Peggy R. "Female Status in the Public Domain." *Issues in Cultural Anthropology*. Edited by David W. McCurdy and James P. Spradley. Boston: Little, Brown, 1979.

Schapera, Isaac. *Married Life in an African Tribe*. Evanston, Ill.: Northwestern University Press, 1966.

Schieffelin, Edward L. *The Sorrow of the Lonely and the Burning of the Dancers*. New York: St. Martin's, 1976.

Bibliography

Schneider, David M. "Abortion and Depopulation on a Pacific Island." *Peoples and Cultures of the Pacific.* Edited by Andrew P. Vayda. Garden City, N.Y.: The Natural History Press, 1968.

Schneider, Harold K. "Romantic Love Among the Turu." *Human Sexual Behavior.* Edited by Donald S. Marshall and Robert C. Suggs. New York: Basic Books, 1971.

Schivelbusch, Wolfgang. *Das Paradies, der Geschmack und die Vernunft.* Munich: Carl Hanser Verlag, 1980.

Selby, Henry A. *Zapotec Deviance.* Austin, Tex.: University of Texas Press, 1974.

Shostak, Marjorie. *Nisa: The Life and Words of a !Kung Woman.* New York: Vintage, 1983.

Simons, G. L. *Sex and Superstition.* New York: Harper & Row, 1973.

Siskin, Janet. "Tropical Forest Hunters and the Economy of Sex." *Peoples and Cultures of Native South America.* Edited by Daniel R. Gross. Garden City, N.Y.: Natural History Press, 1973.

Smith, Timothy D'Arch. *Love in Earnest.* London: Routledge & Kegan Paul, 1970.

Spencer, Robert, and Jesse D. Jennings et al. *The Native Americans.* New York: Harper & Row, 1965.

Spindler, George, and Louise Spindler. *Dreamers without Power: The Menomini Indians.* New York: Holt, Rinehart & Winston, 1971.

Spitz, Rene A. "Authority and Masturbation." *Psychoanalytic Quarterly* 21 (1952).

Spradley, James P., and Brenda J. Mann. *The Cocktail Waitress.* New York: John Wiley, 1975.

Spradley, James P., and David W. McCurdy. *Anthropology.* 2d. ed. New York: John Wiley, 1980.

Starr, Bernard D., and Marcella Bakur Weiner. *Sex and Sexuality in the Mature Years.* New York: Stein & Day, 1981.

Steinberg, Leo. *The Sexuality of Christ in Renaissance Art and in Modern Oblivion.* New York: Pantheon, 1984.

Stern, Philip Van Doren. *Prehistoric Europe.* New York: W. W. Norton, 1969.

Stone, Lawrence. *The Family, Sex, and Marriage.* New York: Harper & Row, 1979.

———. "A History of Sex." *The New Republic.* July 1985.

Strage, Mark. *The Durable Leaf.* New York: William Morrow, 1980.

Suggs, Robert C. *Marquesan Sexual Behavior.* New York: Harcourt, Brace & World, 1966.

———. "Sex and Personality in the Marquesas." *Human Sexual Behavior.* Edited by Donald S. Marshall and Robert C. Suggs. New York: Basic Books, 1971.

Sumner, William Graham. *Folkways and Mores.* New York: Shocken, 1979.

Sutherland, Anne. *Gypsies.* New York: Free Press, 1975.

Swartz, Marc J. "Sexuality and Aggression on Romonum, Truk." *American Anthropologist* 60-3 (1958).

Swartz, Marc J., and Daivd K. Jordan. *Anthropology: Perspective on Humanity.* New York: John Wiley, 1976.

Symons. Donald. *The Evolution of Human Sexuality.* New York: Oxford University Press, 1979.

Szasz, Thomas. *Sex by Prescription.* Middlesex, U.K.; Penguin, 1981.

Tacitus. *The Agricola and the Germania.* Translated by H. Mattingly. Middlesex, U.K.: Penguin, 1948.

Talese, Gay. *Thy Neighbor's Wife.* New York: Dell, 1980.

Tannahill, Reay. *Sex in History.* New York: Stein & Day, 1981.

Taylor, J. M. *Eva Peron: The Myths of a Woman.* Chicago: University of Chicago Press, 1980.

Textor, Robert B. *A Cross-Cultural Summary.* New Haven, Conn.: HRAF Press, 1967.

Turnbull, Colin M. *The Forest People.* New York: Simon & Schuster, 1961.

———. *The Mountain People.* New York: Simon & Schuster, 1972.

Tuzin, Donald F. *The Ilahita Arapesh.* Berkeley, Calif.: University of California Press, 1976.

Bibliography

———. *The Voice of the Tambaran.* Berkeley: University of California Press, 1980.

Uchendu, Victor C. *The Igbo of Southeast Nigeria.* New York: Holt, Rinehart & Winston, 1965.

Van den Berghe, Pierre L. *Human Family Systems.* New York: Elsevier, 1979.

Van Offelen, Marion. *Nomads of Niger.* New York: Harry N. Abrams, 1983.

Vayda, A.P. "Love in Polynesian Atolls." *Man* 61 (1961).

Veblen, Thorstein. *The Theory of the Leisure Class.* New York: B. W. Huebsch, 1924.

Wagley, Charles. *Welcome of Tears: The Tapirape Indians of Central Brazil.* New York: Oxford University Press, 1977.

Wallace, Irving, et al. *The Intimate Sex Lives of Famous People.* New York: Delacorte, 1981.

Wallerstein, Edward. *Circumcision.* New York: Springer, 1980.

Ward, David, and Gene G. Kassebaum. "Homosexual Behavior among Women Prisoners." *The Sexual Scene.* 2d ed. Edited by John H. Gagnon and William Simon. New York: Transaction Books, 1973.

Weatherford, J. M. "Anthropology and Nannies." *Man* 10-2 (1975).

———. "Deutsche Kultur, amerikanisch betrachtet." *Deutschland: Das Kind mit dem zwei Köpfen.* Edited by Hans Christoph Buch. Berlin: Verlag Klaus Wagnbach, 1978.

———. "Kongresskultur." *Freibeuter* 12. Berlin: Verlag Klaus Wagenbach, 1982.

———. "Labor and Domestic Life Cycles in a German Community." *Dimensions: Aging, Culture, and Health.* Edited by Christine L. Fry. South Hadley, Mass.: Bergin & Garvey, 1984.

———. *Tribes on the Hill.* Rev. ed. South Hadley, Mass.: Bergin & Garvey, 1985.

Whiting, Beatrice, ed. *Six Cultures: Studies in Child Rearing.* New York: John Wiley, 1963.

Bibliography

Wilson, Monica. *Good Company: A Study of Nyakyusa Age-Villages.* London: Oxford University Press, 1951.

Wilson, Peter J. *Man: The Promising Primate.* New Haven, Conn.: Yale University Press, 1980.

Wiseman, Jacqueline P., ed. *The Social Psychology of Sex.* New York: Harper & Row, 1976.

Wolman, Benjamin B., and John Money, eds. *Handbook of Human Sexuality.* Englewood Cliffs, N.J.: Prentice-Hall, 1980.

Zilberberg, Bernie. *Male Sexuality.* Boston: Little, Brown, 1978.